WITH

Remembering Louisiana, 1850–1871

CÉLINE

Remembering Louisiana, 1850–1871

Céline Frémaux Garcia

EDITED BY PATRICK J. GEARY

Foreword by Bertram Wyatt-Brown

THE UNIVERSITY OF GEORGIA PRESS
Athens and London

© 1987 by the University of Georgia Press
Athens, Georgia 30602

Designed by Sandra Strother Hudson
Set in Linotron 202 11 on 13 Bodoni Book
by the Composing Room of Michigan
Printed and bound by Thomson-Shore
The paper in this book meets the guidelines
for permanence and durability of the Committee on
Production Guidelines for Book Longevity of
the Council on Library Resources.

Printed in the United States of America

91 90 89 88 87   5 4 3 2 1

Library of Congress Cataloging in Publication Data
Garcia, Céline Frémaux, 1850–1935.
Céline remembering Louisiana, 1850–1871.

Includes index.
1. Garcia, Céline Frémaux, 1850–1935—Diaries.
2. Louisiana—History—Civil War, 1861–1865—Personal
narratives. 3. United States—History—Civil War,
1861–1865—Personal narratives, Confederate.
4. Reconstruction—Louisiana. 5. New Orleans (La.)—
Biography. I. Geary, Patrick J., 1948–   .
II. Title.
E605.G26 1987   973.7′82   87-5939
ISBN 0-8203-0964-8 (alk. paper)

British Library Cataloging in Publication Data available.

To my Célines:

Céline Marie Frémaux McGinn 1886–1967

Céline Marie McGinn Geary 1912–

Catherine Céline Geary 1977–

Contents

✑ Foreword ✑

THIS MEMOIR by Céline Frémaux Garcia provides a refreshing
and significant account of what it was like to grow up female in
mid-nineteenth-century Louisiana. As Patrick Geary's useful
and penetrating introduction makes clear, the autobiography not only
deserves publication but also merits critical attention. There is more art
and honesty in this book than first meets the eye. As in all autobiographies and most novels, the central figure appears in somewhat heroic
proportions. Yet, Céline modifies that image to a degree: she defends
herself but does not hesitate to show us her vulnerabilities, too.

Three aspects of the memoir will especially intrigue the cultural and
literary historian as well as the general reader: the uniqueness of her
endeavor; the cultural conflicts that she describes; and most important,
the psychological detail that she provides. The first contribution stems
from the scarcity of comparably well-written and astute sources for understanding a lost time and vanished social order as seen from a woman's
point of view. To be sure many Civil War and Reconstruction memoirs
were written by women, most of them the wives of generals, diplomats,
or leading politicians of the Confederacy, to memorialize the Lost Cause
with a special claim for the indispensable but unheralded role that
"young ladies" and matrons played behind the scenes. In this sense the
genre of memoir paralleled the fictive romance, dear to the southern
heart. Like the late Victorian novel, the memoir normally serves a hor-
tatory purpose, the upholding of old values by examples from the past.

Certainly Céline was not unaware of that function. She was, however, preoccupied by the details of a longstanding battle with her mother for the possession of her soul. Céline was no social or political maverick and had quarrel with neither slavery, race subordination, nor the glorification of the Confederate dead. She avoids the easy moral lesson and records instead her reactions to events without overflowing sentiment but with a degree of realism that places her, as Patrick Geary observes, as much in the twentieth century as in the late nineteenth.

In addition, very few such autobiographies have appeared out of Céline Garcia's specific level of society—the non-plantation middling order. The Montilly, Frémaux, and Garcia families did not move in the circles of the Beauregards, the Thibaux, and Soulés. Instead, the families from which Céline sprang and into which she married were fairly inconspicuous. They had manners and education but not much money before the war, and like most others, still less afterwards. Moreover, this volume represents one of the very few surviving memoirs written by a woman from Louisiana, particularly a woman whose heritage was Catholic, French, and immigrant, when most southerners were Protestant, Anglo-Saxon, and native-born. For all these reasons this work is most welcome.

Second, we are presented with an unusual story of conflict between generations and between cultures, set in the midst of war. The young Céline is portrayed from the vantage point of a sixty-year-old woman; we cannot believe that the child grasped circumstances and nuances with all the insight that the author as adult attributed to her immature self. Nonetheless, she recaptures the mood of those days long ago. As the secession crisis neared, for instance, war was just a term one heard around the dining table until it crept into consciousness as her mother made an impromptu flag and laughter was heard less often and died sooner than before. The child Céline's experiences with death and destruction have a ring of authenticity and make compelling reading.

Most skillfully of all, the author presents a study in the contrasts between the tiny French world of Creole Louisiana and the enormous one of Anglo-America. She describes especially well the determination of her mother to be both a loyal Confederate, with her husband at the front, and a woman mindful of her French heritage. Throughout the war, her children's education was not neglected. Céline's "Ma" was always the driving force in the family's domestic life. One might be tempted to say that such vigor and ambition for her children was a sign of modernity, but actually throughout recorded history, women in a patriarchal society often made up for the deficiencies of their husbands or simply took charge out of sheer personal will.

Certainly the Old South had its share of such formidable matrons—those whom the Louisiana novelist Walker Percy has described in *The Last Gentleman* as the "lovely little bitty steel-hearted women . . . who sat in their rocking chairs, and made everybody do right; they were enough to scare you to death." Flore Caroline Marion de Montilly Frémaux fits that description. Desperately Madame Frémaux tried to assure that Céline, brother Léon, and younger sister Francine grew up within the close confines of French custom, education, and family ties. With the eldest daughter, Madame Frémaux went to extremes of cruelty to underscore her point. With little provocation, she locked her daughter in dark, freezing rooms, slapped her face in front of outsiders, ridiculed her deportment and petty mistakes—all in an effort to guarantee that Céline would suffer from the same restraints that good bourgeois French housewives knew so well.

Flore Caroline was persistent but doomed to partial failure. After all, as her daughter Céline quickly notes in the opening chapter, Madame Frémaux had come from people who had counted for something in prerevolutionary France. It was not at all easy for her to adjust to the hard, vulgar, and parochial life of southern Louisiana. Madame Frémaux was never the kind, we learn, to take her family's exile from France and her parents' social declension with grace and equanimity. Her "sick-headaches" and her outbursts of temper signified, perhaps, a prolonged case of culture shock. She felt *declassé;* it made her very depressed, very angry. The adjustments as well as the rigidities of the immigrants' experience in America have been treated in many stories and histories, but few of them concern the efforts of foreigners to counteract the liberalizing tendencies of American social life.

Finally, and most important of all, Céline's work has a psychological depth unusual for a family memoir. Historians have come increasingly to recognize the significance of what French scholars, borrowing from Anglo-American notions of "privacy," call "the history of private life" or, in other words, that part of human existence which has been customarily kept out of the public sphere. We need to publish more works like Céline's memoir because they tell us much about the inner dynamics of culture—the persistences and changes of family governance and life over time.

Céline shapes her story around the maelstrom of family rivalries, most particularly her struggles with her mother and younger sister Francine. Recognizing his wife's intransigence with Céline, Léon Joseph Frémaux compensated by giving his daughter a degree of affection and personal attention that no doubt helped the child's development even as it assured Céline's worship of him in a way that his wife did not duplicate and most likely resented. That convolution encouraged Flore Caroline to favor Francine, the younger daughter, a preference that increased Céline's sense of passive rejection which in turn frustrated her mother still further. Insecure herself in the New World and financially threatened with further decline during the trials of war, Flore Caroline sought to make her daughter act in a particular way. When Céline failed to meet that preconception, the mother felt her own self-esteem at risk and lashed back. Sometimes it is hard to tell who is the child in the accounts that Céline gives; the mother has the tantrums, barely stopping short of serious physical mayhem. Meantime all the children were striving for some sense of a separate identity for themselves, not an easy task in light of the intrusiveness of their mother and the strategic withdrawals of the father—and at times, of Céline's beloved brother Léon.

The struggles that emerge give this story a universality and interest that it would otherwise lack. No doubt Céline exaggerates her mother's cruelty, as Professor Geary warns the reader, but very often mothers of gifted children like Céline act in the way that Madame Frémaux did toward the eldest daughter with whom, at some level, she herself competed. My inclination is to accept Céline's rendition of circumstances. In any event, she has the final word since her mother's diary was destroyed by a descendant. What we have here, though, is a record of family strain, whoever was to blame. We also have, though, a chronicle of family love and loyalty. Once in a while we catch a glimpse of the mother who really does care for her daughter, and, for instance, presents her with a handsome family heirloom. Fight though they did as children, Céline and her sister Francine never parted company throughout their long lives.

But most interesting of all is the way in which Céline replicated her mother's character, probably to an extent she never realized. The daughter's choice of husband was similar to the one that her mother had made: a loving, bright, but passive individual who depended upon his wife's skill to manage household and even business affairs. Like Flore Caroline, Céline was less loving toward her husband than he was toward her. She was always ambivalent about men, a confusion that reflected some emotional deprivation which she tried to offset by seeking a dominance generally achieved. Just as her own mother resented the way her parents' failures had held her back, so too Céline blamed her mother for inhibiting her creativity and sense of selfhood. "My education was all I was allowed to have personally," she remarks.

Yet, Flore Caroline's hold upon her was deep. By and large, as child and adult, Céline tried to meet her mother's exacting standards and was proud to do so. Moreover, the daughter was brave at heart, not because she gained that from her father as she thought, but because the battle of wills between mother and daughter had toughened her for the frays of the larger world. She lacked nothing in creativity. Indeed, Céline was her mother's daughter: discipline, education, integrity mattered. For letting us get to know her, we owe a great debt of gratitude to Patrick Geary and the family members who preserved this document.

Bertram Wyatt-Brown

✑ *Acknowledgments* ✑

THAT Céline Frémaux Garcia's memoir has remained so long unpublished is a pity; that I have had the privilege to edit it at last is a pleasure. One might wonder why a European historian would have undertaken the task, but the reason is simple: I was a Louisianian long before I was a Europeanist. My initial involvement with the memoir was fortuitous: In 1981 Wanda Frémaux Harris told me of its existence and urged me to look into it. Although I was at first skeptical, what I found convinced me of its importance, less as an accurate historical account than as an illustration of how a crucial period of our history had been remembered, and I undertook the task of preparing it for publication. In the process I have come to a much deeper appreciation of my native Louisiana and its history.

The project simply could not have been possible without the generosity and assistance of a great number of descendants of the Frémaux and Garcia families. I am most indebted to Thomas Allen, the owner of the manuscript, for his arranging unlimited access to it as well as to the papers of the various families that figure in the memoir. Wanda Frémaux Harris provided invaluable material on the Frémaux and Marion de Montilly families. Her assistance, from first bringing the manuscript to my attention through clarifying many details of the family's history, has been absolutely priceless. Other descendants who provided me with important information and documentation include Netty Lea Triche, Sidney Frémaux, Lillian Garcia Sleet, and Hilda Frémaux Gott.

I have likewise received professional assistance from Stone Miller, Jr., head of the Department of Archives at Louisiana State University; Harriet Callahan, head librarian of the Louisiana Section, Louisiana State Library; H. Mitchell Stockmann of the Louisiana Department of Public Works; Lt. Col. Jacques Vernet, Chef de section des études, and General Delmas, Chef du Service historique de l'Armée de Terre; Marie Mistretta, of Ascension Catholic Cemetery; Nora Lee Pollard, archivist of the Diocese of Baton Rouge; and Mary M. Tanner, of Judson College.

Finally, in placing the memoir in its historical perspective, I have been greatly assisted by a number of historians, in particular by Cheryl Cody, David Chalmers, Kermit Hall, and A. Fred Blakey of the University of Florida; Todd Savitt of East Carolina State University; and Dietrich von Engelhardt of the University of Heidelberg. For his assistance in identifying persons in the Baton Rouge area I would like to thank Charles East. I am particularly indebted to my friend and colleague Bertram Wyatt-Brown who has been unfailing in his encouragement and assistance at every step of the process. I am grateful to the staff of the University of Georgia Press for their support in this project and in particular to Loris Green for the exceptional effort that she has made in its final preparation. None of these persons are responsible for the omissions and errors which may appear in my introduction and annotations; they are however largely responsible for what there may be there of value.

✑ Introduction ✑

ISITORS to the uptown New Orleans home of Joseph Garcia
during the early years of the twentieth century often remarked
on the extent to which writing played an important role in the
lives of the family members. Each morning the family, which included
Joe and Céline Frémaux Garcia, Joe's sister Sara, and Céline's mother
Caroline, retired to their separate rooms after breakfast for several hours
of writing. The most prolific of these authors was Mrs. Garcia. Not only
did she carry on a voluminous correspondence with friends and relatives
in the United States, France, and Belgium, but she also maintained, at
least intermittently, a diary begun in the 1860s, and she wrote a series of
accounts of her travels in the South and vignettes of her early life in
Louisiana. Writing had always been an integral part of her life. Although
it began as an onerous and hated obligation pressed on her at the age of
four by her mother, Céline's writing became a beloved compulsion which
she pursued even in the last years of her life. Crippled by arthritis and
unable to hold a pen shortly before her death in 1935 at the age of 85,
Céline had two sticks bound to her useless hands and painstakingly
tapped out her correspondence and personal testament on a typewriter.

Céline is remembered by her grandchildren as a great storyteller.
Three generations of Frémauxs, Garcias, Allens, and Leas continue to
repeat the stories she told the children who gathered around her. With
her most ambitious and significant project, however, she was remarkably
secretive. Not until long after her death did her heirs find the following

account of the first twenty years of her life, from her earliest childhood memories until her marriage in 1871, and of family legends which she had heard from her parents and grandparents.

The memoir was apparently a well-kept secret, and for good reason. It includes many of the stories with which Céline entertained and instructed her grandchildren, it covers one of the most colorful periods of Louisiana history, and it contains a wealth of incidental detail about life in a middle-class immigrant's family during this period. Nevertheless, its real interest and significance lies elsewhere. The child's-eye view of antebellum New Orleans and Baton Rouge, the vivid descriptions of the violence of daily existence in a no-man's land between Confederate and federal armies during the war, and the melancholy of Reconstruction in New Orleans form only the backdrop for the main drama of the often vicious confrontation and rivalry among members of Céline's family.

Céline was no Mary Chesnut, moving in the highest level of southern political and social elites and commenting wryly and iconoclastically on the southern cause.[1] The individuals with whom Céline came into contact were the perfectly ordinary people of Louisiana and Alabama, and those whom the war brought into this world. For the most part her attitudes toward the region, the war, race, and class were entirely typical of the upper middle class of post-Reconstruction New Orleans. Nor was she a Lucy Breckenridge, the daughter of a wealthy southern planter whose diary records the life of a young woman on a great plantation during the war.[2] Likewise, Céline was quite different from the other Louisiana diarist with whom one might wish to compare her (and with whom she was slightly acquainted), Sarah Morgan.[3] Morgan's father had been a judge and an important member of Baton Rouge society, and her affection for family members loyal to the Union gave her a unique perspective from which to view the Confederate and Union participants in the war and occupation.

Céline's family was from a different social and cultural milieu from that of the Morgans. They were neither members of the old Louisiana

Creole society nor were they part of the wealthy Anglo-Saxon community to which the Morgans belonged. The Frémauxs were middle-class French immigrants. Prior to the war Céline's father owned no land, and the only slave the family owned in 1860 was a domestic inherited from Céline's maternal grandmother. Céline's father had a total wealth of only a few thousand dollars even at the height of his career. Moreover, Céline was a very young child, barely eleven when the war began, and thus poorly informed about the origins or even the course of events in the larger world about her. This isolation was increased by the close supervision that Céline's mother exercised over her circle of acquaintances, at least until Céline moved to Jackson. In New Orleans and in Baton Rouge, virtually all of her playmates and acquaintances were either immediate neighbors or members of the families of engineers associated with her father.

Likewise, Céline's memoir differs from the above-mentioned authors in that, while it was written with reference to her diary, it is essentially a work of a middle-aged New Orleans woman writing in the first decades of the twentieth century. Thus Céline and her memoir are to be compared less with nineteenth-century authors and diarists than with other Louisiana women writers around the turn of the century such as Jeannette Walworth (1837–1918), Ruth McEnery Stuart (1849–1917), Mary Ashley Townsend (1832–1901), and Céline's close contemporary, Grace King (1851–1932). Like many of these women, Céline wrote from a position of social prominence in New Orleans society, and her memories of the 1850s and 1860s are colored by her defense of both the vanished world of which her family had been a humble part as well as of the social order of her own day.[4]

If Céline's memoir presents few novel insights into the public events of the 1850s and 1860s, it is a remarkable evocation of the private life of a Louisiana family. Here Céline parts company with the great majority of her contemporaries who wrote romanticized or idealized accounts of nineteenth-century domestic life. The primary value of Céline's account is the unique view it provides into the domestic life of an immigrant family during the painful years of its "Americanization," and in particular the furious conflict between mother and daughter. The real focus and the real interest of the memoir are the rigid and, to contemporary southern observers, excessively harsh child-rearing practices of Céline's mother; her almost fanatical pursuit of her children's education; the competition between Céline and her mother for her father's affection; and the disappointments of a young girl maturing in a rapidly changing society and ultimately acquiescing to an acceptable but hardly romantic marriage.

Although she was writing some thirty years after the events, Céline's strong emotional involvement in the events and characters had hardly weakened. If anything, her adoration of her father and her resentment toward her domineering mother, her (to Céline's eyes) duplicitous sister, and her sister-in-law had increased through the years. Certainly Céline had had sufficient time and occasion to brood over her relationships with these people. Except for a brief period in the late 1890s, her parents had lived under her roof because her father, a civil engineer who was more a poet and artist than businessman, had never been able to equal the modest success he had achieved as assistant state engineer before the war. Her sister-in-law Sara, after a brief and disastrous attempt to enter a convent in 1869, became a permanent member of her brother's household. Described by Céline, Sara was a depressed and depressing specter, always in black, never smiling, and always ready to expect the worst from family, from friends, and from life itself.[5] Joe Garcia, Céline's husband, had become in time a prosperous stationer and a prominent figure in New Orleans society. He provided a good home for his adored Céline and tried to be a good husband. But while she came in time to love him, it is doubtful that she ever reciprocated the intensity of his feelings for her. He was not her first or even her second choice—in her eyes both of these had been destroyed, although in different ways, by the war. Joe, a wartime comrade of her half brother Léon and a collaborator with her father in White League opposition to Reconstruction, had won the approval of her parents, and their marriage had something of the inevitable about it. Joe was always in and out of the Frémaux home, constantly pursuing Céline with awkward but earnest fervor. Never willing to oppose her parents' wishes overtly, she ultimately simply gave in.

The memoir, then, is much more than an extended version of the stories with which Céline had long entertained the family. It was rather a meditation on the origins of her family and the relationships in which she found herself. It would perhaps be too much to say that the memoir was written in revenge against her mother, sister, sister-in-law, and husband. However, because of the strong criticism it contains, this was surely one text that the other family members never saw, although in the memoir itself Céline repeatedly states that she never hid anything she wrote.

Céline's Louisiana

WITH the exception of a brief stay in Mobile, Alabama, and a year at Judson Institute immediately following the war, Céline lived her entire life on the lower Mississippi. At the time of her birth in 1850, Louisiana was entering a new period in its social and ethnic history. As the census of 1850 indicated, the gradual replacement of Louisiana's Creole-dominated political and social structure by "Americans" from the North as well as from other regions of the South was largely complete. This gradual transition, which had taken more than two generations, was enhanced by the ever-increasing influx of Irish immigrants into the lower Mississippi as a source of cheap, free labor during the 1840s. Thus the dominance of English as the language of trade, politics, and religion was assured at both ends of the social spectrum. The port city of New Orleans, the only real urban area in the state, was essentially an English-language community except within the ever-shrinking circle of old Creoles and more recent French immigrants from the 1820s and 1830s. Even these showed remarkably little hostility to intermarriage and eventual amalgamation with their American neighbors and business associates.[6] Outside of the most isolated and impoverished areas of the bayou country to the west which continued to be characterized by small farms belonging to the descendants of Acadian exiles, English was well established as the dominant language of the region.

These changes, which the social upheavals of war and Reconstruction would only accentuate, were perhaps less obvious in the town of Donaldsonville, where Céline's parents were living at the time of her birth. Donaldsonville had long been an important community on the lower Mississippi and was the major settlement between Baton Rouge and New Orleans. Unlike either of these two, however, Donaldsonville and the surrounding Ascension Parish were almost entirely French-speaking, and were the home not only of Acadians but many Creole planter families and more recent French immigrants. It was the gateway to the Teche country to the west as well as an important agricultural and administrative center and had even functioned briefly as the state capital. In the 1850s a number of state agencies continued to have their offices in Donaldsonville, including the state land office where Céline's father, Napoléon Joseph Frémaux, was employed as a clerk.

Thanks to his younger brother, Justin Frémaux, who was active in New Orleans' Know Nothing Party, Céline's father was able to receive an appointment as assistant state engineer in 1855, an appointment facilitated by his naturalization in the same year. Apparently at this point he had his name changed from that of his father's idol to the less politically charged Léon.

Léon's career in the land office and then in the office of the state engineer took his family out of this small and traditional French community into the very different worlds of antebellum New Orleans and Baton Rouge. Moving to New Orleans in 1853, the family settled on St. Ann Street in the heart of the old French Quarter. Céline's early experiences in the city were different from those that she had known in the country, but the society of middle-class French immigrants in which her family

moved was essentially unchanged. Virtually all of her childhood acquaintances lived within a block of their home on St. Ann, and without
exception the language of her daily life was French.

The move to Baton Rouge in 1855 brought about radical changes in
Céline's world. Although much of the rural population of East and West
Baton Rouge parishes was French-speaking, Baton Rouge itself was an
American town and had been so for decades. In addition to being an
important market town and shipping point on the river, it was the state
capital and the site of the state school for the deaf, dumb, and blind; the
state penitentiary; and an important military garrison. Baton Rouge society was American, and for the first time the Frémaux children had to
learn to function in English.

This initial period in an essentially American society, during which
Céline and her brothers had had their first experience of Americanization, proved to be a great help during the war years. Céline's father had
been elected captain of a local volunteer company, the Creole Guards,
but in 1862 he was commissioned captain of engineers and was sent to
select a site for fortifying the Mississippi between Baton Rouge and
Vicksburg. He chose Port Hudson and began the first fortifications of the
site. When his wife learned that he was again in the area, she moved
with the family to Port Hudson and then, at the beginning of the siege, to
Jackson, Louisiana, where they remained until the end of the war.

Jackson was a completely American, Protestant community which in
the 1840s and 1850s was the educational center of the state. Centenary
College, a Methodist institution which had been founded in Clinton,
Mississippi, had moved to Jackson in 1845 to occupy the buildings of the
defunct College of Louisiana. In 1860–61 Centenary enrolled two hundred students, and Jackson boasted not only the men's college but a
preparatory school and a number of women's academies. Jackson was
also the location of the state insane asylum which, along with the school
for the deaf, dumb, and blind in Baton Rouge, was one of the major
public institutions in the state.

In Jackson, Céline's immersion in Anglo-Saxon society was total. She was the only French-speaking student in her classes and the only Catholic. Yet, unlike her mother who never deigned to form any real friendships in the community, Céline became fondly known to the older generation as "Frenchy" and found her new environment extremely attractive. The enduring friendships Céline made among the people of Jackson lasted throughout her life and resulted in the marriage, years later, of her daughter into one of the Jackson families to which she had been most attached.

Thus, in the first fifteen years of her life, Céline had moved from the secure and familiar world of old French Louisiana to progressively Americanized areas of the state. In spite of her mother's extreme efforts to preserve the French identity of her children through education and through the inculcation of family traditions of social and cultural superiority, Céline found herself entirely at home in this new world. French language, mores, and traditions were never forgotten, to be sure. French remained the language of the household throughout her life. But one finds nothing of nostalgia for France or French Louisiana in her memoirs, which were written entirely in English.

The Families

THE AMERICANIZATION of the family did not destroy the traditions, legends, and sense of self that Céline's parents and grandparents had brought with them from France. Their stories continued to play an important, although somewhat attenuated role. The family legends of glories and riches lost in the French Revolution tempered the later generation's experiences of upheaval and reversal during the American Civil War. The "Lost Cause" was something already familiar to the de Montilly family who had suffered in the Revolution, and Waterloo prepared the Frémaux family for Gettysburg, Vicksburg, and Appomattox. Even the opening stories of Céline's memoir, which attempt to recall (in a language owing more to nineteenth-century romances than to history) the dangers Céline's great-grandmother faced when forced to return to Paris during the Terror, seem to have been echoed in the confrontation between Céline's mother and federal troops when she had to return to Baton Rouge to retrieve family property during the Civil War. Thus the past provided Céline a pattern in which to live and to remember the present.

The past was even more vital to Céline's mother, Flore Caroline Marion de Montilly (1818–1908), who was never able to adjust herself to the social and cultural position in which she lived most of her long life—the wife of a not-so-prosperous French engineer of undistinguished background living in what must have seemed to her a harsh and uncultured American society. Little in her childhood had prepared her for such circumstances. Indeed, one could speculate that her childhood had prepared her for no realistic future whatsoever. Her parents, Jean Dominique Victor Marion de Montilly (ca. 1794–1849) and Anne Françoise Leveque (1798–1857) had married in Paris in 1813. The husband, son of a Parisian merchant, who indicated his profession at the time of his marriage as that of professor of music, brought to the marriage 600 francs of personal effects, 2,000 francs of debts, and an advance on his inheritance of 3,400 francs.[7] He and his parents must have considered the marriage to the fifteen-year-old daughter of the late Jean Louis Joseph Leveque, comte de Fleury, and Marguerite Françoise Grimpreau quite desirable. In addition to the prestige of the family, the girl brought a dowry of 7,560 francs plus an annual *rente* of 77 francs.

The young musician was, as his granddaughter accurately wrote, a disaster as a businessman. By 1822 when his wife obtained a legal separation of property, he was deeply in debt both to a variety of business creditors and to his wife, to whom he owed 8,760 francs.[8] Upon his departure one jump ahead of his creditors all of his remaining property in France was seized and sold. His wife joined him in Brazil two years later and continued to supply him with loans and goods, ultimately raising his debt to her to 20,774 francs, due at 5 percent interest. These later loans went the way of the former, and ultimately she returned to France where she had left her son and youngest daughter. Her husband and older daughter Céline remained in Brazil. Mme de Montilly took a position as governess in a Russian family in order to support herself and her daughter Caroline. Her husband abandoned his hopes of making his fortune in Brazil and, like many other French adventurers before him, set sail for New Orleans where he arrived by way of Havana on 24 December 1825. There he apparently had moderately better luck and was able to arrange for the family to join him in about 1832. However, his financial incompetence continued and in 1840 his wife won a judgment against him for his past debts to her in the amount of $7,264.54.

Caroline was thus raised against a background of sinking financial position, instability, and domestic tension. She probably knew her father very little as a child and was, of all the members of the family, the one most attached to the old world of pre-revolutionary France. Her entire childhood, unlike that of her older sister Céline, had been spent in France, much of it in the aristocratic circles of her maternal grandmother's family, and in the equally aristocratic world of Moscow's French-speaking society. To step from these elevated circles to those of a middle-class immigrant family struggling to make its way in the rough world of New Orleans in the 1830s must have been difficult for her.

These woes were probably compounded by the continuing tensions between her father whom she had hardly known and her mother. Apparently the strain was not limited to that between her irresponsible father and her long-suffering mother. In addition to Caroline's older sister Céline and a brother briefly mentioned in the memoir (he apparently died under mysterious circumstances sometime in 1847 while traveling between Natchitoches, Louisiana, and Texas), the family included a sister who was never mentioned. This sister, Adrienne Felice Marion de Montilly, had been born around the time of the family's hurried departure from France and in 1840 had married a paternal first cousin, Isidore

Pinsard. The marriage ended in divorce and Adrienne Felice later married Henry Robert. Her divorce and subsequent remarriage was a stain on the family name which was never forgiven. The reasons for the divorce are unknown, but the fact that Pinsard and his subsequent wife Pauline Adam (Aunt Pauline in the memoir) remained extremely close to the family as did Victor, a son from the first marriage, indicates that the family placed the blame entirely on Adrienne Felice.

To the crime of divorce, Adrienne Felice added the insult of having herself named the administrator of her father's estate in 1851 and attempting to have her mother declared mentally incompetent. Her mother retaliated by disinheriting her from her own estate.[9] Her name is not mentioned in any family record, and it appears that from the perspective of the de Montilly, Pinsard, and Frémaux families, she had simply never existed.

In this strange world, surrounded by a stranger family, Flore Caroline never ceased to believe that she was intended for better things. The better things however seemed less likely than spinsterhood, and by the age of thirty she was apparently resigned to the tolerable but déclassé life of a tutor and governess.[10] Her mother had led this sort of life during those seven years in Moscow, and in the late 1840s Caroline was serving as governess in a wealthy Anglo-Saxon family intent on acquiring a patina of French culture for its children. She was rescued from this fate in 1849 as a result of the death of her sister, Céline, who left a husband and a small infant, Léon Victor Frémaux. Caroline left her position in the Shields household in Natchez to assist her brother-in-law with the infant, and within a year had become the new Mme Frémaux.

'The Frémaux family too had left France for a better future, but it was less burdened by its past. François Etienne Frémaux (1788–1841) had been an enlisted soldier in the Eighty-second Line Regiment, and had risen from private to fourier by 1811 when he was severely wounded in the right arm while fighting in Portugal. His injury forced him to retire from active service on a modest pension. He remained a staunch Bonapartist however, and during the Hundred Days returned to active service in the Third Battalion of retired soldiers. In 1812 he had married Aimée Adelaide Lebrun, a licensed midwife, and the couple had six children, only two of whom, Napoléon (Léon, 1821–1898) and Justin Augustin (1831–1901), reached maturity. Like many other *demi-soldes*, retired soldiers of the Napoleonic army, François was apparently severely affected by the crisis in restoration France during the late 1820s and following the revolution of 1830 he emigrated to New Orleans where he opened a book shop. His wife opened her practice as a licensed midwife. Apparently the Frémaux family had some financial success, since Etienne was able to send his eldest son Napoléon back to France for his education in the Collège Louis le Grand in Paris.

Upon his return to Louisiana, Napoléon Frémaux went to work as a civil engineer in the state land office and in 1846 married Marie Céline Marion de Montilly, the widow of Louis Schmidt. Céline had one son, Léon Victor, and died of yellow fever at the age of thirty-two on 27 February 1848. Within fourteen months, Frémaux had remarried, this time to his sister-in-law, Caroline, who would never quite forgive him either his humble background or, apparently, his playful, irreverent disposition. When their first child, a daughter, was born, she received the name of her late aunt, Céline.

The younger Céline remembered her childhood home as one filled with tension, rivalry and bitterness. Most of her anger was focused on her mother, and one would dearly wish to know Caroline's side of the story (her diary was burned by a granddaughter). Certainly Caroline's ideas of child-rearing were strict by nineteenth-century southern standards, which tended to extoll discipline in theory but in practice allowed girls as well as boys a great amount of freedom, at least until puberty.[11] Girls were allowed to roam widely and to play as roughly as boys, and in general were disciplined very little lest their aggressiveness and toughness, necessary for the future rearing of male children, be broken.[12] The description of child-rearing practiced in Céline's cousins' homes conforms to this image of permissiveness. Caroline however had very different views. Raised in conservative European society and determined to civilize her offspring in spite of the prevailing values of the American South, Caroline sought to control her children's every moment and to break their wills to her own.[13] Her efforts earned for her the epithet of martinet among her American neighbors and the disapproval of other Louisianians of French descent (such as her brother-in-law Justin) who were more a part of southern society.

Caroline's determination to inculcate her aristocratic social and cultural ideals in her children were most evident in the educational program she undertook with them. A mother's primary responsibility for her children's education was normal in the South.[14] Increasingly in the nineteenth century an education was considered essential both for boys and for girls, but while every town boasted academies of the sort that the Frémaux children attended in Baton Rouge and Jackson, their general low quality and frequent disappearance placed the burden of education squarely on the shoulders of the mother.[15] However, the daily lessons to which the Frémaux children were subjected almost from birth were seen as excessive by community standards and certainly constituted a desperate effort to preserve and continue the sense of social and cultural superiority in the next generation. Who else but Céline's mother would have given her daughter a French grammar as a fifth birthday present or would have forced her children to conjugate the verb "to escape" (*échapper*) as the family fled before the advance of the Union army?

Nevertheless, one should not too quickly accept the harsh, brutal image of Caroline presented by her daughter. The harshness of her discipline seems to have most affected Céline—the other children managed in time to escape either by leaving home (as did her brother) or by simply ignoring Caroline's more excessive orders, as did her sister. Céline emerges as an almost willing, cooperative victim of her mother's rages, goading the poor woman with her haughty silence. Moreover, Caroline's sacrifices to insure that the war would not disrupt the continuity of her children's education must also be seen not only as clinging to a vanished past of aristocratic tradition but also as an attempt to provide them with some measure of security. Teaching had been the only honorable means by which she and her mother had been able to support themselves, and she no doubt wanted to provide her children with this safeguard against the vicissitudes of fate and fortune. The wisdom of her foresight was confirmed after the war when Céline was able to help support the family's meager income by teaching in the New Orleans public schools.

Céline obviously adored her father, who had died shortly before she began the memoir, and throughout her memoir a constant theme is the competition between her and her mother for his trust and affection. Nevertheless, the image she presents of him is of a particularly weak head of the family. If, as has been suggested, the Old South was a true patriarchy, the Frémaux family was a notable exception. Perhaps had Léon been a stronger presence in the family, Caroline's excessive impulses might have been tempered. However, not only was Léon's artistic temperament little suited to the role of stern master, but he came into his marriage at a severe disadvantage. He was marrying a woman older than he from a distinctly higher social background. Moreover, before the war his work kept him away from home for months at a time on state business, leaving Caroline alone to cope with the growing family. During the war, his absence became even more prolonged, although Caroline took the virtually unheard-of step of demanding to move to Port Hudson to be with him. Even when he was home, however, he appears never to have stood up to his wife, and although he did undertake a program to "toughen up" his eldest son (which apparently had a greater effect on his daughter), he does not seem to have made any effort to modify his wife's child-rearing style. Perhaps Caroline, who had grown to maturity with a legally emancipated mother and a ne'er-do-well father, simply found that she was forced by circumstances to follow the model of wifely comportment she had learned as a child.

The War

As WITH ALL MEMBERS of Céline's generation, the Civil War was the great, central event of her youth, and one which continued to affect her throughout her life. Not only had she experienced firsthand the horrors of war, but the subsequent social position of her family owed much to the involvement of her father and husband in the White League movement of Reconstruction and post-Reconstruction Louisiana. Céline, like many other socially prominent Southern women, was herself very active in Confederate veteran organizations. Thus her memories of the war were molded and transformed by the events of the subsequent forty years. Nevertheless much of their immediacy and freshness remain.

Although an eyewitness to the Battle of Baton Rouge and one of the few civilians to inhabit Port Hudson immediately prior to the siege, her memories of these events are frankly confused and not particularly enlightening.[16] The real interest of her account is rather in the view it gives of civilian life during the war. The town of Jackson, located twelve miles north of Port Hudson, was the scene of frequent raiding and skirmishing between elements of the federal army and irregular Confederate units. The constant uncertainty of life; the brutality and hatred of the Confederates for the black troops active in the area and the similar brutality of the federals toward suspected collaborators; the moral dilemma facing mothers who needed to cross Union lines for food and supplies but who would then be forced to take an oath of allegiance to the enemy; the humiliation of the local noncombatants through wanton destruction of their property; the casual cruelty (and occasional kindness) of the Union soldiers; the generosity and courage of the local population—all made deep impressions on Céline, and she portrays them with great immediacy.

The Memoir

THE TITLE Céline chose for her memoir, "My Life As I Remember It," is entirely appropriate. The text, which she wrote during the first years of this century, is in no sense either an unreflected narrative or an objective history of her first twenty-one years. Readers who approach it looking for a "factual" account of antebellum Louisiana, the Battle of Baton Rouge, or Reconstruction in New Orleans will find numerous errors and inconsistencies. It is rather the result of years of living with her memories, telling her children and grandchildren about their family's past, and attempting to record on paper both the significant events and feelings of her first years as well as the meanings that these events came to have for her during the decades that separated the naive young French girl of antebellum Louisiana from the mature New Orleans matron of the twentieth century.

Exactly when she began writing the memoir is unknown. She had already written a number of sketches previously, and probably began writing the memoir in earnest sometime between 1900—two years after the death of her beloved father whose memory she enshrines in the account—and the death of her mother in 1908. At one point she speaks of her mother as living. She was apparently finished writing when in 1914 she corrected a detail concerning her family's flight across the river from Baton Rouge in 1862.

Her primary source was her remarkably keen memory. She could recall the most minute details of sixty years previous with amazing accuracy: the hat she wore in New Orleans in 1856; the names of the steamships on which she had traveled or on which her father had worked before the war; the names of casual acquaintances from her childhood. She also recalled the emotions of those early years: the terror of crossing a dark field at night at the age of three; her anger and resentment toward her mother; her scorn and defiance toward federal soldiers in war-torn Jackson.

Not of course that all the details she recalls are entirely accurate: some, such as the casualty figures in Jackson and Mobile, have grown with the passage of time. Others, such as her paternal grandmother's occupation or the details of her grandfather's legion of honor, have been "improved": the licensed midwife has become a physician; the old veteran who saved General Bonnaire at Condé has in the memoir saved Napoleon himself.

As aides-mémoire she used a variety of written materials, especially her own diary, the reminiscences of friends, and the series of associations that were evoked by the presence of various mementos from her childhood. The books, furnishings, papers, and pictures which she had been able to save across the years touched off a flood of memories which account for the most vivid portions of the memoir. Time and again one encounters, either in the family papers or preserved by various of her descendants, these objects which had formed the guideposts of her memory: the cross of the legion of honor, and the sketches and watercolors done by her father before, during and after the war. But also carefully preserved are such insignificant objects as the fashion plate from an 1857 magazine given her by her childhood beau Camille Bercegeay to comfort her during a particularly traumatic punishment by her mother; pages of her lesson books copied as a child at Baton Rouge; the last piece of furniture brought by her grandfather de Montilly from France, a linen chest of drawers; the identical Lépine watches apparently purchased in better times for her mother and aunt that she and her mother carried; the books damaged through her brother's carelessness as he was attempting to rescue household possessions from occupied Baton Rouge.

All of these and more seem to have precipitated a flood of memories, not only of people and events but more importantly of emotions, which she recorded in her memoir.

Among the written materials which assisted her in the preparation of the memoir, her diary was probably the most important. Only fragments of the diary survive and it is impossible to determine when she actually began keeping it or for how long she continued. What does survive suggests, however, that while the diary may have been a help in recalling chronology of events and incidental details, the memoir is in no sense a revised version of the diary.

The remaining fragments include original entries from the period of 1 January 1870 to 13 October 1871 and a copy of entries from 1 January to 24 May 1869, which begins with the notation "copied from old book." A later diary fragment dated "New Year 1878" begins: "As it happened, through mere chance I came across my 'Diary' left off somewhat before I married and a sudden impulse came over me to continue it and even to take it up where it was left off." There follows a series of summaries of the years 1871 through 1889 written at various times with considerable lacunae. All of these fragments are written on lined paper measuring $10\frac{1}{2}$ by $8\frac{1}{4}$ inches apparently torn from a book or books similar to one in the Garcia family library. This volume is a leather diary book embossed with "Céline L[eonine]. Frémaux" on the cover. How many such books had originally existed and how extensive the diary once was is impossible to know. Some sections of the remaining diary from 1870 concerning her wartime beau Scott Worthy have been cut out, and Céline may have destroyed the other portions of the diary, possibly after having completed the memoir.

To judge from the remaining portions, the original diary was not a privileged source for the memoir, nor is it likely that the diary contained intimate details not found in the later memoir or in the vignettes of her life she wrote prior to writing the memoir. The reasons for this are not hard to determine. The memoir is the carefully constructed work of a mature adult and contains attitudes and interpretations which had been molded over the course of a lifetime. In addition, as Céline so often mentions in the memoir, her mother insisted that no secrets be kept from her, and in particular Céline reports that she never attempted to lock up or to hide anything that she had written from her mother. Even if she had been successful in keeping such secrets from her mother, her sister seems to have made prying into her affairs such a habit that she would have quickly found out the contents of a secret, personal diary and reported them to her mother. Thus Céline could have hardly included in the diary any of the feelings of anger and resentment felt toward her mother and sister, her growing concerns about her future sister-in-law, or any but the most guarded and indirect comments about her relationships with Camille Bercegeay, her childhood sweetheart; Scott Worthy, the Jackson youth who fell in love with her during the war; or about Joe Garcia, her future husband. Thus the diary entries contain primarily details about the weather, social activities, her short career as a substitute teacher in the New Orleans public schools, and other petty details of her life. Only occasionally does she record her frustrations with Joe Garcia, whom she grew to love only very slowly in spite of his awkwardness and timidity, and even then nothing appears which would have been objectionable to her mother or fuel to her sister.

The diary did, however, have a role in the writing of the memoir, one not unlike that of the physical objects from her childhood. Within the laconic entries in the diary were sufficient comments with strong associations which could trigger fuller and more emotional accounts of her feelings later when she could write in safety. An excellent example of the relationship between the diary and the memoir is the treatment of her trip to Jackson, Louisiana, in the summer of 1870. It had been during the family's stay in Jackson during the war that Céline had made her first real friends other than among the narrow circle of her father's business associates, and she remained extremely attached to the Leas, the Worthys, the Millers, and to other East Feliciana families throughout her life. As a thirteen-year-old she had fallen in love with Scott Worthy, then a dashing cavalry soldier seven years her senior who had been severely wounded in battle and by 1865 when the Frémaux family left Jackson he was obviously in love with her. She had returned to Jackson for a visit in 1868 and had seen Scott, but by then the rumor that he "drank" led her to spurn his advances. He assumed that the reason was another man, and in anger and spite concluded a hasty and unhappy marriage. Shortly after the wedding he abandoned his wife and went to California. He returned in the summer of 1870, apparently to see Céline, who became a close friend of his wife although she feared spending any time alone with him. The story ended tragically a few years later: In the summer of 1873 Céline again visited Jackson. Apparently Scott's family forbade him to pick her up at the station or to spend time with her alone, and in a fit of depression he committed suicide the day before her arrival.

In 1900 Céline wrote a rather florid account of her "affair" with Scott Worthy which she entitled "A Love unto Death." In this account, one of several vignettes she had written over the years in anticipation of her memoirs, she went into considerable detail concerning the visit of 1870 and in particular concerning her relationship with Scott and his wife. She mentioned this vignette in passing in the memoir but did not elaborate on the relationship in the longer work. By comparing the diary entries covering the visit with the 1900 account and with that contained in the memoir one can see the role that the diary played in writing the others.

The diary entries themselves contain only a brief sketch of her visit. She records her departure on 21 June, her trip up the river to Bayou Sara, and her social activities in Jackson during the ensuing month. About Scott she says little. She records meeting Scott's wife Lavilla and adds that "If she loves Scotty I think I will like her." She reported on Wednesday, 29 June, that Scott was due back from California but did not yet know if the report was true. Thursday she recorded: "We all . . . went to the dinner but unfortunately a quarrel which occurred took a great part of the charm from it." Concerning Friday, 31 June, she wrote: "Went round home saw Mr. Scottie and his wife. . . ." In a brief postscript added six months later she notes that by the end of her stay, "I have gotten so that I feel sincerely attached to my new friend Mrs. Scott Worthey." This is the full extent of her discussion of Scott and his wife.

Only in the 1900 account do we learn that Scott returned Thursday, 30 June, and before seeing his wife and family went directly to a concert that Céline was attending in order to see her. Only when she pointedly told him that she objected to having him accompany her did he return to his family. Likewise, the description of her brief visit with Scott and Lavilla disguised a concerted effort of several days' duration by Scott to involve her in the selection of a homesite for him and his wife given him by his father upon his return. The single entry for Tuesday, 4 July, "Today Jessie (the daughter of Scott's sister Sally) had a spasm," disguises the events around the one moment when Scott and Céline were entirely alone together: the two of them had worked together to save the child and after, as she held the child, he made an unambiguous declaration of his love for her.

Other entries in the diary similarly touch on issues which would become important in the memoir. She records that on Sunday, 9 July, "Pa arrived this evening late. Says sister has a sprained [ankle]." In the memoir she describes vividly and with great emotion how her sister humiliated and embarrassed her in front of her friends by pretending to have a sprained ankle in order to gain the attention of the local youths, only to forget all about her supposed injury when given the opportunity to dance for an audience. This minor episode that one might take simply as evidence of coquettishness Céline saw as part of the pattern of her sister's duplicity, lack of propriety, and cruelty, a constant theme in the memoir as a whole.

One can conclude from these examples that the diary entries, while not entirely candid and written apparently with the knowledge that they might well be read by her prying mother and sister, nevertheless contained veiled references which, years later, could bring back the emotional confusion of the young Céline confronted by a determined lover, or the anger of a shy girl tormented by a willful sister. It is almost as though the diary had been written with this in mind—as the briefest of outlines to be fleshed out, reconstituted as it were, when at last it would be safe to say all that the Céline of long ago had silently felt.

The Edition

THE MEMOIR itself is contained in ten signatures of lined paper written in a clear, strong hand. The orthography is in general quite clear and presents few problems. Pagination is somewhat confused, but Céline herself recognized her errors and attempted to correct them. The work is divided into chapters, but the manuscript provides only vague indications of just where the actual chapters were to begin.

Capitalization, punctuation, and paragraph division present certain problems for the preparation of the edition. Essentially, the author used very little punctuation and often began sentences without capitals. On the other hand, capitals are often used within sentences for emphasis. The text is divided into paragraphs, but the reasons for the divisions are not clear. I have modernized punctuation and paragraph divisions, as well as capitalization, where it might otherwise cause confusion.

As many other authors educated in the nineteenth century, Céline took a refreshingly free approach to spelling, particularly of proper names. I have preserved the spelling, which is of potential interest to anyone wishing to better understand the art of letters as learned by the fireside, in the schools, and in the colleges of antebellum Louisiana.

I have attempted to keep to a minimum the explanatory notes which accompany the text. Essentially I have attempted to identify those persons, places, and events necessary for the understanding and appreciation of the memoir's content. No attempt has been made to identify all of the hundreds of persons who appear in the text. Likewise, I have attempted to avoid editorializing on Céline's moral, political, and social views or changing her language, some of which, like her use of the epithet "nigger," are frankly offensive to modern readers. As mentioned above, she was no radical or even progressive in her views on blacks, Mexicans, or federal soldiers; she does not challenge the accepted notions of her day concerning the roles of men and women in society; her religious views (more carefully recorded in the diary than in the memoir), are unexceptional.

One might have wished to find the memoir of a radical abolitionist, feminist or reformer, but such a document would provide less insight into the society of the descendants of French Louisiana than the one at hand. Céline speaks with a very human voice. Her values and her prejudices, her loves and her hates, are spoken with a force which brings to life, across the decades that separate us from her and her from the child that she was, a world that brought forth our own.

My Life
As I Remember It

❧ Beginnings ❧

TO BEGIN at the beginning—the first name I think I ever heard of as ancestors was the name de Grimpeaux.[1] They were my great, great grandparents; all I know of them is that they belonged to the old nobility of France, that they had two daughters: the eldest married a Prince of Polignac.[2] The younger—my great grandmother—married Mr. Joseph Leveque, comte de Fleury.[3]

Both ladies were of the house of Marie Antoinette. I do not know what their duties were, but their love and devotion to the unfortunate queen was unbounded.

If there were others in that heroic family, I never heard of them. History tells the life of the Princess of Polignac, my great grand aunt.[4]

Mrs. de Fleury had been reared, as was the custom in their class, in a boarding school for the nobility. Much care was bestowed on their looks and form, much on accomplishments, very little on learning. For instance: every night her feet were put in stout linen boots laced up the sides—lest her feet spread during sleep. A linen corset was also worn at night that the body might develop just as became her "Station."

The girls there were taught embroidery. Once a week there was a class of sewing. It was rough sewing for the poor, or alms house. As to ordinary sewing as might be *useful* to them, it was not to be thought of. Were they not to have seamstresses at their command?

History was insisted upon, so also languages, géography and arithmetic were very much neglected. Were they not to travel with a retinue?

What need a lady with knowledge of roads and countries? Would they not have "Piqueurs" and guides to know for them?

However their hearts were well trained. Bravery, Valor, Honour, Patriotism, and Duty were developed to the utmost, as shown in the many demands of their eventful lives.

Great Grandma was a young woman, very young, when the Revolution began. She was alone in Paris on some sort of political or devotional duty. It was in an awful time; blood was flowing everywhere. For safety she wore the dress of a Breton peasant. It seems that her appearance was not quite plebian enough to deceive; a band of ruffians caught her and "a la lantèrne, a la lantèrne with the aristocrat," came from the mob.[5] She was lost; she thought her moments were very few, but just then a *water carrier*, himself a "Sans Culotte," who had for years carried water for the de Fleury's, made his appearance on the scene. He had known her from birth. Many instances show that hers was a loveable nature, for many were the servants devoted to her. This man, then, rushed to her. Her hands were tied behind her and a noose was being prepared. She was being hustled beneath the dreadful Lantèrne. The man hustled her nearest foes, and roughly shaking her, began to abuse her for being on the street saying, "I told you not to go out. I told you that uppish look would be the death of you."

"Citoyens, this is my wife's niece just from Brittany. I understand your error, but this girl is a fool, not an aristocrat."

"But look at her hands—has a peasant such hands?" objected one. "And the fair skin of her neck," said another, snatching her kerchief from her shoulders."

"Yes, I know," said the man. "Her mother was a fool before her, made a Lace maker of her, kept her in a cellar making Lace—instead of teaching her something sensible. Here, get out of this—" shaking her again "—and keep indoor, washing dishes for my wife, and make no more trouble for good Citoyens."

He was known to the roughs as a true revolutionist. Alas! Maybe he had denounced many aristocrats. Be it as it may, he saved our ancestress and we do not know his name! He scoldingly took her away, hid her in a low, dark coal-bin under a stair of his house. He did not trust his household with the knowledge of her presence. At night he brought her food. Five days later he smuggled her out of Paris.

But that was not all: her mission had not been fulfilled. She must go in again under some better disguise, but go in she must and did. Her home had been sacked, and the windows, bare of sash, showed the inner devastation. She managed to conceal herself for weeks in its emptiness.

One noon as she was returning to it, she found a crowd in her street. They were yelling and gesticulating, trying to find some vent for their bloodthirsty turbulence, and when one proposed: "Let's burn that house, it belongs to a ci-devant.[6] Bring fire, let's have some fun."

She did not hesitate; in her house lay the secret of her mission and the names of several persons, whose death would have followed discovery. She pushed through the crowd, mounted a pile of stones, and harangued the crowd, saying: "Look there! Citoyens that is my house, it was looted when it *did* belong to the ci-devant Marquis. I bought it with an aristocrat's money, and I expect to raise a brood of Patriots in that house. So have a care don't burn my house, Vive la France, Vive la Patrie!" The tide was turned, the disorderly horde went elsewhere for pillage.

At many times *she* wore man's attire, and many times it saved her from detection. Once she had worn the dress of a "Sans Culotte" and on retiring had left the garments in a front room together with her feminine attire of the day before. It seems that she had been traced to this dwelling, and that night a lot of young "Servants of the Republic" were sent to arrest her. They broke into the house and came upon the two sets of garments. It struck their vicious natures that the aristocrat must be in company with someone of their coarse set, and they decided to go no further but to let this true son of the Nation have his visit out. With many horrible jokes called out to the darkened inner room they wished them well, and departed, knowing they could arrest her any time with or through her plebian lover, whose clothes they marked. However, she was never caught; she noted the mark and evaded her enemies.

Years Later

HER SON was 27 years old and she nearly 50 when her husband died. A few months before it had become known to her that she would again be a mother. She retired to one of his properties outside of Paris, there to have and to care for this posthumous child. The child came—a girl, she who was to be my grandmother. The names of Francine, Anne, were given to her.[7] She was nursed from her mother's breast—quite an unusual occurrence in those days. For hundreds of years back no lady of that house had even dreamed of caring for her child herself. The family was then: the mother; the son, Joseph Vicomte de Fleury; a daughter 12 years old, who later married a Marquis of La Vallee; and the baby Anne Francine.[8] The Vicomte belonged to the Diplomatic corps, was sent to Louisiana, and died of Yellow fever a few days after his arrival.

Anne Francine was reared in wealth, and had quite a dowry when, at the age of 15, she married Jean François Dominique Victor Marion de Montilly.[9] I spelled out the long, long name many times in my early years—on the marble slab which marks his last resting place, in the St. Louis graveyard on Claiborne & St. Louis Streets. He was also rather well off in money, had one brother ("Old Uncle Marion," mother called him), and two sisters, Eugenie and Evrenim. The latter had been named Minerve during the Revolution, but in more peaceful times the name was reversed to Evrenim. Grand-Pa was very young to marry (not twenty) and too young entirely to manage money. In a few years he and Grand-Ma found themselves with three children and nearly ruined. Grand-Pa was a linguist knowing six languages, and a fine musician. At the age of four years he played on the Piano the most difficult operatic music. Grand-Ma was more highly educated than most women of her times, and was very practical. Grand-Pa was *not* practical. He put all the rest of his fortune in a ship (a sailing vessel) and its cargo, a variety of goods which he *supposed* would sell in South America. Their son Ernest was left with his Uncle; their youngest child Caroline was left in a "Pension" and in care of her Grand-mother & Aunt. Céline, the second child, they took with them to Brazil. [10] The trip was made in 93 days. The whole venture was against Grand-Ma's better judgment.

To dispose of the Goods—which were not in demand—took over a year. The ship was also sold. For some business or other Grand-Ma returned to Paris 13 months after leaving it. She was to collect an inheritance, take her children, and with them return to Riojanero.

It happened that as she reached Paris a Russian nobleman—through one of the diplomats at Paris—was seeking a governess as chaperone for his daughters. He wanted a person of a birth and social standing which would admit her on a footing of equality in his household and among his friends. The compensation was princely. It was offered to Grand-Ma, who accepted. She found the life there to her taste and hoped in a few years to benefit her children with her savings. The family was that of the Sheppeleoff: there were two girls, Annette and Lisi, and an adopted daughter, Lizette Dourneoff. [11] Six months later Grand-Ma sent for little Caroline, whose grand-mother had died. The child left the Pension— well chaperoned of course—for the long trip across Germany to Russia. Caroline was later to be my Mother. She often related the incident of that trip. They travelled two months. They were in a private coach and travelled easily, leisurely, stopping at night in the best "hostelleries." In St. Petersburg her mother met her, and a month later they entered Moscow, where they resided. Ma's life there was very happy. She was much petted and loved. Nearly 7 years they spent there, until the Russian girls were presented at Court, and were engaged to be married.

Arrangements were made for the young ladies to live with their Maternal Grand-Mother. My Grandmother desir[ed] to come back to her children, especially Céline, who was by now almost grown. This time the trip was taken by sea from Cronstadt to Havre, from there to Paris, where she once more—and for the last time—saw her people. She took her son, and the three sailed for New Orleans, where Grand Pa and the daughter awaited them. Grand Pa had amassed something. He had put most of it in a Book Store run by a manager. It proved a successful venture. Grand Ma brought quite a sum with her, but she had taken a taste for teaching, and she opened the first Finishing school in New Orleans. All went well with them for several years. Céline had married a Mr. Schmidt, only son of rich Parisian parents who had come to America in a fit of anger. He seemed to live in anger most of the time. A fall from a horse caused his death two years later. His parents wished his wife to come to them. promised to leave their entire fortune to her. But she did not accept. A few years later she married again—this time a very pleasant-tempered young Civil Engineer, Mr. Léon J. Frémaux. [12]

Meanwhile Caroline had grown up, and considered it her duty to earn her own living. Her parents opposed her in this, but she persisted, and her 1st venture was going as instructress in the family of Mr. Shields of Natchez. [13] Mrs. Shields was a proud, disdainful woman. That was Ma's verdict at the time. Later, 50 years later, we heard from a very reliable source a tale which might have made Ma think, that Mrs. Shields—born Surget—was perhaps less mean and more unhappy. If mother had known at the time she would not have remained.

Ma's Sister had now moved to Donaldsonville, where her husband was employed in the State Land Office. They had a little son. [14] Four months later she caught scarlet fever and died in seven days' illness. [15] On receipt of the news Caroline left Natchez to come to her mother, who sorely needed her at this time of grief. At the time of Mrs. Frémaux's death a Governess was being sought by Mr. and Mrs. Bercegeai. This situation Caroline accepted at once. [16] At the Shield's she had two intelligent pupils with a mean mother. At the Bercegeai's there was one pupil, almost an idiot, and the most lovely parents. A happy home was theirs. And Ma looked after the welfare of her sister's child, who lived with his wet nurse, a French woman, Mrs. Rogomme. Eighteen months later Caroline Flore Marion de Montilly became Mrs. Frémaux, and the baby became her own son.[17] He was 2 years old.

The Frémaux family was also French. The father, Etienne Frémaux, had always been a soldier, as his father before him. Under Napoleon, Etienne Frémaux fought, and worshipped his Emperor who, on a battle field, with his own hand had pinned his own cross of honor on the breast of his bleeding soldier.[18] A cosack's lance had torn that valiant breast as he carried his wounded general from the melee. At another battle a bayonet thrust scaled a piece off the precious cross, but the iron deviated and only a flesh wound resulted. He received seven wounds in that one encounter. In the hospital a new cross was offered him, but he would not exchange. I have now the glorious cross—once worn by the great Emperor—with its piece of white enamel nipped off.

Mrs. Frémaux, also French, was born in Normandy. She was Aimée Adelaide Le Brun, of Normandy.[19] She was a beautiful woman who spent the years of her husband's soldiering in the study of Medicine—quite a unique profession for a woman, in those days. She was passionately fond of the work, and also took a complete course in surgery, took high degrees in that line, and, during the troublesome time of Napoleon the 1st, gave the best of her work to her country's soldiers.[20]

After the death of Napoleon Mr. & Mrs. Frémaux moved to Louisiana and to New Orleans. And in this democratic land it came to pass that the Aristocratic De Montilly's and the plebian Frémaux intermarried. Mr. & Mrs. Frémaux had had, and lost, six children before my father came. He was Léon Joseph, born in Paris in 1821.[21] The next [was] Justin, born in N.O. eleven years later; and the next—and last—Aimé, also born in N.O., died of yellow fever some times in the early "40," I think 1842.[22] Father was a Civil engineer; Justin (my Uncle), a Politician. Léon Joseph Frémaux and Caroline Flore Marion de Montilly were married on the 26th day of April, 1849. She was 32 years old and looked 18. He was in his 30th year. They soon took little Léon with them. They boarded with the Bercegeai family, and in that house I was born, on the 21st of March 1850. The first arms that held me, the first one to kiss me, was Mrs. Bercegeai (Madame Aimé, we always called her).

The half idiot daughter Victorine Blanchard had married, and was chosen for my God.Mother. Victorine brought Mr. Warren a dowry in money, land, and slaves of sixty-two thousand dollars.[23] Long years later, she died a pauper in a Charity Hospital. The younger sisters (half sisters) were my most loved and loving friends; they were seven and five years older than I was, and the brother six months older than Léon.[24]

Mother had begun to teach when quite young. It had grown to be a necessity of her being: She began to teach Léon even before she had me, and I dare say that lying on Mother's bed I must have heard Léon Recite some sort of lesson. I have always heard that before I could talk plainly, I knew quite a bit of Bible history.

Mother was positive, very serious—a perfect slave to duty—as she understood it. Life had been serious to her, she made it a serious affair for us.

❧ Donaldsonville to ❧ Baton Rouge

I WAS NEVER TOLD that I was a *little* girl. I was always a *big* girl. A big girl 3 years old should not do this or that; then a Big girl 7 years old should be able to do so or so—and thus it went through life.

The first thing I remember of the kind—I was not quite three years old: we were dressing to go to a marriage. I owned a cat, which cat was my constant companion; that night the cat took a fit, and was ordered killed. Of course I cried bitterly, and then it was I remember for the first time Mother's voice telling me from the next room—that big girls did not cry for cats, that I would have many more subjects for tears later on— and that she wanted the foolish tears Stopped Immediately.

I do not know how quickly I "stopped"—I know the bride was named Eleutere Landry, that father lifted me to his shoulder as she passed into the supper room, and that was my first knowledge of a bride.

After all, my cat was not killed. The servant threw a bucket of water on it and it never had another fit. We kept the cat from Ma's knowledge a long while.

I was destined to cry again for that cat—a year later we moved to New Orleans, and the servants being superstitious about moving cats, I was forced to give it away. I left it to the woman who had saved her for me, promising myself that when I was a lady in a house of my own, I would buy Leonora and have my cat back with me.

My very first remembrance of anything was of going into an unoccupied house. There were many jars and bottles on the floor. Mother took up one that had a snake coiled up in it and took it out somewhere: I have had a horror of snakes ever since. The mention of them makes my flesh creep.

Next: I remember standing on a raft of great logs, father rolling my one garment about my armpits and dipping me in the river, to my great delight; then he would look at my toes and remark: "You are not good bait—no shrimps have come up." There were "gunny" sacks with meat—for bait—fastened to the logs, and a negro was fishing. Pa, then, had a saw mill; he furnished cord wood to the Steam boats. There were great piles of yellow sawdust, and goats round about. I remember Pa having the goats milked and giving me the milk. We were living in our own place then, next to the Bercegeai's, there was a large flower garden, and then a little side piece which was ours Léon's and mine—we could *pick* flowers there: a trumpet-honeysuckle, a pink crape myrtle, a purple althea, and "Mary" golds, as we called them.

Once a hen and her chicks were scratching up things there. Léon drove them out and in doing so killed one of the chicks. He threw it under a tree. Ma saw it lying there; on being asked about it Léon said, "Céline had it in her hand, and she did not go to do it, Ma, but it squeezed and it died. She is so little. Ma, don't whip her. Please, *please* don't whip her." I can remember that I felt myself lost. I *knew* I was going to be whipped. Ma called me to her and asked why I killed the chick. I denied having done it. She said, "Tell the truth now; I know you did it. Why did you do it?" I was silent; Léon was in tears begging her *not* to whip me. Ma took him by the arm and put him on the gallery and came back to me and *did* whip me. The old cook, hearing me cry, came in told Ma how it had happened; she had seen the killing, it seems, and Pa, arriving just then, gave Léon quite a spanking. In my immature mind, I thought it unfair—only one of us had killed. Why should both be whipped? Ma has since told me that I was not $2\frac{1}{2}$ years old at the time.

I remember too the fun it was to be put on the back of *John* (a grey plow-horse) and to ride about in the horse lot. We also had a play fellow, Guess, the dog. We had a swing and we loved to swing turn about. Guess had his turn too, and he took such a liking to it that we often found him on the swing seat in the morning.

I remember also once, of seeing a runaway horse. He was saddled and bridled, and the wooden stirrups and broken bridle reins seemed to fly around and strike him at every step; Féfé held me up to the fence to see the horse.[1]

My first loss was one day of a black-berrying party. All were going in carts. Our cart was blue. One of the laborers carved me a wooden spoon of red cedar. My dear friends Féfé, Franka, and Camille Bercegeai were in our cart with Léon and I, and the man Mr. "Carco" did the driving. I lost my spoon during the trip through the woods and cried about it. Mr. Carco then said he would make me another one, but Ma said "no"—if a big girl like me could not care better for her things, I certainly could *not* have another made. To make me forget the spoon Féfé carried me in her arms around the lot to play. The Play was walking up the shafts of the cart and jumping in and out at the back. In some way the dumping arrangement was not secure and the little finger of my left hand was badly mashed. It was the first real hurt that I remember.

A very few days later—my hand was yet bandaged—Ma and Pa, Léon and I got in the buggy and went across the bayou to see a sick lady—her name was Mrs. Superviélle; on the way, Ma told us that we would have to be very quiet, and not talk at all because the lady was in sorrow, as the thunder had killed her baby.[2]

I can see that house yet: all vine-covered and Bees around, humming so loudly, I thought. Ma went directly into the lady's room. I was left in the parlor. Pa and Léon stopped on the gallery. There was a very old person kneeling beside a little crib in the middle of the parlor. In the crib was a lovely little dead baby with white flowers all around it. I kept very still. Presently several gentlemen came in, Mr. Superviélle carrying a little white coffin. The baby was put in it, the lid screwed on (with a screw driver), and they went out with it without a word. The old person took me by the hand and led me to Mother. Mrs. S[uperviélle] seemed to have cried; she was lying in bed with a very handsome night robe. She was holding two little baby dresses. One was pink. She gave them to Mother and we soon left. Pa began to whistle a tune as we got on the road, but Ma silenced him. She seemed very sad, so Léon and I on our little bench in front of our parents kept very still.

When we reached home Féfé was there, and we had great romps. Mme. Aimé was there too, and she undressed me and put me to bed that night. Very early next morning Pa called out to me, "Get up, Céline, and come see something." I tried to get out of my crib but got so fast on the edge one foot on each side and I stuck there. So Pa came to me. He had on a dressing gown and looked very tall—I had never seen him in that sort of garment he lifted me in his arms. My gown was damp and he looked at me with his kindly eyes open quite round and whispered, "Mme. Aimé did not do her duty by you last night, but Mama won't know it." And he carried me inside his gown, only my head sticking out, to Mother's bed. And, lo, there was a little bit of a crib there, and in it is wee bit of a babe. It was a little sister. I was told this was on the 3rd of August 1853.[3] I was 2 years and 4 months old.

I was very much afraid of "The dark;" a dark room was a thing of horror to me. Léon was afraid of nothing. Ma never sent him in dark places, always sent me. One day she wanted something for the baby who was unwell and she sent me to Mme. Aimé's for it. It was night. To get there I had to cross the lot and a field. I have known since that the field was only a half-acre plot. But to me, then, the corn was a big as a tree and the plot seemed an endless forest. I begged and pleaded not to go. I got a whipping and threatened with another if I did not go, and be back in 15 minutes by the clock. I did not understand clocks but I looked up at it. It seemed formidable. Its big face scared me. I felt it was my enemy. It would help Ma compel me to this horrible thing. Finally I started. In the lot it was not so very dark. I could see the horse John at the other edge. I ran across. John was my friend, but then after passing him there was the field, the wilderness! I crossed the bars and lo my blood seemed to freeze. I was about to crouch down against them. My back seemed cold on that summer night. I thought of that clock. It would *tell* if I stopped. The furrows went from home to Mr. Aimée's. I got in a furrow and put my apron over my head not to see the "Dark" but my hair hurt and every strand seemed to be trying to pull out its own way, and *things* touched me. Of course it was the corn leaves, but I thought it was Things, awful Things. My throat went dry, and great beads of sweat were over me when I reached the other fence with a bump. My apron was still over my head. My fear of Ma and the clock deserted me; I called out loudly: "Féfé, Féfé." A door was opened, a stream of light came my way, and with wild bounds I threw myself into Féfé's sheltering arms. I got the Camomile tea and Féfé took me in her arms to carry me back. She knew Ma must not see her, so in entering the lot she drove old John before her and only let me go on our gallery.

That trip did not cure my dislike for the Dark, it only compelled my obedience to orders. I felt that Ma was adamant. She was the law, and inexorable. I never attempted to beg off after that night, never!! Baby as I was, the "iron entered my soul." I *knew* I was a slave. I felt a sort of gratefulness to the clock for not telling on Féfé. I kept a sort of respect for that mysterious ever ticking clock, but I knew it could be merciful.

In the fall of that year there was an epidemic of Yellow Fever and Cholera. Pa had always been employed in the Land Office at a salary, and he [had] run the Saw Mill besides. Well, one day he was at the Mill and saw a Steam Boat coming down the river, as if drifting. Something seemed wrong; he got in a skiff and with four niggers rowing went to her. He shouted. No answer came, so he clambered aboard and found that many were dead and all others sick on board. The Captain was living by lying on the pilot house floor. With his men Pa took charge. They shouted to the Mill hands to notify Ma, and they took the steam boat down to New Orleans. When they reached the wharf only 3 men were living—The Captain, Pa, and one negro.

In New Orleans Pa met his brother and others who told him they intended presenting his name for Assistant State Engineer, if their party won the campaign. Uncle was a "Know Nothing;" Pa was a Democrat.[4] I think I heard them say that the Democrats won, but anyway Governor Hebert was elected.[5] Louis Hebert (a cousin of the Governor) was nominated State Engineer and father Assistant, at a Salary of two thousand a year.[6]

Why it was necessary to remove us to New Orleans I do not know. I think a crevasse had necessitated the building of a new levee where the Saw Mill had stood. I *do* know that in a few years the whole of our home place, and a part of the Bercegeai's plantation, had been swallowed up by the ever changing river bed.

I was 3 years and a half old when we moved to New Orleans. My grief was very sincere: I had to leave my cat and many of my playthings, among which was a long, narrow jug, which I called my child; it could stand up and be dressed, as I thought, quite like a child. But the jug could not be taken. I left it in Féfé's care. And my dear friends who protected me so often—how I would miss them!

New Orleans

OUR NEW HOME was on St. Anne St. between Marais and Villeré. Our landlord's name was Mr. J. Joubert, a little thin man whose reputation seemed to be that he was a miser, and very hard on his tenants.[7] However, as our rent was always promptly paid, Ma found him quite a gentleman and his family very agreeable. He had a very pretty daughter who died young, may-be at 17 or 18.

We lived in New Orleans two years and a half. During that time these are the facts which remained with me.

First, the day of our arrival Léon fell in the gutter, walked right backward into it. His suit was so ruined that he could never wear it again. A city gutter was a new thing to us. A ditch we understood, but a reeking, filthy gutter we did not know, else he may have been more careful. I see him yet, dripping from that "dip." Boys then wore embroidered ruffles showing below the trousers at the knees, and ruffled, turned-up cuffs over the sleeves. The "jabot" and collar of the shirt were likewise of ruffled embroidery. Ma had Léon taken in through the gate by old "Uncle" Green, an old, very black slave, and stood under the hydrant of river water—as a first wash. Léon screamed lustily all the while, and when he was clean enough to touch Ma took him in hand, stripped him, "cuffed" him, and put him to bed on a mattress on the floor—the beds had not yet been put up.

I had a like experience a year or so later. Ma had a scrap of pink-striped organdie that I thought very beautiful. For my 4th birthday Ma made it up into a little slip for me. I was very small for my age and yet there was only enough for a short-sleeve, low-neck slip. As March was too cool to wear such a garment it was put away for later use. Finally one warm evening it was put on. Oh, the happiness of that moment! Then an organ grinder played a tune at the corner and I began to dance around and around with the tune, ballooning the scimp little dress all I could. I unwittingly reached the gutter edge and over I went. Mother got me in the corner of the step and called to the girl to fetch a pail of water. It was poured over my head. The little slip and mud were swept off together and I was sent to bed in disgrace. I do not remember to have been whipped.

About that time I had scarlet fever. People did not seem to fear disease as they now do. Mother had a class of French pupils, all little children like ourselves. There were then four of us; a little brother had come.[8] During the class hour the baby generally lay on the foot of my bed, and after class the children would often stop and speak to me, when my head did not ache too much. Not one of those children had scarlet fever; neither did any of ours. We wore white stockings then, and as I was to stay entirely in-doors till the "scaling" was over Ma bought me two pair of slate-colored hose so that I might see myself when my prison time could be over.

Being a scary child, as I have said before, Ma took much trouble to break me of senseless fear. If she required me to fetch anything from a dark room and I showed reluctance she would light a candle, take me by the hand, and lead me to the object required. Then she would put out the light and go once more with me in the dark, touch the object, then return. Then I was sent alone in the dark to fetch it. I would go; in my little-inner self I *knew* there was nothing to hurt me, yet the fright was just as strong. Upstairs the attic rooms were more than a terror to me. The night that the little brother came I felt myself carried up and found myself in the arms of a stranger. She whispered, "Keep quiet, your Mama is sick," and she put me in a bed where brother was already asleep. I had never been upstairs at night. The room seemed immensely large and full of frightful things. I covered my head with the bed clothes but could not sleep. There was a something that looked like a big white goat at the foot of our bed. Once in a while I would risk one eye out of the sheet, and it was still there. It seemed to move its head, but it was always there. I was wild with fear; brother slept. All at once I heard a sound or a cry. Of course I knew the "Goat" was springing on me. I must have moaned or screamed, for a servant ran up and with trouble found me wrapped in the bed clothes. I told her about the dreadful "goat."

Léon woke up and sleepily said, "Goats do not hurt if they do get in a room." He turned over and went back to sleep. Ruth (the servant) said she would drive the goat off. She lit a lamp and went down. I did not see any more goat, but every now and then I hear its—to me—terrifying cry.

It was years before it came to me that the cry must have been that of the infant downstairs, but that goat remained (to me) hidden in the recesses of the dark closets of that attic.

Once I was sent up to carry some soiled clothes in the basket. I went up as usual with my back scraping the wall and my eyes glued to the cabinet door. Just as I was about to open the clothes basket it turned over. A great "Boo oo oo" greeted me, and something living moved among the scattered clothes. I don't know what happened then. I next found myself in Ma's room, and before me was Mrs. Avril and her daughter Fannie, about 14 years old.[9] It seems that Fanny had found a communication door unlocked between her attic and ours and had come in our side. Hearing my footsteps on the stair she hid in the basket and, seeing who it was, made a great Boo "for fun." I know she was scolded both by her mother and mine. The attic communication was locked, but so long as we lived there I lived in terror of "up stairs."

The two first weeks of brother Paul's life were happy times to us. Every morning Aunt Pauline Pinsard[10] sent a servant for us, before breakfast (3 of us), and we stayed at her house until dusk. On our return we generally found Aunt Honorine Frémaux[11] at our house. She would see that a lamp was left with brother and I upstairs, and through her influence Ruth also slept up there. We loved Aunt Honorine, but our adoration and our heaven were at Aunt Pauline's corner of Orleans and St. Claude. Aunt Pauline was quite wealthy, I believe. She was not our aunt at all but the wife of Ma's first cousin Isidore Pinsard. She had one daughter by a first marriage and he had a son by a first marriage.[12] There had been a little girl baby who lived two years. I once heard my mother remark that Aunt Pauline had lost her child 3 years before. If she had said the child died I would have understood. I can not remember how young I was when I understood death, but lost, why should a person lose a child; why did they ever cease to look for it? I would often ponder over this thing. I don't know where the expression "Virgen Forest" had been pronounced before me, but anyway it got connected in my mind with that lost baby and I would look up into Aunt Pauline's beautiful face and wonder why, oh why, did she not go in the virgin forests and look and look for her baby before it died of fright at night or starved to death. I wondered if she knew how *very* scared that little thing must have been. That thought was the only check to my adoration. I was very timid and very much of afraid of mother, so it was long before I dared to make a remark to any one about Aunt Pauline. I finally mentioned it to Pa—no one was ever afraid of Pa. Unfortunately his occupation kept him for months away from us, at times.

After Pa had explained I was very remorseful for my thoughts of Aunt Pauline, and ever after I was always my very gentlest with her, as a sort of atonement.

When brother Paul was christened she and Uncle Pinsard were his sponsors. She offered Ma her lost baby's beautiful rose wood crib. She cried when making the offer, and it was quite a while before she got composed. Ma did not take the crib and some 7 or 8 years later aunt had use for it herself.

With all that, I was in such fear of Ma and punishment. (I deserved it at times.) I once spilled some ink and water on the floor—playing with an old ink bottle. Ma saw the wet spot and called out, "Céline what is that on the floor?"

"Water, Ma," I answered. It seems to me yet that a whirlwind struck me just then: Ma jerked me about cuffed me right and left till my ears were ringing then turned me up and spanked me with a piece of jumping rope. It was not for the spot, but for the lie! As a cure, Ma hit the right remedy, I do not remember of having ever tried to disguise the truth after that day. What puzzled my little brain then was how Ma knew that the wet spot was other than water. And the conviction came to me: "Ma's, of course, know everything, like God does, so it is no use lying."

Aunt Honorine and her children we saw very seldom. Just on stately visits now and then. She had two little girls of sister's and my age, they were both beauties.[13] Sister was also an unusually pretty child.

Aunt has told me since that she seldom came because Ma was too strict. She said she never paid one visit that Ma did not punish one or all of us before it was over, and she (aunt) could not bear to see children punished for insignificant things such as noise or the upsetting of a chair or slamming of a door.

The fact is that once, in getting under a bed to hide (Beds were then made fully 2 feet high from floor to mattress), well, getting under one I cut my knee on a piece of glass that happened to be caught in the seam of the matting. Ma bandaged me up and gave each of us, Léon and I, the verb "To crawl" to write on our slate. That meant at least 2 hours penance.

Don't stare, reader; yes, I was not yet five years old and I wrote French verbs. For my 5th birthday I was presented with a *Grammaire de Laumont*. Before that, I had been taught orally. I remember reciting a piece of 10 verses entitled "Oh Dieu qu'adore mon Père," on the New Year before my fourth birthday.

A little thing happened that day which made no impression at the time, but which I remembered as I did all that happened out of the daily routine. We were on our way to wish Grandma a happy New Year when we met our cousins going on the same errand to *their* Grandma. One of them announced, "We are going to move soon."

"Yes—where to?" we asked.

"Right here" Mémé said. "Right in this house, as soon as the Spaniards move out; we will move in, I think next week." I looked up at the house and just then the Spaniards were coming out all dressed up. There were 2 or 3 boys in black velvet suits with long curly hair falling well below their collar, and a little girl my size. I don't remember her dress, but she had on a red silk hood or bonnet. That was all. We passed on. Years afterward, I married one of the little Spaniards and the girl Sara has had her home with me.[14]

Mémé and Hortense were dressed in plaid silk that day, and sister and I wore white cashmere trimmed in pink silk galloons. Our hats were pink plush with a bunch of little rosebuds half hidden in tulle on each ear. These pompons were tacked on the tie ribbon of the hats. Elastic was not used at that time, and the tie ribbon was 3 inches or so wide and tied in a rosette under the chin. We also had on bronze-colored prunella gaiters made to order. I remember the man taking our measures. We were very proud of the shoes.

Grandma lived on Royal St. near St. Louis St. That was the fashionable quarter then. Every Sunday we took dinner there. It was always a very ceremonious affair. There was always company, gentlemen and ladies, so we children had a pretty lonely time on Sunday. Ma generally left home at 1:30. Dinner was at 3 o'clock sharp. I don't know what time it was finished but I know that in winter the candelabras were placed on the table with the roast. The dinner was served in French style in courses, and I was always very sleepy before the dessert came. On one day I did go to sleep and was carried up stairs. I woke up to find myself lying on a rug, my head on a cushion—a red ground with a tiger worked on it. The tiger had yellow glass eyes. I felt very much rebuked, and was afraid Ma would scold, besides, so I stayed upstairs and played with the tiger until Ma was ready to go. Pa was there that day, and he remarked, "Well, little lady, you won't sleep on the way home tonight; you have slept enough." And he took my hand in his strong, warm grasp. When we reached the Congo Square the nine o'clock cannon was about to be shot off, and Pa pretended that it was a battle, and he *would be* very scared if I had been sleepy and could but hamper him in his flight, and when all of a sudden it did go off he said, "Oh how brave we are; we did not run." I felt happy, as I always did with Pa.

But the very next Sunday I went to sleep again. I woke up this time in a corner of the dining room. The servant was putting the room to right. She helped me out of the narrow corner and volunteered that Grand-ma was vexed at me, and I had better not go in the parlor. She also said she had kept me some dessert. "Did Grandma say to keep it?" I asked.

"Why, no, child, I told you her war vexed."

So young as I was, I did not take the dessert. "No, Odille," I said. "I don't want it. Grand-ma might not want me to have it; dinner is so long here," I added by way of explanation.

Occasionally Grandma gave us playing cards and a big coral beaded pin to perforate their outlines, that we might look how pretty they were by lamplight or firelight. Once an old maid took dinner there—she was not good looking, very thin and sharp looking. They called her Miss Gautier.[15] We saw her there often, but this was the first time we had met her. She played with us some, and I heard her tell Grand-ma that we ought to have toys or some sort of amusement at her house. Grandma acted on the advice and we always found some sort of toy or game for our use after that. We liked Miss Gautier. She always made us laugh at table and no one rebuked us. We did not feel sleepy when she was there.

Once during our stay in New Orleans we went to see a dog and monkey show. Sister was with us too. And once I went with Grand-ma and Pa to a real theatre—the Orleans Theatre—to see *Les Amours du Diable*. Cahiée was the star actress. I was very delighted, and many of the scenes are present in my memory. I have never seen the piece played since and I don't think I would like to go see it now. My remembrances are so pleasant.

After a while Father thought best to have us in Baton Rouge, as he was there most of the time when not on duty in the parishes.

Just before we left there was a great balloon ascension in the Congo square. A Mr. Gadart was the "Balloonist." We went to Aunt Pauline's to see it. Pa explained the process of inflation as it went on. Aunt Pauline's was our place to see all the sights. The Congo square, then surrounded by a high iron railing, was the place for all out door sports, festivals, fireworks, etc., and sitting on aunt's front gallery we commanded a perfect view of every kind of show that went on in the square. Climbing a greasy pole with prizes at the top seemed to be a favorite amusement. Then there were races in gunny sacks and other things perhaps not participated in by *nice* people, but very enjoyable to us from the safe shelter of aunt's balcony.

When the time came for our departure, Pa said we would go on board the *Algerine* which was a "State boat" then undergoing repairs at the Algiers' Dry Dock.[16] We moved aboard five or six days before she was ready for the trip. It was great fun living on a boat high out of the water. If Ma had just let us off with lessons during that time!! But Ma never left off lessons. We did not know the meaning of vacation: only Sunday was without school, and then we had "duties" to write.

After two days on board the *Algerine* was floated. Then came the work of fitting her with a powerful crane.[17] Father was among the men on deck. Mr. Hebert was also there when a rope gave way which would have caused great disaster if not held rigidly. Father grasped it at the same moment the hook of an immense pully broke, fell to the deck, and rebounded to father's face. The men scattered in terror, expecting the whole framework to fall on them, but, Pa bleeding and spitting his teeth to the floor, held on to that rope. He could not talk or call and only his eyes appealed. Mr. Hebert was first to realize the state of affairs. He took the rope, calling the men to their senses. As Pa was relieved he fell in a swoon. As soon as possible was carried to the cabin and laid on a table. A doctor from Algiers was summoned, also a barber to shave Pa's mustache. It was found that every tooth, upper and lower on the right side, had been crushed and the lip split up in two places. Passing by the door of the cabin I could see the blood dripping from the table to the floor and spattering the feet of all the men who were helping. Ma was very busy and for the first time of our lives we had no regular lessons that day. It was weeks before Pa could take anything but liquid food and his face was bandaged quite a long time.

The state boats were small, stern-wheeled steam-boats used for all State work such as opening Bayous or closing them. They were not intended for passengers or freight but had deck place for lumber, tools, and electrical apparatuses. Bunk rooms for the laborers (State Slaves) and 3 rooms for the officers—Captain, engineer, and any state official who directed the work. As the boat was being repaired Pa, for the time, replaced every officer, and we occupied the whole cabin. An old negro was Cook and his cooking was very different from what we were accustomed to have. For instance, he acquainted us with ham & eggs, bisquits, and "greens & salt pork." The latter Ma could never be induced to taste and we young ones did not like. How little we thought that in the Sixties we would have thought a "mess of greens" quite a sumptuous feast.

One thing this old cook made that was a joy to us: they were little dried apple pies. He made them just for us. As a kind of "spoil," he would even let us see him make them. He would roll out a piece of dough round, put in the stewed, dried apples, and wrap them in just as grocery men wrap a five cts. worth of peas in a paper. We thought it fine and delicious—we who never set foot in a kitchen, to be allowed to be there and see things. We were having that freedom on account of Pa's sufferings, but we did not realize it at the time. We did not speak a word of English and only one of the "hands" spoke creole, which we understood almost as little as we did English.

In the dock just next to ours was a large ship. I do not know its nationality, but it was not French (I knew a French flag when I saw it). The sailors were always trying to be friendly with us, especially sister who was so very pretty. They would give us shells and apples and little wooden carved dolls, etc. They would tie them to long twines and swing them further and further till they reached our deck. My first gift was a pretty sea shell. Ma would not let me accept any more—"A *big* girl, a *lady*, was not to take from sailor men." I remember wishing I was *not a lady*. Sister got so many little things, and Léon so many nuts and apples—all of which he would have divided with me, but he had to eat them surrepticiously. Ma was not allowing eating between meals. Being a boy he was at times out of Ma's sight, but we girls, never.

Finally the big ship was finished and all decked with bunting, and the sailors were in gala dress. There was a big feast spread out on deck. We all were invited to come aboard for the launching but we did not go. Four niggers held an awning over Pa, who was in a big rocking chair. He bowed and pointed to his bandaged face as an excuse for not going over.

The big ship glided out of her dock and passed so close to us that the sailors left two red handkerchiefs of things on our rail for sister and I. Cakes and raisins and fruit and candies. In mine there were all the little trinkets Ma had made me refuse. "My Sailor," as I called him, was a large, young man that was always laughing and singing. The day they left he wore a bright colored sash about his waist and took it off and waved it till the ship had turned the point. Sister's sailor was a little old man and he sent kisses to her, and it made Pa laugh; and set his face to bleeding. Poor Father—he suffered very much at that time. He did not talk for weeks; he would write on a white slate with a lead pencil. It was my first acquaintance with a white slate. If the Yankees had not stolen it from me during the war, I would have it yet. Pa gave it to me when he was able to talk.

In New Orleans we left few friends, as we children were not allowed to visit at all. There was a little girl one year younger than myself; she lived just across the street from us. She was mourning for her mother and was raised by two old ladies, very small, very thin and very solemn. I never knew their name but the child's father was Mr. Cairon. She was a spoiled child but I was allowed to play with her occasionally.

Brother saw a good deal of the Joubert boys, but I was afraid of them. They had gotten me in trouble once and I was ashamed to meet them. It was this way: they had what creole children called a magic lantern. It was a soap box in which were two revolving uprights on which were wound a certain length of pictures, maybe a yard or two. A little piece of lighted candle illuminated the interior. A small hole in the back of the box permitted the happy owner of 2 pins to see the picture once. I had never seen one before and, having procured 4 pins and Ma's permission, we went to see the thing. They had it on their front steps, four doors from ours. Well, there were several little children ahead of us. Only one could look at a time. The wind rose and put out the candle several times. So when it came to Léon's time to look, Joe Joubert took the box in on the table in the front room. I felt dubious about stepping in, but the three Jouberts laughed and said I took my mother for an ogre. What difference did it make, three steps inside a room? Against my better judgment we went in, and before Léon had seen half Ma was calling for us, and we had to leave. Léon got his ears pulled and I was whipped and sent to bed for having let boys persuade me to do against my judgement. That was bad enough, but those boys came over to explain to Ma that I had not seen anything yet and etc. They were just in time to see me chastised and undressed.

I never looked at or spoke to them after that, so I was not going to miss them by leaving. But there was one I grieved to leave. A young girl, nearly grown—Luciana Dubuch. She also lived opposite, in a big, two-storied house. She was very kind to me, gave me scraps for Doll's dresses and even made a few for me. She would kiss me and pet me and altogether protect me from her brother, who was a great tease and three or four years our senior. I had given her my whole little childish heart. I thought her beautiful. Once she went to a party, and ran over to show me how she was dressed. Her dress was white tulle trimmed in roses, and a wreath of full-blown roses crowned her pretty brow. Her hair was long and curled. Yes, I regretted to leave her.

Pa had bought almost an entire outfit of household goods, and every day some would be brought aboard the Algerine. Finally she was all ready and we started up the river. At Plaquemine we stopped 3 hours. Pa had some state business there. At Donaldsonville we also stopped. Our friends the Bercegeai's came aboard and stayed several hours. How my friends had remembered me was proven by the fact that Féfé brought me my precious Jug well wrapped in paper and we had quite a deliberation to know if it was safe for me to take it. Would not Ma object to it again and throw it overboard? So we decided that our friend the cook would keep it in the kitchen and put it with Pa's private tools when they would be landed in Baton Rouge. Having decided this momentous question, we indulged in all the fun we could possibly crowd in a few hours. Then again we were under way.

A house had been secured by a friend of Father's, but when he and Ma saw it, they found it not at all suitable. With many recommendations Ma & Pa left the four of us aboard and went house hunting. By noon they had secured a very pretty one very nicely situated one block from the State House—where the Engineer's office was. Into it we moved and remained till driven out by the Bombardment in June (I think) of the year 1862.

Baton Rouge: The Halcyon Days

TAKING IT ALL IN ALL, our life in Baton Rouge was perhaps the happiest of our existence. It certainly was Ma's halcyon days.

If it had not been for Ma's idea that her duty to us rested mainly in educating us herself, we would have been as happy as other children. But she *would* teach us, and teach us incessantly, in this way: we never played out of her hearing, so if we played "ladies" and pretended to go traveling, we *had* to go to some place that really existed in that special part of the globe. If we mentioned a name of a city or a lake, she would call out, "Where is that city? What river runs near it? What is manufactured there?" and we felt as if we had an extra lesson on hand. Then again our little friends often refused to come and play with us because it was always as if we were in school. And she very seldom let us go to their house to play. When she did we were given an hour to return, and woe betided us if we missed the time by a fraction of a minute. If we did, our punishment was generally from 25 to 100 lines to copy. And when copied, we had to read them out to her. And they had to make sense if we had to write 2 or 3 lines more to come to a period. I do not suppose any children on earth ever copied as many lines as we did. One of the most frequent causes was for speaking English among ourselves. No one around us spoke French, and Mother feared we would forget it. To others we *had* to speak English (after we learned it) but to each other it was positively forbidden, and she never missed us for a "Yes," or "Come here." She would call out, "Five lines, Léon," or "Céline," as the case might be. The younger ones, Francine and Paul, 3 lines, or when Paul was *too* little to write she would tie a handkerchief over his mouth for five minutes by the clock.

Ma had always suffered from headaches which lasted two or three hours. By this time they increased to lasting five hours, and later still seven hours. Any outdoor exertion brought them on besides the regular ones every seven or eight days.

Notwithstanding, our lessons were as regular as clockwork. Breakfast was at 7:30. Léon & I both had to have our verbs written before then, or a piece of dry bread was brought to our desk and we could nibble it while finishing. Father never interfered. Pa *supported* us but Ma *raised* us, and she did it "by hand." Dickens did not invent Pip—there were several of them at our house.

Pa was our play-fellow when he was home. He built us swings and safe see-saws, and we had a tightrope to walk on, and jumping ropes and stilts. He was a great play-fellow. When Pa was playing with us we expanded; we became, as it were, intoxicated with joy. We forgot that it had to end, and it always came as a positive shock when Ma would call out, "Time for this-and-thus now—get quiet," and Pa would stop us, maybe in the act of a sumersault or a pirouette, and stand us correctly upright, and with as much good humor go back to his reading or other occupations.

On winter evenings Pa would sometimes solemnly get up from his occupation, walk out, and return with the Buffalo Robe (he never sent a servant for it, always got it from the closet himself). We knew what that meant: we would hurriedly take off our clothes and put on our night-gowns, and then we had a romp. Oh, such romps: pillow fights and etc. I was in my glory, for I must say, naturally, I would have been wild. I loved to climb, to run, to shout, to jump and etc. Léon was very silent and quiet; it even worried Father, and many of our rough toys and games were offered as inducements to *wake him up*, as it were. Pa had him a fine pair of stilts made. Léon did not take to them at all; I did.

I can remember Father putting a gum drop or a bun on the front gallery balustrade and starting the little neighbors, Léon, and I, all on stilts to go around the house, the first one around to get the candy. Léon seldom, or perhaps never, reached there first. Léon was very intelligent and had a remarkable memory, but he was slow of movement and *hated* lessons. I could not blame him then; I did not love them myself, considering study time as so much taken from my rightful play hours. Other children of my age played all day. I had not known that in New Orleans, but here in Baton Rouge we had the Larguier children next door. The three youngest, who were respectively one year older than we three, had not yet started to school when we met them.[18]

I had learned early that repining about lessons brought longer hours and various punishments, so I never repined. Léon could not take things that way. I have seen him sit before his slate holding his pencil till the breakfast bell rung, without having written a single word of his verbs. At times I could write one tense of mine and one of his alternately, to keep us even, and then he would get behind on the infinitive tenses. Ma never detected the different writing. I suppose both were as bad one as the other. If Léon was punished it was almost as bad as if I were, as I never played alone. I would sit disconsolate and wait for him. The worse was, he did not even hurry with his lines to copy. When I was eight years old Ma began to start me on abstracts of ancient history. I would read a chapter and write it from memory on a slate. Ma corrected it. I had 3 lines for every mistake of any kind, and after lessons the slate work was copied in ink on fool's cap paper. Oh, those abstracts!! How many tears they cost me. I have them now, the dreadful things, and how blurred some places are. And well I know it was where big tears splashed, maybe because my fingers were so cold. There was no fire in the school room, only the rising sun till about 10:00 A.M. Maybe because some children had come to play, and they had to be turned off because we were at study, or maybe—as often happened—Ma had cut out a whole leaf for a blot or a skipped sentence or a mistake of some sort. A leaf meant two pages!! Sometimes it was the very last line that was bad and two pages meant two hours writing and when in tears, any amount longer.

We had been in Baton Rouge about a year when we had another little brother.[19] When he came I was six years and six months old. Paul had been in a way given to Léon and called him little father (Tite pop's), and Ma gave me that one—Eddie—and for years he called me tite mama. When we found Ma in bed with the baby she called me and said I must be housekeeper while she was disabled. Mine was the business to give out meals and to see that the children behaved at table—that was not much, as Pa was home and he always made the meals a joy, so no one thought of *not* behaving.

The third or fourth day of her sickness (Eddie had sore eyes) Ma asked me for some soft lint out of her top bureau drawer. I could not open it, so she got up and opened her arms to reach the handles, and there she remained perfectly still. I called father and the nurse but for several days she was as one crucified with her stiff arms wide open. Then commenced my ministrations to Eddie. Holding him to Ma's breast was quite a hard performance and caring for his eyes was another. But he was *my* baby; I could not do too much for him. At that time I became acquainted with cupping. Dry-cupping they did to Ma, and blood-letting cupping was used on one of the slaves during that week.

We certainly said fewer lessons just then, but we would come to Ma's bedside and recite and our written exercises were done as usual.

The same day of Eddie's birth there was a little sister born to the children next door.

When the time came to christen Eddie Grand-ma came on a visit. I liked Grandma before, but that visit made me love and admire her. She was a small woman and the generations of gentlewomen showed in every line of her aristocratic face and hands. Her hands were beautiful: so white and soft, and the nails so pink. Grand-Ma loved dress and she had beautiful clothes. Her hair was nearly white—she must have been 61 years of age. She wore beautiful morning caps of embroidery, and her morning dresses were opened down the front on embroidered petticoats. She embroidered a great deal of the time. Her thimble, I remember, was tipped in coral, and her needle was never lower than that tip. She told me "Ladies" always sewed with short needles and touched them with the very tip of the thimble. I tried for years to sew like her but to the present day the second row of dents on my thimble shows that I am less a "Lady." All Grand-Ma's things were beautiful. Her writing case was beautiful, of ebony inlaid with pearl and gold finishings. During her visit Pa employed the evenings engraving her monogram on every piece, and on the seal he cut a steam Mail boat with the Motto "Tu pars. Arriveras tu?" (Thou startedth; wilt thou arrive?). The pen holder was beautiful and had a gold clasp to receive and hold a quill pen point. The outer case or box was of tortoise shell inlaid in gold. My daughter Florestine now owns the case, which is much over 100 years old and looks as if just bought.

The christening was quite a gala affair. Mr. & Mrs. Louis Hebert were sponsors for Edouard Charles Frémaux, and my little baby I thought beautiful in my own christening robe and a white cloak lined in pale blue silk.

Pa took Grandma to visit all the places of interest about the town and vicinity, and I went everywhere with them. One place visited was the State Penitentiery.[20] Here are the memories it left me: great high, white walls with turrets every now and then with armed men walking from one to the next and back again. Then a queer gateway like a cistern with a stave out. We got in it turned and we found ourselves in a little yard surrounded with high iron bars. A turn key opened a ponderous lock, and we went into the place proper. The big lock clicked behind us and Pa remarked that we were just as locked up as the convicts. It soon was the dining hour. All the convicts marched into a long hall. Each stood before his own cell. They were each given a tin bowl of soup, a plate full of beans and a piece of salt meat. A big piece of light bread covered the bowl. Then each man entered his little cell. The doors were locked then a man passed around big tin cups of coffee which the men took through the gratings. At that time convicts were not allowed to speak to each other. This dinner was a revelation to me. I had always believed that prisoners had only bread and water. Yet this locking up of silent, great big men made me silently cry. Then we visited the looms. They were employed in making cotton drilling and heavy canvas cloth. The looms were noisy but there again was silence of voices, only the foremen cried out an order now and then. We did not visit the women's department. When we passed through the office Pa bought several little brass bound pails made of alternate strips of white and red Cedar. They would hold barely a pint of liquid and were very well finished off. They were made by a convict and sold for the benefit of his two children who were in an aunt's keeping. Pa bought quite a number. I have mine yet, with a "C" burned in one of the white strips. Pa put the "C" there. Pa left an order for a quantity of the canvas sufficient to make a sail for a "cat boat" he owned.

Grand-ma's visit came to an end and I went with Pa to see her to the boat. She took the *Eclipse*, which showed a brilliant sun with golden rays between her smoke stacks. Pa made some kind of remark about its being hard to represent an eclipse so they had done their best. Grand-Ma laughed, and we left. That was to be the last time I should see her on earth. On the way home Pa explained to me all about eclipses of sun or moon and took me in the state house in a room where there were celestial globes and appliances where he fully illustrated his teaching, and I went home feeling very proud of having learned something without having to *study* it.

Pa's lessons were so easily learned, and were always object lessons. Long before that, when we lived in New Orleans, he had taken me to a foundry on the Algier's side and explained and showed me the process of molding for and casting iron. I can see yet the great cauldrons of molten iron almost white, with sparks as big as nuts crossing and recrossing the brilliant surface, and the great crane swinging slowly toward us. Pa sat me on his shoulder. Then a sort of a hinged door under the cauldron was opened and the contents sputtering sizzling and hissing spread into the prepared moulds in the earth. And blue and yellow flames seemed to come out of everywhere. Men with long iron bars were going and coming. The casting was to be balcony railings. The scene reminded me of the "hell scene" in the only opera I had then seen.

The evenings at home were spent very uniformly. The servant would light two or four candles and place them on the dining table. She would then bring Pa a large cupful of hot "Bouillon," which he ate with strips of bread cut lengthwise; while eating he would talk of the different news of the day and talk to us. Then when he had finished and the crumbs well brushed away he would spread his drawing or painting apparatus on the end of the table. Ma would seat herself half-way down the length of it with a book, and read out loud to Pa till long after we had gone to bed. That was our time of silence; we sat around that table and played, but it had to be silently. We played with paper dolls most of the winter. We made and painted dolls and dresses. We had our own common paint boxes, but if Pa was painting we often got a dip of his fine paints. He was very liberal with his chrome yellow and Prussian blue. When seven o'clock began to strike Ma closed the book (she always used a few strands of red floss as a book mark) and made a sign to the youngest to come and say his prayer at her knee. We older ones would quickly put away the toys, then in turn said our prayers and went to bed.

Those prayers! I hope God heard them and registered them some-where. I could not remember when I learned mine, so Léon and I were all right about that, but Francine and Paul, and later Eddy—it was dreadful. They seemed to go to napping the minute they knelt down, and Ma would shake them and scold and have them in tears every night. If the siege was unusually hard Pa would get up and go outside, or go around locking up the house. It only came to me when I was grown that it irritated him and, not wanting to interfere, he fled the field.

Sometimes I would get interested in the reading and listen attentively, but the next day I was all lost and could not fit the new names to the old, and I felt very ill used. Sometimes I would copy the name of a book on a little slip of paper, to get the book and read when I was grown. Oh, the many, many things I was going to do, and the many I was NOT going to do, when I was grown.

Our friendship for the Larguier children began with our first day and lasted till the war separated us as to the others. As to myself they are my dear friends yet. I never lost a friendship once acquired. I was very fortunate. I gave a lot of love, and reaped a lot of friendship.

I remember the first day of our arrival. In the evening the children came to our front fence. There were Callie, Isidore, and Willie, and a negro girl called Felly. They spoke to us, but as we did not understand one word of English, they soon left in disgust then came back with an old nurse, "Aunt" Gawt, who spoke creole, and through her they learned whom we were and the impediment that stood in the way of a better understanding. In a comparatively short time we could communicate with each other, and for years our games were together—however, with a fence separating us. It was an old-fashioned cypress split picket fence. There are very few in existence now. They were not very close, and we were on our side and they on theirs. Dolls and toys passed to and fro for about three years, after which our mothers allowed one picket put on hinges for our convenience. Even then there was no promiscuous going and coming. When we were allowed to go over we had our time to return. And if we came home sooner to get a toy or anything, Ma made us stay, saying people did not make two visits to the same persons the same day.

Ma never became intimate with Mrs. Larguier. In fact, I never knew her intimate with anyone. She had pleasant acquaintances, but there it stopped.

In April, which followed Eddie's christening, Ma was written to to come to her mother, who was quite ill at a friend's at Bayou Goula. The letter reached her early after breakfast and at 2 P.M., having made all recommendations, Ma was ready and left aboard the *Laurel Hill*. She took with her Eddie and his nurse. Father was also on his way down the river to some Bayou. Ma has since told us that a servant slept in the house by her orders, but at the time we did not know it, and Léon and I had the responsibility of ourselves and of the two little ones.

We had our duties all mapped out for us. We were to recite to each other 3 fables each, write so much, and recite so many chapters of catechism, I to Léon, he to me. Francine had so many lines to copy a day. I think it was 7 lines. Paul then 2 years and 7 months was the only one exempt from any duty. And we were neither to visit or have visitors so long as she would be away.

I remember that time perfectly distinctly. The only undiscipline we allowed ourselves was to call out in reciting to each other "Grande tête de veau bouilli."[21] Who made you? And the other would answer "Grande tête de veau bouilli," God made me! Of course it made the lesson longer, but it was such fun to say foolishness without rebuke. We would snatch up little echoes of babyishness when we could. *Fun* seemed so elusive and fleeting to us. I can remember very few days when our gladness lasted until we were in bed. It always seemed as if we must pay for any little joy we might have had through the day.

I remember one perfect day. It was a picnic day. I have written it up separately.[22]

Mother was away just eight days. Grandma died and was temporarily buried on the Sigure plantation.[23]

Before this, maybe the summer before, we had had a pleasure trip to Donaldsonville aboard the State Boat, *The Walker.* Pa's work was to be for several days in Bayou Lafourche, and we spent those 2 or 3 days at the Bercegeai's. The very first evening I got in trouble. We were all running around the dining room table, and in and out of the house. As I started down the steps a servant was coming up with a soup tureen of hot "Sagamité," boiled cracked corn in milk. I was in short-sleeves, and both my arms went into the hot mush above the elbow. Féfé caught me, carried me to the pump and tried to save me. I was quite burned but not blistered. I made no outcry for fear of a punishment, but alas! Féfé had not cared for my dress; it was all wet and dabbled with the milky starch. Ma *must* know. During the supper nothing was said. Féfé put me on a big napkin and my red arms were not noticed; we little folks were at the foot of the table. But after supper it had to be known. There was to be a visit to some of our neighbors. Ma put on my gown and sat me behind a door, to be punished till they returned. I heard Mme. Aimé tell Féfé to stay home and see that I did not cry too much, and was not frightened. When all had gone Féfé came and played with me. I did not leave my lowly seat but she fetched a doll and a doll crib. And we played "Madame" till we heard the gate click. When Féfé picked up the things, and Ma being almost on us, she had just time to slide under the bed with the toys. The Dimity spread reaching the floor—as was the fashion those days—hid her completely. Ma gave me a long scolding about rough games and added. "I will not whip you because you were really alone. I was afraid Féfé was with you, and of course you would not have been very punished."

Féfé knew me, she knew that in my duty-ground mind I was going to confess that she *had* been with me. So she raised a tiny place of the spread and silently beseeched me not to confess. I did not, so we both escaped that time.

In the night Mme. Aimé came and anointed my arms with something and the next day they felt less hot. During the morning Féfé took me to see a relative at the other end of the town—then not nearly the size it is now. As we passed along, persons would call out, "Whose little girl have you there, Féfé?"

And three or four times she answered, "Mrs. Frémaux's little girl; this is Céline," and we would have to stop and be questioned. It was all very kind, but annoyed my guide, so the *next* time a query came, she answered, "Mrs. Monkey's little girl. You don't know her." And we would pass on. It struck me as very foolish that grown people would believe *that* was a name. And Féfé replied "Oh, yes, lots of these people are very foolish."

My first word on getting back was, "Mme. Aimé, the people here are so foolish they. . . ." I never got any further. Ma snatched me up, cuffed me well, took off my hat and top dress, and said I would spend the rest of the day in the dark garret alone for calling people foolish whom I came to visit. Probably if she had heard me out she would have been less angry.

Up in the garret she took me with a piece of dry bread. Oh, Ma could not have known what dark meant to me. She shoved me in, shut the door, locked it and put the key in her pocket. In the first moments I thought I would die with the fright. I had fallen on a pile of newspapers, and the rustle of my stiff petticoat against them sent cold chills all over me. I kept my eyes shut for fear of seeing the dark. After a while I heard the dinner bell, and as I was directly over the dining room I could hear the people and dared to open my eyes. And behold! it was not so very dark. Both windows had cracks above and below the shutters and I could see to distinguish objects pretty well. I sat up more comfortably and ate my bread.

After the meal downstairs Camille ran up to the door and whispered, "Push the left shutter open—*not* the right one, the left one. I can't stay here; your Ma will catch me. Don't cry." I had not cried before, having been too frightened, but at the words "Don't Cry" I gave way completely and sobbed aloud. I did not push open the shutter. I was too scared to walk about then. I did not know which was the left one, so I stayed on, it seemed to me, hours and hours. Finally all noises in the house ceased, and a moment later I heard a thump, a heavy thump.

I was frightened into saying, "My God, Ma, come and *beat* me, but please come."

Then I heard Camille at the window. "Don't scream like that," he said. "Come here and push the shutter; I can't open it from outside." So I went, and almost fell out in my violence. He was on a ladder—that was the thump. He came in and explained that all had gone up the bayou in a boat and would fetch Pa back to supper. Then we played. There were many books of pictures and many colored fashion plates. He made me choose one (I have it yet) and he read me tales. And when he thought the folks might be coming back, he would peep through the crack in the right window, which was in view from the road.

Finally he saw them coming, so he fixed me on a little broken chair right by the door. He pushed the left window shut. Oh, how dark it was. I heard the ladder's thud as it struck the ground. After a while Pa came to get me. He took me in his arms and kissed me on the neck, murmuring something. I never knew what, but it started my tears afresh. He took me straight to the bed room. When Féfé came to bed—I slept with her—she brought me a lot of crullers and some honey and milk. And she said, "Don't mention this supper, but it is a secret between your father and me." Dear Féfé, she had helped me get in that punishment. But how many and many times she helped me out of scrapes. And always with Pa's knowledge. It never dawned on us till we were nearly grown that perhaps Pa would have been more lenient in "raising" us.

When we travelled home Ma had some sewing for me to do that I might not be idle during the six-hour trip. My possessions were increased one doll, one doll cradle, one picture, one squirrel tail, and a little glass mug by that trip.

✑ Childhood ✑

WE WORE very deep mourning for Grandma. I had been to a children's party two days before Ma heard of Grandma's sickness. I had worn a blue barège dress trimmed in wavy satin ribbons. Sister, being too young, had not gone. Ma finished her dress after our mourning was made and gave both dresses to a Mrs. Allain, relative of the Heberts.

When a year and one day had passed, Father busied himself to have Grandma's remains moved to the family tomb in New Orleans.

In the meantime, Ma had inherited what she could find of her Mother's things. There was a slave woman named Odille, and many things.[1] It seems that in breaking up house-keeping for the summer, Grandma had stored many articles with friends. The Delpeuch family had the bookcases and books, which they returned.[2] The Choppard family all the glassware and crockery, also returned.[3] A lace chest of drawers was also returned, and many things, but the actual furniture of a five-roomed house, together with a square piano and family portraits, were never heard from. Grandma's business man, having robbed some persons, had in his distress committed suicide a few weeks after Grandma's demise, so all trace of many things was lost. Grandma, in her will, had left to Miss Numi Locke (Mr. Gustave Breaud's 1st wife) a pearl necklace; to Mr. Farnet (testamentary executor), a very fine emerald ring;[4] to his wife (Seraphie Delpeuch), a gold bracelet studded with diamonds; to Aunt

Pauline, an amber bracelet, the amber of which had been picked up by Grandma on the shore of the Baltic sea at the time of her trip to Russia. If anything else was given, I never heard. Ma gave Mrs. Sigur's eldest daughter Grandma's coral-tipped thimble and the pearl-trimmed one to another friend.

When all was ready for Pa's trip, solemn though it was, he said he would take me with him and keep me ten days in New Orleans. A little black leather trunk was packed for me. I was in due time dressed and my hat tied on. We were sitting on the front gallery waiting for the signal from the man Robert, who was to notify us as the boat got in sight. The weather was cloudy and it began to rain just as Robert made the signal. Ma quietly took off my hat and announced that I might go on some other trip when it did not rain. Pa suggested that it would not rain ten days and Robert could carry me to the boat, but I had to stay. Presently Robert returned with the little trunk on his head, and that was all. This was my first great disappointment.

Trip to New Orleans

LATER THAT SUMMER Pa took Léon on a trip to New Orleans. They started late in the evening. Léon told me he felt sick at his stomach but he did not tell Ma for fear of having to stay home. Ma always deplored his secrecy, but Léon never did. He had no sooner gotten aboard than he gave up his dinner and was put to bed. When Pa retired later he found the boy had high fever and in the morning when they landed in New Orleans he had a fine, fully developed case of measles. Father bought a blanket from the boat, got a closed carriage and took him to Aunt Pauline's. Both Marie and Victor were off at boarding school, whereas at Aunt Honorine's there were four little ones.

Well, Léon was petted and spoiled. They gave him fine toys, bought him a fine magic lantern, had little boys come and play with him and in every way made his six weeks' imprisonment a time of joy. Meanwhile, at home, we were all four in bed with the same disease.

When Léon returned we were all well again and more than ever I desired to go on a trip to the city. My time came at last during the following winter. It was a very cold day and the wind was blowing. The little black trunk was again packed and after Robert left with it and Pa's valise to watch for the *Laurel Hill,* I whispered to Pa that we had better go. I was so afraid Ma would think it was too cold as we were all five recovering from the whooping cough. Maybe Pa had some sort of a misgiving, too, for immediately we left the house. On the levee it was bitter cold and so dark. There was no landing house or shelter of any kind so Pa walked up and down the wharf. Then he told me to put my hand in his pocket but the pocket was too high. My hand would not go in. Presently we saw the chimneys of a boat round the point. Pa said, "Here we are." I told him that was not the *Laurel Hill* and he pretended he thought it was. He rolled a paper like a spy glass and told me to look well and see if there were not great carved leaves on those chiminies. Of course, I could not see leaves but instead saw the Indian figure suspended between the plain edged smoke-stacks and I said so. Pa took the paper, looked, and said, "Well, we do not want the *Natchez.* Your name is not Pocahontas." So we turned off the levee and went under a shed. An Italian sold fruit there and he had a parrot in a tin cage. I had never seen a parrot nearby, and the man made it talk for us. Then Pa told me all about Pocahontas.

Presently the *Laurel Hill* hove in sight. We left the shelter and went to the water's edge. We walked up and down to keep warm and Pa was singing kind of under his breath, "Oh que nous nous amushames [sic] Chez le père Godichon. Nous n'étions ni hommes ni femmes. Nous étions des auvergnats."[5] I had never heard the foolish thing before and he sang it with such a comical twang that I was in high glee and not thinking of the cold. Then Robert picked me up and carried me across the gang-plank and into the beautiful cabin.

There was one empty stateroom in the Ladies' cabin. Pa engaged it for me explaining that when a girl was big enough to travel without her mother she should be reasonable enough to stay alone in a stateroom. The chamber maid, I think, was amused. She came to help me undress, and I asked her if it was very dark in there when the door was shut. "Why, bless your little heart," she said. "We never put out the cabin lights and by opening this transom you can see every part of your room." She went out and I heard her talk to some one in the next stateroom. I had gotten in bed when she came back with a beautiful young lady. The young lady asked if I wanted her to sleep with me. No, I did not wish it. I was too timid to sleep with a stranger and too proud to own that I might be afraid. So she sat by the bed and told me a fairy tale and then went out, shutting the door. It was darker than I had expected so I crept to the upper berth and fixed my pillow right by the transom in the light. Later, I coughed and coughed, and in doing so fell out of bed. I did not get hurt and made up my mind to stay on the floor the rest of the night. When I woke up it must have been very early morning. I combed my hair and dressed quickly for fear the pretty lady would find me unclothed if she came in.

When she did come in, she looked even prettier than before. She was surprised to find me dressed. She was going to New Orleans to be married and would have two little girls to dress every day and she thought she would practice on me. I thought, "What manner of little girls could they be, if at seven years they did not know how to dress?" I had been dressing for years, and braiding my hair that was far below my belt. I had been standing with my back to the wall, my dress hooked top and bottom a little each way. Finding that her little girls did not know how to dress at all, I finally turned and she fastened the remaining hooks. I never knew her name. She was very beautiful. Her mother was with her and a gentleman, middle aged and fat. I hoped he was not the one she would marry because I did not like fat men. They were very friendly to me. The old lady gave me the largest red apple I have ever seen, said it grew on her plantation.

Pa thanked them for their kindness to me and gave the young lady some candies in the then fashionable bags. It was blue and gold, very pointed at the lower end, and at the top a gold cord drew the blue satin closed. When we landed each went their way and I have never heard of those persons since.

I spent three happy weeks in the city, the first week at Aunt Pinsard's. Marie was home from school that week. She was quite a big girl, seven years my senior. I slept with her in a little alcove room off her mother's. It was the custom at that house that Marie and I, after dressing, ran downstairs to the little dining room and were served with cafe au lait and toast. A white French servant attended to us. She had come from Europe and was to return to Europe with Aunt in a few years. Uncle had bought one man-servant and two women, a cook and a washerwoman. On buying them, he had told them that his stay would be of about seven years, not more than ten, anyway, that he wanted Aunt and Marie served irreproachably, like queens, that if they did as well as he wished them to, they would all three be freed on his departure for Paris. And surely those three slaves had an easy time and Aunt and Marie and their guests were "treated as queens." Let me say right here that they were made free three years before the war.[6]

Pamela bonnets were then all the vogue. Maria had a pink velvet one with darker velvet roses on it and the ribbon ties hung to the hem of her dress. She was always dressed beautifully. One day we were going somewhere and just as I was putting on my hat, Aunt said, "Come here. You will wear this for dressy occasions." There, in a diminutive bandbox, among many sheets of white silk paper, nestled a Pamela bonnet for me. As I was in mourning, it was black and had a black satin rose and a spray of blackberries around the low crown, and a black ribbon bow like

Marie's that went to the tail of my skirt and flew about in the wind. I have had many hats and bonnets, but the pride I took in that one had never been equalled. Pamelas were just imported from Paris. Very few children had them as yet. Marie went back to boarding school and I was taken to my own Uncle Justin's house.

Aunt Pauline's household was a much richer one than ours, but it was conducted about the same way. I was well acquainted with all her ways, but Aunt Frémaux I knew very little of, having been there maybe four or five times when in New Orleans before.

Uncle's line of occupation kept him out very late at night, so he stayed abed till eleven every morning. The house was kept quiet on his account and to accomplish this end the children were dressed in double wrappers over their gowns and taken to the other end of the house to play. Aunt never scolded, never wanted to scold, so Bridget, the nurse, had to use her own judgment about keeping Mémé and Hortense quiet. It was very poorly done by promises, cakes, pull candy, or letting them do just as they pleased so long as Uncle was not awakened. I was more than surprised at this mode of raising children. They hardly knew how to read nor how to sew or, in fact, anything. Hortense was six and a half years old, Mémé eight and a half, as I was. They rolled over the floor, played in water, smeared in flour or coal or ashes. They never seemed to really play. I knew so well how to play. I had an all over china doll that Marie had given me, so Aunt bought the girls new dolls and we played some, but Bridget had to make their dolls' clothes. Once, while she was thus employed, Mémé took a pail of soft soap, put reddening into it, and with her father's clothes brush painted the whole stairs. Her clothes, shoes and stockings were ruined. Another servant was called to clean the stairs. Aunt said not a word. She seemed not at all surprised or displeased.

She had a very delicate baby, Blanche, and to that baby she and a young nurse gave most of their time. Aunt sewed a great deal. Her children had numberless garments. I remember she went out once to buy a silk dress for the girls and she came back with a plaid piece as she said the girls had six already and she could think of no other color.

Hortense, for some reason, had been christened only a few weeks before this visit of mine. Her dress had been of rose colored silk trimmed in tiny narrow black velvet. The underskirts were many and of the most beautiful embroidery.

When Uncle was up, a general breakfast was served. The children came to that meal dressed in clean clothes from top to bottom. Their dresses were pretty tight at the belt and so uncomfortable that most of the time they wore them unfastened.

By dinner time the girls were so soiled that a big bib was put on for that meal, and directly after it we were dressed up for an evening walk in Jackson square. Many times we did not get out at all. It would grow too dark before those two girls were dressed, they would "carry on" so. Mémé had long curls. How often did I see her run her fingers through the half just curled and undo Bridget's work, and by the time the second half was finished the patient woman would have to start again on the first side, and so on, several times. If Mémé was willing to be dressed or tire teasing, then Hortense was found to be hiding somewhere under a bed or in some dusty bin. Once, trying to elude Bridget, she stepped off a bed onto a rack by putting her foot in the pocket of Bridget's dress that was hanging there. The dress tore, the rack broke and Hortense landed on the wash stand, turned over the wash basin which also broke, but Bridget caught her in her arms and the child got no hurt. That was the all important thing. Aunt gave Bridget a new dress, bought a new wash basin and the episode closed.

At home I had no money; I did not need it. Here the children had five cents apiece to spend when out so Father gave me money too, but I very seldom spent it.

Once, Hortense broke my china doll. I cried. Ma had told me that if I broke any of Marie's toys, she would know it and I would be punished when I came home. I implicitly believed Ma would know about that doll, which I was not sure was my own or Marie's, only lent to me. I was dreadfully distressed. Hortense said she knew how to mend it. She got a whole bar of soap. Yellow soap, then, came in bars one and one-half feet long. She got a table knife and some water and such a mess as she made with those things, but it did not mend the doll. For months I was haunted by the fear that Ma would ask me about Marie's toys. I would have been just that timid as to tell, but she never asked.

I paid many visits with Father and went often to the theater. Twice we took Caroline Tacon, and her father came once, but he did not come in with us.[7] He came in the middle of an act and wore white pants and a velvet round-about coat. He was very excentric and that time it caused quite a stir in the parquette and several hisses were heard. I felt mortified because he came and sat with us, but Caroline did not care. Once we went to an opera, I think it was the *Sylphide*. We had an open box quite in the middle of the house. Mémé and Hortense were beautiful in pink silk and lace and jewellery. During an intermission we were taken in the foyer for ice cream and cakes. Aunt had specified we were to have nothing or only lady fingers. Uncle took us out, however, and we got safely through ice cream, but Hortense cried for cream puffs. Those cakes at that time were the size of a saucer and contained three or four spoonfuls of the cream. Uncle got some in a bag. Hortense insisted on having the care of them. She tripped on the stairs and was picked up bathed in cream. All the front of her dress and chemisette and her gloves were ruined completely. Uncle laughed till he was red in the face and with his and Pa's handkerchiefs wiped her off, and that was the end. Aunt never said one thing. The next day I saw her ripping the trimmings off but Hortense was not even remonstrated with for her willfullness.

I really thought that those children would never come to any good, when, in fact, no lovelier, more reasonable, active and ingenious women ever adorned a home. They both married and made their families most happy. Aimée (Mémé), in a fit of anger at the age of four years, had put out one of her eyes with a pair of forbidden scissors. Uncle was very proud of her beauty and was almost crazed by the accident. The best medical aid was procured and only as regarded the cure of her eyes was Aimée ever coerced. So well were the doctor's orders followed that for years no one could detect anything unusual in Mémé's black eyes. Now past fifty years of age she seems slightly cross-eyed.

During this visit to New Orleans I saw the famous Rovel Bros. in their plays and I went for the first time in a restaurant. It was a bitter cold night. After leaving the theater at Orleans street, Pa and I walked down Royal Street. Royal Street was then The Street of New Orleans. I was freezing and told Pa so. "Oh, are you?" said Pa. "No, you are not, say you are." While speaking he had pushed open a door and thrust me in and sure enough I was no longer freezing. We were in a big room, well heated and well lighted, and Pa ordered some hot oyster soup for this young lady. I looked for the *young lady*. There were many there but none came to our table. All at once it dawned on me that I was a young lady to a waiter, and I was very dignified and only laughed and babbled about it to Pa when we left. Pa fastened me up snugly in my cloak and made a muff of his silk handkerchief. Because I had no hand out to give him to be led through the night, he made me walk front of him and held my plaits as guiding lines. It was great fun. Everything out of rule was fun to me, and thus we went to Canal street where the omnibusses had their stand. Canal street, then, had a canal in the center. It was a mud, unpaved street with hardly any lights. I saw it only that once. It looked like an ugly, muddy wilderness. Pa lifted me into the omnibus and home we went to the corner of Esplanade and Rampart. This was during my stay at Mrs. Chopard's. I slept there two nights. To be occupied during the trip home Pa gave me *Robinson Crusoe* in two volumes and illustrated. I shared Pa's stateroom this time and when we reached home I was surprised to find all the children coughing yet. I had forgotten my whooping cough, having not been troubled since that first night on the *Laurel Hill*.

I found the home folks in a state of discontented excitement. The nurse had been changed. Instead of Dora, Susie had been installed.

Léon had penances for days more and Sister and he seemed to be at daggers point. I was dreadfully mortified when I heard about it. I knew it would not, could not, have happened if I had been home. Here is the shameful truth.

Among the negroes was one Sterling, a long, thin, yellow man who was always hungry, always eating, and always had eatables in his cabin. It seems the nurse and Sterling were not friendly, so more to play him a trick than for desire of potatoes, the nurse and Léon got in and took a few of his raw sweet potatoes. Sister was sworn to secrecy according to rules then. The thing, I think, was something like, "I cross my heart and kiss it too that I may never tell," and she stood near the cabin to tell if Ma should appear. Ma did *not* appear and it was only the next day that they dared try to eat the potatoes. Sister did not like raw potatoes. It choked her and she said she was going to tell. Sterling had found some potato peel in the yard, counted his goods and missed the stolen ones. He came to the "big house" with his complaint. Nurse and Léon denied any knowledge of them, but Sister volunteered all information. What incensed Léon was that no suspicion had rested on her at all; she just volunteered to tell. Ma gave Sterling one peck of potatoes, another nurse was installed, and Léon paid dearly for that affair. He had often before said that Sister tattled on us and many of our punishments had come through her instrumentality. After the potato episode, Léon *never* trusted her, even after we were grown. Léon felt very sore also, because *I*, who always took from him and helped him, did not at all condone with him. I was ashamed, mortified, hurt awfully, to think he had stolen, actually taken things. And from a nigger! And with a servant! We, none of us, ever forgot those two potatoes. I deeply regretted having stayed so long in New Orleans. Two days less and our honor would not have been dimmed.

Also at this period arrived my first love letter. It announced the fact on the first line: "Dear Céline, I write you this love letter to ask you if you remember how we scared the geese by shooting peas at them the last time I saw you." The letter was from Camille Bercegeai. A week or so later Ma said I ought to answer my little friend's letter as it would be a good exercise in spelling and grammar. I did not care at all about writing. I had written several letters to Father when he was off and one or two to Grandma before she died, and my experience was not of the pleasantest. Always a scolding, two or three attempts, and lines to copy for each blot or misspell. No, I did not want any correspondents, but Ma, of course, had her way. A slate was ruled for the rough copy and even then I tried to beg off as I did not know how to write a *love letter*. To which I was told that that kind of love letter was easy to write but that, however, girls never wrote love letters. So, my letter and all those that followed began "Dear Friend" and they were as short as Ma would allow. He wrote once a month and I found out later that his school demanded a letter by way of composition the first Friday of each month. I also found that whatever personal news was in the Post Script. Well, mine were painful duties too, but had no P.S.

The sixth letter had quite a fancy flourish after the name and it ended with very, *very* small letters which spelled *your loving beau*. Ma did not notice it; neither did I, but brother, in trying to imitate the flourish, discovered the words and showed them to me. Sister was there and straight away went to Ma with the information. It did not disturb me at all as I had no idea what a beau might mean and it was perfectly natural he should love me. We all had loved each other always.

However, the next Saturday, when I should have answered, Ma said I had better write to Féfé as I was getting to big to write any longer to a boy. That suited me very well as it was much easier to find things to say to her than to Camille. Léon had been sent to school but took French lessons with ma, every day besides. He hated those lessons worse than anything he could think of. "Poor Lélé," as I used to call him, he had his ears pulled so often that he was hardly ever without little scabs at the back of them and his head would be bumped against the wall so often that he used to say, "As soon as I am big enough, I will run away." That idea of his running away made me give in to him ever, so he would remember me kindly wherever he would go. We were perfectly in earnest about it. That was our first secret from Sister.

No, there was another that we had kept ever since I was four years old. At that time, several ladies had called on Ma and as we were being kissed, one of them said, "Caroline, which is Céline's child?"

Ma said, "Scht, not so loud, the *boy*, but they do not know. If they did, they might not love one another as real brother and sister." We both had heard. We both ran out to the yard under the big quince tree and such a talk as we had. We did not know that Pa had married twice. We were still small but we knew Céline was Ma's sister and that she was dead. We promised each other never to tell anyone else and never to let Ma know that we knew. We kept our word. Ma told us the day Léon married and we never let on that we had known before, seventeen or eighteen years before.

One day Léon was making a toy steam boat and on the wheel house he wrote Bird, and told me that meant Bird, the name of his boat. I pondered long. To me, it did not spell Bird but "Beerd." He made fun of me and thought himself very superior because he could spell in two languages. I was deeply mortified and determined to learn English. There were two Larguier girls older than Callie. We called them "Miss." One, the elder, was Miss Cora, perhaps five years my senior. To her I went for help which she was very kind in giving and *that* was my own secret. I soon passed Léon but kept my knowledge to myself. Not that I knew so much, but that he knew very little. He did not apply himself at all to study and in fact seemed every year to be more and more apathetic and strange. For instance, he never felt the difference of weather. Ma would put on or take off some of his garments as she thought best, but of himself he did not care. He could not tell by the taste if batter cakes were corn meal or flour made. This state continued until 1860 when he became suddenly very ill. Doctors were puzzled and one day thought him dying. The next, his eyes showed clear, fever was gone. He was well but weak, and that soon wore off and ever after he was like the rest of as to activity, acuteness of perception, and far above the average in intellect. No one has ever known what brought about the sickness and the complete change. But the fact was there and Ma and Pa were very thankful to Providence.

Somewhere in 1858 Uncle Pinsard came on a visit to us. It was in summer, in June, I think. He stayed a week and it was a happy week to us. Pa was at home and many boating parties, picnics and long tramps in the woods we had. The tramps were taken by Uncle, Pa, and myself. I was always ready to go and never tired. The springy loam of the forests were a joy to me, to hear the crunch of leaves under my feet, to breathe great free breaths, to laugh loud unchecked, to even sing, sing out loud as I walked holding Pa by the hand, to be jumped by the two over logs or across ditches, etc., etc., etc., all without rebuke. No lines to copy when I came home. Nothing, nothing but the joy of living in the safe care of my pleasant, ever gladsome Father. He would take me sailing with the boat full of young girls and I would make myself small between the big people and listen to the songs and maybe sit between Pa's knees and learn how to steer the boat or Pa would tell me of the stars and show me the different constellations. Of the boating parties I remember one particularly. It was a Saturday afternoon. There were quite a number of young people going and they had all met at the house. One of the young ladies asked if I could come too. First, Ma said I was not dressed up enough, then she said yes, but she must speak to me first. I knew what that meant. She would tell me to say I did not desire to go. I had had to do that many times, so that time I only waited for the yes and slipped out in the crowd and gained the head of the line where Pa and my friends, Trevanion Lewis and Jim Cooper, took charge of me.[8] We went up the river then came down and stopped at the Valentin Dubroca place. Everybody got out and we had watermelons on little tables hidden in the shade of two large petasporums. There were about five little tables in each. I never saw anything like them in any other garden.

Then we went down the river some and one young man went to sleep.

He was Adolph Kent.[9] Some of the girls wanted to tickle him with the feathered tips of their fans but his father said, "Better not, girls. He is a sleep-talker and sleep-walker. He might say something rough." Just then Adolph got up and stood on his seat. Everybody laughed, thinking he *feigned* sleep, but he walked right over the gunwale into the Mississippi river. Immediately, all was commotion. The sail was let down, two negro sailors half stripped and jumped overboard. He came up once and went down again, then came up on the other side of the boat. His father caught him by the hair and two of the young ladies reached under his arms and, others helping, he was drawn in. He was not unconscious but chilled. It was the fashion then to wear petticoats. (Hoop skirts were not yet in general use.) Several petticoats were produced and Mr. Kent wrapped up as best he could and we came to the shore immediately. Adolph Kent was never known to talk or walk in his sleep after that. He died the death of a brave soldier, shot in the breast in the early part of the Civil War.

Ma was very averse to letting us see Processions, Masquerades, Political Parades, Flambeaux Marches, and so on. We heard of them through the Larguier children who went to every thing of the kind. Their father was Captain of a fire company and once a year the engine came into their property all bedecked for the occasion and Cora, the eldest daughter, presented a wreath or banner or something. If we were at our lessons, we only heard the Hurras. Once we saw a little through the cracks of the fence. Ma always refused the invitation for herself and us to witness and join in the festivities. Callie and Isidore generally saved us some of the refreshments, but it was a sort of surreptitious feast.

Once there was a barbe-cue. It was during the Buchannan campaign. Pa took Léon out with him early in the morning. Later in the day he sent word to Ma to send Sister and me, with a grown nurse, to meet him as there was to be some spectacular feature that he thought we would enjoy. To our surprise, Ma dressed us and sent us! Just as we got on the grounds before we met Pa there was a vociferous hoorahing and a man was lifted above the crowd on a thousand hands, it seemed to me. All seemed commotion and noise. The nurse turned right around with the remark that surely if Madam had known how fussy it was she would not have sent "Ti-Mamselles" and she took us straight back home. Ma said she had done well as barbacues were no place for little ladies. It turned out that what we saw was the end of the last speech and that after that colored balloons were sent up, then a real balloon, then fireworks, etc.

The "hoodlum" element did not, at that time, exist and, Baton Rouge being a rather small place, the whole population was acquainted and joined in every sort of public demonstration. Ma had lived so many years in European big cities and heard so much harm of the common "Populace" that she never went to see if in this country things were different, and, by reasons of slavery, it was different. The slave represented the low class and took no part in anything and the whites, even the few laborers, were not coarse as in other countries or in our own since the freedom of slaves.

When Mr. Larguier died, the firemen attended with music and furled banners. The coffin was carried on a ladder truck. Ma would not let us stand even at the windows to look. She made us feel ashamed of our curiosity, got us all in tears of sympathy for the grief of our neighbors and kept us all reciting prayers until the funeral had passed and the music died away in the distance. Ma was right in this instance and in many others but her way was harsh. It took almost all our childhood joy from us. In justice be it said, Ma was as strict with herself as she was with us. She seldom took a pleasure and then it was under protest or not to be always refusing Pa's entreaties.

Pa was always trying to "wake up" Léon and he once took him up Red river on a two month's survey. Léon enjoyed the camping as he enjoyed everything else at that time. The greatest joy was "No school." When he came back he told me that he had met an old negro who had worked for his mother and who told him that Pa had been married first to Ma's sister and a whole lot of other things that we afterward found were only more or less true. I tried to get him to say if the old negro had mentioned that there were two of us, for in my heart I was beginning to think that I was not wholly Ma's child. She treated Léon and I exactly the same, the same severity. Sister and Paul seemed at times to find a sort of forgiving spot in Ma. Léon and I never. We never felt hard about Paul for he really was the best of us all, so if the poor little fellow could escape some punishments, why, well and good. We two big ones often took little blames that Paul and Eddie might not be suspected. With Sister it was different. She always turned state's evidence and was generally informer as well. And alas can I say it: it was not always true information.

My position with Ma was peculiar. I knew that Ma trusted me in many ways. Ma would have soon believed the heavens would fall as to think I would disobey or repeat what was not meant for my ears, or shame her in company or such. I was what she called reasonable. I felt myself trusted but not loved. I craved love and sought it everywhere and got it too, most of the time. Few women can count more friends, from babyhood up. The worships of my life were Pa and Léon.

We got so that we feared Sister and she was quick to detect it, and she abused it shamefully. If she wanted any of our possessions, a marble, a candy, a piece of doll rag, she would say, "If you don't give it to me, I will scream and Ma will think you hit me and you will be punished."

Long before I was nine, I had grown very sensitive. I felt that my *past*, note the word, that my past gave me the right to be believed on a simple assertion. If Ma questioned me, "What did you do to your sister?" I would simply say, "Nothing, Ma." and that ended my plea. Sister, or whoever it might be, could tell the tale after that. I *knew* I had to be punished. The sooner the inquest was over, the sooner it would begin, the sooner it would be finished. My head was philosophical, but my heart bled. Oh, how it bled, and how the tears hardened my pride. I got so that I would hide Sister's peculiarities to our little friends and even to Ma, because I was ashamed for her, and I knew, or thought I knew, how mortified Ma, a descendent of nobility, would be when she realized how unworthy a daughter of hers could be.

This line of my conduct I utterly condemn now. I could have enlightened Ma on many points and it would have been beneficial to both of us. Ma would have probably corrected her and she would have lost the power to make me shoulder half of her untruths. She did it in this way. She would tell some extraordinary tale so distorted and embroidered that if there was some foundation to it, it was engulfed in the trimmings, and if anyone doubted her she would say, "Of course it is true. Céline was there. You know she never lies," and that generally settled the matter.

If some skeptic *did* ask me, all I would say in my mixed pride and cowardice was, "I don't remember all these details. I did not notice particularly." In fact, I *was* lying and *knew* it. As a child, it saved me from a long "fuss." When grown, it saved me from the mortification of declaring my sister a falsifier.

Don't think that my conscience was easy. I shed many and many tears about that very thing. But as a young lady how could I say Sister lied? What would have been the opinion about me? I dropped many acquaintances for that cause. If Sister was ever found out once in a house, I never went back, and again, if I found that people loved to hear Sister recount or "took to her" very much, I quickly left her to their friendship and retired. Poor girl, she lost all her friends one by one, but I was never a witness at any of the "breaks." Sister made friends quickly because she is obliging, generous, and very quick and active, tender-hearted, and impulsive. Yet she could not *retain* many loves.

I have gone way ahead of my narration. After Léon started to school I said my lessons alone. I recited while the little ones wrote. Once, Uncle Justin, Pa's brother, came to Baton Rouge. He arrived at night and was to leave the next night. I suppose Ma lost a little time over the breakfast. Be it as it may, I was sitting on a stool near the fire (it was bitterly cold), Eddie was asleep on my lap, and I held a big atlas preparatory to reciting my geography. Ma said, "Now, take your grammar first." I closed the atlas and slung it toward the dining room table. Well, sometimes an atlas slides on a table with a sort of swish, but this time it hit the table flat on its side like a slap. Ma was on me in a minute. She took the baby in one arm and with the other hand gripping my shoulder, she shook me till I bit my tongue, and slammed me around generally. Uncle slipped out of the parlor and tried to help me by asking Ma to refrain on account of his visit and offered to stay indoors all day and play with the bunch of us so she, Ma, could rest easy. Ma had a migraine that morning. Uncle had better done to have ignored the shaking. Ma was perfectly furious. Uncle left the house for Pa's office.

Ma then marched me upstairs and sat me on a trunk in a dark attic which ran over the back gallery the whole length of the house. It was sleeting. The house was slate covered and it sounded as if beads were being poured over the roof. The slates were not six inches above my head. I was freezing and to add to my terror, the door at the further end would open and shut a little crack at each gust of wind. I imagined all sort of terrors and even prayed, actually prayed that I could have a Fairy Godmother sent to change me into something that would not feel the cold. After awhile Ma brought me a blanket. If I had dared I would have kissed her. As it was, I only asked if I could get off the trunk. "What do I care where you sit?" she said. So I slid to the floor and covered myself head and all and shut out the darkness. I must have gone to sleep.

Next thing I knew, Uncle came up to get me, saying, "Your mama says you can come down, but you will have to copy lines." The cold school room felt warm at first, yet my fingers were so stiff and I was mortified that Uncle had seen me in penance that I made little headway with the lines. It was two o'clock and Ma said if I got through before dinner I might come to the table, if not, not.

My lines were in Segur's *History of Greece*. They told of Leonidas at Thermopylae. The dinner came on at nearly three P.M. I heard them all sit at the table. The slate was so cold that my hand had lost all power of motion. All at once I heard a chair pushed back from the table and Uncle said, "Caroline, I don't know if brother could stand this if he were here but I can *not*. If that unfortunate child doesn't come to dinner and get warm, I will leave immediately and, so help me God, never again step under your roof."

Mama came after me, sat me before my soup, and said, "Thank your Uncle. For his sake I forgive your impudence." Uncle left directly after dinner, and Ma put me to bed and made me drink hot elder tea. I was dazed and crazy-like. That was the worst punishment of my childhood. Ma had taken the slam of the Atlas for an exhibition of anger and impudence. I had not uttered a word, and she never referred to it afterward.

Of course, all our days were not black days. One winter there was to be a fair for the orphans. Pa made a little house to be raffled. It was all made of bristol-board, hand painted. It occupied many evenings in the painting. We made the wall paper designs diminutive, but just like those of our own home. We were very interested. My share of work was to clean the color plates, and both Léon and I were allowed to suggest the coloring of the outside, cisterns, banister, etc. We also went to the fair and I heard Pa say that the toy netted $300.00, having been raffled three times. The third time, Miss Mollie Castleton won it and kept it for her own. At most of the fairs Pa took a prominent part. He always managed the tableaux. He always got up one of his very own, and helped the ladies with theirs. Once Pa's tableau was Rebecca at the Well, in three poses. He painted the whole background curtain. There were three camels, palm trees, servants, etc. The whole thing came near failing because Rebecca wanted to wear shoes and stockings. Pa insisted on bare feet and sandals, and so it was at last, and people had the tableau again and again that night.

Once, his pet tableau was of Bluebeard, also in three tableaux. Mr. Alven Reid was Bluebeard and a most beautiful deaf and dumb girl was his wife. She was a very wealthy young girl being educated at the Deaf and Dumb School in Baton Rouge. Her costume was very fine, and she sparkled with gems. In the tableau representing the chamber of horrors, the seven wives to appear hung around the walls were standing on narrow shelves hidden by the folds of their winding sheets, a rope around their bloody necks, hanging to seven great hooks in the walls. When the tableau was over Emma Larguier, forgetting that she was on a little shelf, stepped over and hung sure enough. Of course, Pa unhooked her, but she would not step up again for an encore of that scene.

Once, in tableaux, I represented the Queen of Flowers and once, Spring. That fair took place during the legislature. One of the members, a tall, good looking gentleman, was at the fair and asked someone to send out to him the child, Spring. Pa took me to him and he explained that he had to leave the hall as his boat was in sight. He was leaving for New Orleans. He had been so pleased with my personification that he desired to leave to me all his chances to the various lotteries; there were twenty-seven in all. They won three or four prizes but the ladies at the table told me that as it was a charity fair I must leave the things to be re-raffled the next night. So I did not get anything, but for years I wished and wished I knew the name of "My Legislator," but I never did. During the war when men passed us, wounded or half-starved, I always eagerly scanned the faces to find "My Legislator." My grateful little soul kept his memory green and ready to do him a favor if it ever could be.

We went to children's parties occasionally. A servant took us and to her Ma gave the hour for our return. We were exceedingly well-bred children, never rough, never accepting refreshments more than *once* an evening. If bon-bons were passed we took one and never the largest on the plate. I never knew Ma to have a word of condemnation as to our behavior outside of home.

At Christmas time of 1858 I received a pretty piece of music composed and written for myself by Mr. Aimé. On the reverse was a Polka he had composed and named for Franka. They were too difficult for me at the time. I did not play them till the following year. With the piece I had a letter from Camille saying he had a locket for me but had found that only the top was real gold so he would not send it. He would have me a tortoise shell ring made and a monogram cut from the *real gold* part of the locket and inserted in the ring. He had broken a piece from his mother's tucking comb to have the ring made. I never got the ring as the comb was an heirloom and the piece was taken from him and the comb mended with little gold rivets from the aforesaid locket top. He sent me instead a Cornaline ring which Ma took away from me saying little girls did not need rings.

Léon was going to school, as I mentioned before, and he was getting very wise there. He informed me that rings meant engagements and that Ma would not let me wear one from Camille till I was " 'Most going to marry." I asked him if I was ever going to marry Camille. He said, "Why yes, it was all fixed the time you were born, didn't you know that? But you will have to learn a great deal before that, and go to school. He knows a great deal already so you have to catch up, and you never will till you go to school in English, and can play the pieces he gets his father to compose for you."

I accepted Léon's say about Camille, as I did everything else Lélé told me. In the books Ma read at night, all French novels, girls were betrothed from infancy. In history I had learned how so many princesses, lords and ladies had been promised in marriage by their fathers even before birth. And, in fact, right in Baton Rouge was a lady whose marriage to one of her cousins had been arranged by the parents and on leaving school she was married to him. She had seen him only during the two weeks preceding the ceremony. So it was not so very strange that I would accept the theory as a *fact* and never ask Ma about it. I knew, so why enquire? And I applied myself with renewed vigor both to lessons and music. Time wore on.

There came a time when the State Land Office was transferred from Donaldsonville to Baton Rouge. All the employees were to reside in Baton Rouge, hence I was to once more meet my friends. They finally arrived, the girls I loved so well, their old father, so kind to me, and the boy in whom I was so interested. I almost cried the first time he came to the house. I thought him so ugly. He had on a blue linen suit and after playing awhile, a spot of perspiration began to show in the back and broadened and broadened till he looked very wet by the time he went home. I did not like that and I resolved that when we were married that he should wear clothes that would not show wet in summer. I told Ma that I thought him ugly, and she only remarked that it made no difference about a boy's looks, that his father was the ugliest, but also the best, of men. I never mentioned his "looks" again. He was very nice to me. Every cake, candy, nut, popcorn, picture, ribbon, or colored piece of glass of which he became the possessor was saved for me. Once or twice a week he came with a cigar box closed with a padlock heavy enough to close a trunk. The key was produced and mine was the right to open it and become the owner of the contents of the box. The trash that I ate those days!

During that year we frequently spoke of our marriage, of the profession he would follow, of where we would live, etc., etc. There was no kissing or love making. We were too young to think of that, but he always took up for me in any discussion. When I was punished, he forebore play, carried my parasol from church and my music book to and from Mrs. Garlinski's twice a week.[10] We played "Greeny" and he always lost and always paid the fines promptly. Once, I remember, it was a little silver paper Lion and Unicorn such as is on every bolt of Lawn or Swiss Muslin, once a little Marquis cut off a broken fan of his sister's. I still found him ugly, but he was certainly good.

✌ The War in ✌ Baton Rouge

RUMORS OF WAR began to spread through the land. Companies of soldiers were being formed. Father was First Lieutenant of the Creole Guards; a Mr. Pierce was Captain; Trevanion Lewis, Second Lieutenant; and my friend, Jim Cooper, was an officer too. Captain Pierce did not seem to take much interest in the company. Father devised the uniform. The flag was made at our house. It was a U.S. flag. There were thirty-two states then, so thirty-two young girls, each representing a state, met every Saturday at our home to sew on the flag. The stars, I know, were put in by Miss Adèle Arbour and Miss Emma Rotnaski. Finally, when the flag was done there was a parade, a serenade, and a ball. Young Walters was the flag bearer. We youngsters were allowed to go and look at the decorations of the ball-room. It must have been in spring for Magnolia flowers and Dogwood blooms were used. There were ornaments on the walls made of bayonets and flags. It was the first ball-room I saw, and as the girls all met at the house, I saw a number of ball dresses. I thought them beautiful. All wore white dresses and across the breast a broad blue sash with the name of a state. I remember Ohio was a small person with red hair, Miss Mamie Kent. Father had guilded the names on the sashes. He used gold leaf and the white of egg as he did to guild the letters on the bow of his sailboat.

Captain Pierce wanted Ma to let me come and take a peep at the ball, but, of course, that was too absurd. I was not even disappointed. I *knew* that could not be. The next day we had a lot of pink ice cream, some lemons, and a lot of faded wreaths. We played we had a ball and supper, and had a very fine time.

The next day some gentlemen were talking with Father about the war. Presently, one of them turned and asked, "Little lady, suppose there is a war, would you rather it were now or in twenty-five years?"

I answered without hesitating, "Now. In twenty-five years I will have sons and they might get killed." Without knowing it, I loved my future children. That I should have them I did not doubt. My mother and grandmothers had had them. Of course, I would also in time. The men laughed and I felt timid so left them and went indoors.

Time for my first communion was nearing. The next June would be the time. I began to think more seriously of things religious. I played less and sewed more and better. Little twin niggers having come to our cook, I made their christening cloaks of white cashmere with fancy stitches of blue floss. Ma praised my handiwork and the cook was immensely proud of "Ti-Mamselle's" work, and the twins.

January 1861 came to us children just as any other New Year. If our elders felt themselves on the verge of a catastrophe, we children had no tremors of evil coming. There were more and more companies in pretty uniforms. Oftener we heard drums and music.

The Governor was now Mr. Moore,[1] and my dear friend Gov. Wickliffe; his daughter, Miss Maggie; and his lovely niece, Miss "Dachie" Dawson and her sweet looking mother had all retired to their plantation back of Bayou Sara. Father was renominated State Engineer. The office force was about the same.

Léon had been sent to Spring Hill College, Mobile, Alabama, in Sept. 1860, and in my life had come the first painful parting from him. I played more with Callie and less with Isidore. We had our play-room upstairs. Callie's was also upstairs and the fifty feet of space between our windows had for years been bridged by our "Telegraph," a double twine running through staples on each window sill. Mrs. Larguier did not furnish Callie with scissors. We had a pair. We were poorly provided with thread or colored silks. Callie was bountifully provided with those necessities, etc., etc. Our box at each end of the line was alway exchanging places. Our doll visited by that aerial route; our pet kittens even crossed over once, but our anxiety for their safety was so great, we never tried it again.

We were great circus players. All Cora's and Emma's old ball finery was given to Callie and immediately became common property. I was the "alterer." Léon and Isidore covered the hoops with newspapers or maybe kite paper. They also trained the dog "Fingal" to jump through them or over bars, etc. We would prepare them sometimes for weeks, then when Father returned from some survey, he would put up his big tent on the lawn and the circus came off. There was no audience. We needed all our force for acting. Fingal was a horse, an elephant, a camel, in fact, a whole menagerie. The kind Newfoundland lent himself with great patience to all the masquerading we put him to. Not a turkey feather was ever wasted; we always needed them for Indian costumes. We worked hours and hours to make beaded moccasins and medicine bags, so that, when vacation should come, we could surprise Léon by our gorgeous apparel. We could not dream that May would cut short our childhood, never to return.

Of course, we heard of the war that was sure to come, but war was only a name to us. Then there came a day when a flag was brought to Ma to alter. There were to be blue stripes to be inserted between the heretofore red and white bars. Ma did the work and that night she had a beautiful serenade given her. If that was war, well, it was very nice. We heard the music and had the silk scraps to trim doll's hats, but all at once it changed. Ma's eyes were often red, the men came and went in groups, and there seemed to be less laughter in the air.

Trevanion Lewis had married Miss Estelle DeRussy. I thought it strange that people said, "Poor Estelle, she should have waited." I was glad she had not waited, as Pa, being home at the time, took me to church to see the marriage. Miss Estelle was the first bride in Baton Rouge to wear a big square illusion veil covering her to the hem of her dress.

A day came when father brought home several tin models of pecularly shaped figures not unlike ill-shaped squares, and a lot, a great lot, maybe a cart-load, of brown paper, and several lead pencils. "Children," he announced, "a soldier's children are young soldiers. I want all this paper cut up into pieces, like these tin models. The country needs them." That evening many young men and ladies came and all fell to work marking around the tin models with a pencil, making no waste and cutting with scissors on the mark. We knew later they were to be made into loaded cartridges for the soldiers. We cut for a long time, then we rolled them on little wooden molds, and finally they were filled and became real war implements.

Then Major Hastings came to see Father and there was great handshaking.[2] He said perhaps they would not meet again as friends, and in that case, some written directions which he had left with Pa were to be carried out. Major Hastings was in command of the Barracks and Troops of the United States stationed in Baton Rouge. It seems that he had been requested to evacuate the Barracks to which his answer had been that he could not do so to a handful of citizens, that he could hold out against twice that number with the cannons he had, but that if a sufficiently overwhelming force was shown, he would prefer to retire than to cause useless bloodshed. Before night there were 5000 men camped on the Boulevard. By morning there were twice as many and every boat that landed brought in companies. To be sure, they were not equipped and in some cases the uniformity was only in hats or caps or shirt sleeves. One company had jeans pants, common 75 jeans pants over their tailor-made trousers, but all wore a determined look. From New Orleans there came, among others, a company of Zouaves led by Captain St. Paul. They were fully equipped. Be it as it may, Major Hastings surrendered the Barracks. The New Orleans troops were the first to walk in to the garrison grounds much to the chagrin of the Baton Rouge boys and the spontaneous volunteers. Thus the real war began around us. It did not seem very terrible. All the ladies, beautifully dressed, were on the Boulevard and on all the promenade grounds. Every other house, almost, was serenaded. *I* thought it fine. The next day all was laughter and feasting. The next week tears began to flow; the soldiers had been ordered to Camp Moore.

My first Communion was to be made on the ninth of June. Father had to leave before then and he solemnly blessed me and prayed that all would be well with me until his return. The war, at this time, was supposedly going to last two months. The men, most of them, volunteered for three months. The roll of the Creole Guards was answered by 180 men. On the day of their departure, just as they were about to cross on the gang plank, old Mr. Rotnaski claimed his two sons. Captain Pierce, for some reason had resigned and Pa was Captain. The old man made a tearful plea claiming that they were Poles, etc., etc. The whole company was indignant. Father was furious. He reminded them that they had voluntarily become naturalized, that one of them had been sent to West Point by the recommendation of Mrs. Hebert and Gov. Hebert, that all three were earning a living in the state's offices, that the state that cared for them had a right to the best that was in them, etc., but nothing told on their feeling. They both stepped out of ranks, being perhaps the first renegades of the infant Confederacy. At the same time a very young man named Palms asked for transportation in place of one of the deserters. Mr. Palm's command had gone on an hour previously and for some reason he had been left to follow by the next boat. We left the landing only when the boat had rounded the lower point. Ma looked as one stricken unto death. At the house she sobbed aloud. Then her face was set in a sad stern mold and never, till the long four years had passed, did one ray of hope or merriment relieve the stern tension of her features. A half hour later we were reciting our lessons as if nothing had interrupted. We had lost about an hour. The Jesuits had closed their college and Léon had come home.

I began diligently to work at my first communion dress. It was of very fine India Swiss trimmed with a number of tucks and a real valencienne edging an inch wide. The veil was of the same material and same edging. My white slippers and wax candle had come from New Orleans several months before. Ma had also bought me a wreath of white roses, but a friend, Miss Cecilia Choppin, had given me one of the white jasmine flowers. I wore the gift one and the roses were given to a poor child who had not the means to get one of any kind. Ma came with me to the Communion Mass and Mrs. Charlie Ilsly accompanied me to the High Mass.[3] It rained during the Mass and a servant was sent to pin up my skirts and change my shoes and otherwise care for me on the homeward walk. We were confirmed many months later.

We heard from Father quite frequently for two or three months. From Camp Moore the Creole Guards had been sent to Virginia. They stood as Company A, 8th Regiment of Louisiana Infantry. Their Major was Major Kelly who died years after the war.[4]

Every day for months companies formed and left the town and state. Presently, all was very quiet. Only old men were seen about and boys below eighteen years of age. When ladies met it was to sew for the soldiers or to make lint and bandages. Ma never went to the sewing bees, but sewed at home, and we children made lint and rolled bandages. They were made five yards long and of three widths, one and one-half inches, three inches, and three and one-half inches wide. The lint was put in one-pound packages. Every soldier's knapsack contained a set of bands and a package of lint.

After awhile, all the old scrap iron and every atom of brass was gathered and sent to the army. Ma had sold most of Major Hastings things and the money was kept till he could be heard from. His heirs were found in 1879 and the money mailed to them. His furniture and other effects were packed away in the attic.

The three months had passed and the war lasted on. On the sixteenth of November, 1861, another little brother came to us.[5] Ma had me come to her bedside and write to Father about it, saying we would call him Henry pending Father's ratification or rejection of the name. Only in January did we receive Pa's answer. Mail had become more than irregular. Henry was not christened early as is the general custom.

Christmas of 1861 was a wonderfully mild day. Our friends, the Bercegeais, took dinner with us and I remember that all the doors were wide open and the evening was spent on the lawn. The whole winter was mild and the poor suffered little from the scarcity of fuel.

Sorrow had entered many homes by then. Cora Larguier and her cousin, Juliette Holmes, had both lost their betrothed. They were both in Fenner's Battery.[6] I never knew their names. Cora considered herself a widow from that day. Juliette married years after, a Mr. Roy. She lived and died ruing the day.

With Pa's first letter from Virginia came a little drawing, "The First Mass at Camp Pickens," Manassas. And, from time to time, he would send me either a pen or pencil or a water color picture of some interesting spot or event of his military experiences. Most of them came from Virginia and only one, a pen drawing, came from Tupelo. I put them all in an album which Pa got in Richmond as he was leaving for Tupelo. After the second battle of Manassas, there were so few of the Creole Guards left that they were incorporated in some other company. Before that, however, Father had been transferred to General Beauregard's Engineering Corps and it was in that capacity that he served to the end of the war.

January 1862 had come and gone. Mourning seemed to be the ordinary dress of women. Alas! later they could not even get that, and many families, having not been able to get mourning for their soldier loved ones, have never put it on for any of their mourned ones to this day.

Baton Rouge Under Fire

LÉON could not remain idle all these months so Ma had put him to school at the Baton Rouge Academy.[7] She now decided to send me to the primary school to learn English. I had gone two months when one morning we were all startled by the sound of cannon.[8]

New Orleans had by this time been taken by the Yankees and it seems that gunboats had been sent up the river and were even then bombarding the town. In a moment the greatest excitement prevailed. From my seat at my desk I could see the boys of the Academy rushing pell-mell down the stairs, some even jumping from the lower windows, among them Léon and Camille. They were hatless and bookless. Camille turned toward his home. Léon came straight to our room to get me. I had, meanwhile, gathered up all my books, slate, pencils, etc. Miss Gill, the teacher, seemed very composed.[9] She allowed all girls having brothers to accompany them to go at once. Others she kept till sent for by their parents. I tried to induce Léon to go for his books but he demured. Finally, when he did try to go back to his classroom, the door was locked and those books and that hat were never recovered. I cannot recall the name of the Academy's principal, but he was about the poorest sort of a man to teach youths. At the first cannon shot he screamed, "Save yourselves, boys," and he himself lit out. Hence the disorder, loss, and hurt to the scrambling boys. Miss Gill was a young, frail looking woman. She remained three hours in the school-room and had everything closed and snug before leaving with two little girls whom the parents had not sent for. She took them home and finally went to her own home. By then the cannonading had ceased.

We lived two blocks from the school, by way of the sidewalks, but by going through Mrs. Larguier's back lane and over our fence we were not on the street one minute. At the street we met Sister. She had on a sunbonnet and one side of her hair was braided and the other loose. She said Ma wanted us home at once and that we must come through the Larguiers! Until then I had not been moved at all, but I began to think something was going to happen when Ma, the ever quiet, let Sister out uncombed and made use of her neighbor's passage-way. And indeed on our street all was confusion.

There, just before our block, were several gunboats which boomed out their shells or cannon balls into or over the town. The river was low just then, and the town crowns the hill, so the cannons had to be trained upward to shoot at all. In this way most of the shots were harmless and fell in the fields and woods at the back of town. There were no high turrets to war ships then. People seemed to be beside themselves. Old men, women and children passed at a run or weighted down with their most precious belongings, going, going, and ever going, they knew not where. To the woods, they said. Catfish town, a small part of the town between the foot of the hill and the back of the levee, was abandoned. Every individual had gone to the woods. Ma and Mrs. Larguier had gathered their money, silverware, and a few necessities into wheelbarrows, baby carriages, and baskets, and calmly awaited with their slaves around them until they saw that the danger warranted leaving their homes. And then their plan was to go quietly into Catfish town near the levee where no possible projectile could reach and return as soon as the danger was passed. We children, of course, wanted to go. Children always want to be on the go. But Ma sat us down in a row and started us to reciting fables, verbs, and multiplication tables. After a while the cannons ceased. Only one shell had hit the State House, one-half block from us. In the morning the boats had gone. Some of the people were returning; others remained three days and nights away. All had suffered greatly from mosquitoes, principally. Several old persons and sick children died from exposure.

Three babies had been born in the woods. Many persons had lost money jewels, and utensils of all kinds, but, notable was the fact nothing had been disturbed in the momentarily abandoned houses. Our friends, the Bercegeais, had gone to the woods, but returned in the same hour. There was no mother to restrain them and they had gone till they became hungry.

About this time there was a planter 3 miles back of the town who announced that he wanted to close up his sugar house, and that he had a quantity of sugar which he would sell at 5 cts. a pound. The usual price at that time for "clear open kettle" sugar was 7 cts. and 7½ cts. a pound. Ma and Mr. Aimé decided to get a barrel each, and a barrel of molasses to divide between them. So, Léon and Camille, with a wagon, went with the money for the sugar. Several hours later Léon came back with the whole purchase. Ma asked him why he had not left Mr. Aimé's share at his place as he had to pass by there to come home. Then it came out that there had been a dog fight at the plantation and Camille had got frightened, thought the dogs were mad and he had run away, leaving poor Léon to load his wagon, make his bargain and return alone. Camille had driven before in the cart, but Léon had never touched a bridle in his life. Léon was then 14½ years old; Camille, 15. Léon said he was so mad at Camille that he would not pass before his house. However, Ma had our sugar and our share of molasses put away and sent Léon to fetch Mr. Aimé at his house. Of course, he *had* to do it. Ma sent a servant with Léon. Of course, Camille had not yet reached home.

When Léon and I had our next talk he informed me that Camille was a coward and that he would never feel kindly to him again. I was very much mortified and asked Léon never to mention the episode to any one, and I think he never did.

It was becoming very evident that the war was on for a very indefinite time. We lived very economically; goods were getting scarce. Ma spent a goodly sum to fill the pantry and buy plain dry goods to last a long time.

Letters from Pa were less and less frequently received and when they came they were often three months old.

All the boys who had reached their eighteenth year had gone to join the army. They had some difficulty in doing so since the City (New Orleans) belonged to the Yankees, and these latter tried their best to keep the new recruits from reaching the Confederate army.

Spring had crept into summer when the news came that there was to be a battle soon, to take place in Baton Rouge. The gunboats had come up once or twice more, had sent a few shots at the town, but as yet, no blood had been shed among us. War was a thing away from us. We did not seem to be actors in the turmoil. Ma's face was set and serious, her eyes were often red, but the way of our household had not changed. Meals were at the same hour; lessons went on surely as the sun rose and set.

Over the River

ONE DAY the gunboats were known to be coming up the river and it was reported that the town would be burned or shelled. I *think* it was in early June.

A friend of Father's, a Mr. Dubroca, living in a princely home one and one-half miles above Port Allen on the opposite side of the river, came across to see Mother and invite her to come to them with all of us and two servants, and stay until after the nearing battle should have been fought.[10] Ma did not wish to go. She resisted all she could. The argument that decided her was that after the Yankees occupied Baton Rouge no news at all of the Confederate army could reach us.

We went over taking a few clothes and things, just one trunk full. Sister and I each took two of our dolls, but we never played with them over the river. Ma took one slave and her child, Odile and Alice. According to custom, or law of the time, Alice had been given to me at her birth and I was her god-mother, but she could only be my very own at my majority.

Mr. Dubroca gave Ma as a dwelling two of the three rooms of the

"Garçonnière," his boys' cottage. They had all gone to the army, four or five of them, leaving him only Maurice, the youngest, fifteen years old, until such time as necessity took him also, if the war lasted long enough.[11]

Mr. Dubroca himself was an old man. There were in the house at that time: old Mr. Dubroca, a widower; Mr. and Mrs. Gus Dubroca and baby girl, Zozo; an old maid aunt of Mrs. Dubroca, Miss Julia Cade, an old person, very kind and much loved by all. There were also Miss Alzire; Miss Corinne (Colo); and Lily, a girl just my age; and Miss "Titine," Celestine; Maurice, age fifteen; and a governess, Miss Dillon; then Mother and her six children.

Mr. Gustave Dubroca belonged to some corps of the army just then located in the vicinity. Miss Celestine was betrothed to a Mr. Favrot, then in the army. Miss Corinne was engaged to Mr. Cade, also in the army.

So many were interested in news that if any sort of rumor passed through the Yankee lines we were apt to hear of them.

Ma was supposed to come back to the house the next day to fetch a few more necessaries, but the fleet was all over the river and she could not get across.

The town was shelled in an irregular and almost harmless way, but every day or so one or more houses were burned down, presumably, on account of their interfering with the sighting of the Confederates from the fleet's outlook. This was the usual way of procedure. A number of men with an officer would be sent to the doomed house. The officer would call for the lady of the house and make known his errand. At the same time, the men were igniting the premises in the back, and when the interview was closed at the front door, or in the parlor, the back was all in flames and nothing could possibly be saved. The inhabitants, if upstairs, had narrow escapes with their lives and only the clothes they wore. After a while most of the people had bundles ready prepared for immediate flight, but in many cases the bundles were too heavy for women to carry or were stolen by the incendiaries. It was more than a woman could do when finding her home in flames in the night hours, to save her children, and anything besides. Very few houses were burned by the shells. In every yard pits had been dug, into which people took refuge during the bombardments.

The battle did not take place as early as it had been expected. It only took place on 6 August 1862. We all knew that the Confederates were approaching. We had seen and heard many, many men pass in the fields back of the house, or creep silently along the river, back of the levees. We children were in a constant state of excitement; we were actors in the war. We helped. We fetched water, corn bread, and potatoes to the marching troops. Ma was like a Sphinx. Her hopes, her fears, her anxieties, her despairs, she must have had all these experiences. Every emotion was buried in her breast and only a sort of haunted look testified that she felt at all. We had gone over the river in the evening, after lessons. The next morning we said our lessons with Ma as usual. Then, in the afternoon, we took lessons in English of Miss Dillon.

Miss Dillon was peculiar. In that wealthy house with meals served to any one at any time, she could never get ready to have breakfast with any of the members of the family. Then, of all the bounteous supply, there was never a dish to her taste. She would order this, that, or the other, to suit her momentary desire. Miss Alzire did not mind it but the servants did not like her. Nigger slaves of kind masters were prouder than even their masters. That a governess should find "Old Marster's" table not good enough was a fault not to be forgiven. Every morning for breakfast she would fix a freshly laid, raw egg with fresh butter, a spoonfull of honey and a teaspoonfull of sherry. A half hour later she ordered her breakfast. In every other way she was, or seemed to be, all right. Very learned, very talented, very amiable, she was. After two P.M. an honored guest, she lived as one of Mr. Dubroca's daughters.

We had been with the Dubrocas perhaps two weeks and were at our lessons when Miss Celestine walked into the room without knocking. We children were very surprised. "Titine" wore a riding habit and gauntlets;

her veil was thrown back. She said, "Miss Dillon, do you know where I could find my riding whip? Have you seen it at all?"

"No, Titine, I have not. You had it yesterday morning."

"You are sure, Miss Dillon, that you have not it in your room?"

"Why, the idea!! Of course not."

Titine walked straight to the table, lifted the chenille cover and there lay, disclosed, the pearl and gold jewelled riding whip. She took it up and said, "I would tell you to hide it better, if there could be a 'next time' to a case of this kind." Then to us, "Children, lessons are over for today. Run out and play." We flew.

Downstairs, we fell into another scene in the hall. The washwoman had a lawn dress on her arm and was saying, "Yes, Miss Colo, I knew it the minute I ironed it. The hem was begun by hand, you know, then Vic took sick and Nora finished it on that machine your Ma had just bought." The Dubrocas were then wearing deep mourning for their Mother and the muslin dress had never been worn. Miss Dillon had purloined it from a trunk in the attic, changed the sleeves a little and *worn* it, right in the house. The girls had not noticed it. Anyone can own a sprigged lawn, but the servants had found it strange and the ironer had recognized it. Respect for "white folks" was so strong that they had said nothing "at the house."

But when Titine, one evening, lost her whip and the house-girl, feeling something under the table cover, had been ordered, "Let it alone, Nora, the table does not need dusting," they decided to tell all they had observed.

At dinner, Miss Dillon's meal was served in her room, breakfast, the same. Directly after the meal the carriage drove up to the very steps of the gallery. Mr. Dubroca, père, handed Miss Dillon into it. Old Polyte, the boatman, got on the seat with the driver and I heard the order given. "Polyte, you will row Miss Dillon across, see her trunk *in* the hotel office, and you will immediately return." That was all. She went out of the plantation and out of our lives, but not by a good deal, out of my remembrance.

It was the first time I had known of a grown person doing what was wrong. It was the only time to the present day that I found myself under the same roof with a felon. I felt "shamed" for weeks. I have never heard her name mentioned since. The grown people forbore; we did likewise. We all knew, but we felt that it was too awful to mention. After that, there were no more English lessons.

At Dubrocas' we took a good deal of outdoor exercise. The place was immense. There was a miniature forest, a little mountain, four great hot houses where tropical fruits were made to grow and mature, flower gardens, truck gardens, two orchards, and, of course, the cane field, uncultivated the next year, but at that time in perfect running order with its hundreds of slaves and its numberless servants.

Each girl had her own maid. Then there was Mammy who saw to the clothes presses and two half-grown girls who seemed to have no other occupation than to be around in case they were wanted. In the dining room was an old, white haired butler, a young negro boy and a young mulatto girl, and lastly a little piccaninny in a long white shirt who pulled the cord of the fly-fan. Of the outside servants, cooks, washers, yard men, etc., I know nothing. Our ramblings never could take us in their district.

Of the seamstresses, there were five. They occupied a pavillion of two rooms with a gallery in the front. Each had her own particular splint bottom low chair. The place was overhung with flowering vines and shaded by two immense cedar trees. We read near there very often, Lily and I, seated on two old chairs which had become so entwined by a wisteria vine that they were as one piece, chairs, tree, and vine. In that way we saw a good deal of the "sewers."

They were all five yellow niggers and wore real gold or coral-headed pins in their fancy Madras "Tignons." In a room just off the pavillion were ranged great cedar tubs with hoops of brass as bright as gold. They were bath tubs and every evening Mammy marshalled us, girls first, boys later, to take our bath. A young woman attended to our toillette while Mamie, from the doorway, gossiped or chided the "sewers." After the bath all walked out onto the levee or took a horseback ride. Sister and the little ones never went horseback, but Léon and I were always in the cavalcade. There were some days when a gunboat hovered very near the shore; then the ladies stayed indoors. But especially on those days the boys, Léon and Maurice were sent out, and generally returned with some message from some Confederate corps. Probably, they had taken some warning message to the scouts in the parish.

Once the scouts camped in the sugar house, had a meal and departed. An hour later, at eleven P.M., a gunboat was anchored opposite the front avenue and a regular bombardment of the place began. Everybody was called up and dressed. The most precious of our few possessions were all gathered, every vehicle on the place prepared. Mr. Dubroca desired all the family to go to safety at the Duralds' place. In great silence the departure was effected. The horses' and mules' feet were muffled in clothes and bagging. The chains of the wagons gave a deal of trouble to swathe and silence. At last we left. Léon rode a pony, so did Maurice. Ma and the five others of us had been assigned to an old carriage. Miss Alzire and Lily were in a topless buggy while Mrs. Gustave Dubroca, Miss Julia, Colo, Titine, and Zozo were in the family carriage. Servants followed in wagons and carts. Slowly and silently we filed out down the avenue and along the road sheltered by the levee. At the Duralds' lane we discovered that the shells were falling in the woods between the river and Duralds', so the direction was changed, the cloths removed. We were too far to be heard by the vedettes, and we traveled much faster. To occupy our time, or for fear that we might miss our next day's schooling, Ma kept us reciting geography, verbs, fables, and mythology. I found it unpleasant but *natural* at the time. Schooling was the *one* thing to Ma, as far as we were concerned. Ma called Léon to ride at the side of the carriage and recite the verb *to escape*. He did not want to do it and said he could not keep the horse so near the wheels in the night's darkness, and he rode off. I was appalled!! Not to obey!! Gods of Olympus!! What would happen to him, I wondered. When we reached Mr. Sasthène Allain's place to which we were going, fifteen miles lower, I could see Ma was very angry by her tone of voice and my heart was beating like mad. Flying from danger in the depth of night had not moved me. In fact, I felt rather bad at leaving. Mr. Dubroca had stayed at the plantation. I wondered if Pa, in the army, would approve of this "flight." It hurt my pride. Reciting lessons was nothing to the uneasiness of my conscience about it. Had I been a free agent, nothing would have moved me. Of course, I was not a mother then. I understand the flight now.

Finally we reached the grand old place. Mr. Allain was an uncle of the Dubrocas, a widower, who lived alone there with his slaves.[12] If he had sons in the army, they never returned, and his body servant, Soulouque, became possessor of the beautiful home. There was a lot of hustling about the silent house as our large party arrived, beds to prepare, rooms to make habitable, etc. I remember how surprised the old gentleman was when he discovered that his house was not by far in any condition for guests. Of course, his own room, parlor and dining room were as they had always been, but in the twelve or fifteen years of his loneliness, he had never looked into the other rooms. So the big billiard hall, which he and his friends often used, was made into a dormitory for our immediate needs. Almost pell mell, everybody tried to take a nap and most of them succeeded.

In the morning there was another hustle about the kitchen. The weather was fine and we children scattered over the immense gardens. There I saw the first jujube trees. They were in bearing and the housekeeper gave us many of the fruit. This place was much larger and of more importance than Mr. Dubroca's. I think we remained there a week, but I enjoyed only the first day. That night I slipped on a fruit peel and fell on a cracked porcelain basin. The jagged edge ripped across the small of my back about five or six inches. I bled very profusely. Colo saw me first.

I had fainted. They lay me on my stomach and two persons' hands were required to hold the wound closed. There was no way to bind it just at that place and no sticking plaster was about the place. A negro was sent three miles to the nearest store to get some. All the while he was gone, Colo and Miss Alzire knelt on the floor near me holding the cut closed and the blood oozing and running on each side of me in two little pools on the floor.

When the sticking plaster did come, it was almost useless, so dry and old as it was. They fixed me up the best they could, slipped me on a table board and lifted me to a bed, and there I stayed six days on my stomach. Oh, they were long, long, those six days, but I could see the river and a beautiful house on the other side. The young ladies from there and our young people visited every evening. I could see them rowing back and forth in the great long skiffs, two negro rowers to each skiff.

Mr. Allain, "Uncle Sasthène," the Dubrocas called him, was very loth to lose his guests. He tried every device to convince them that great danger awaited them at the Dubroca place. But one evening, the whole Yankee fleet filed down stream, and we immediately went back. Léon kept out of sight so much that he was never found to say lessons. I was so hurt that I could only recite things that I knew. But Sister and Paul and Eddie had their lessons everyday. Ma mingled very little with the other ladies as she would not leave me to the care of a servant.

Well, it was a Sunday morning that we returned to West Baton Rouge. Mr. Dubroca was glad to have his folks home again, and he told Mother that the much spoken of battle was very near and that a C[onfederate] S[tates'] gunboat was to be down to help the land troops. He opined that Ma go over the next morning and fetch across many things that we really needed. No ferry boats were running—there were no men to run them. Ma went over with two skiffs. She found that the Yankee officers had lived in our house during their stay, had used our belongings and quite a number, especially of our toys, were missing. She packed a few things in a cart, thence to a skiff and sent it across. As the cart was returning to the house, the Yankee fleet reappeared at the bend and Ma had to hurry to the mooring; otherwise, she might have been detained indefinitely, or made a prisoner. At any rate, she could not have returned without taking the "Oath." Had Ma taken it, she would have adhered to it, but she did not want to be forced to that extremity. How could she take an oath of allegiance to the United States, when Pa was a Confederate officer? And Léon was being raised in the idea that he would have to go to the army as soon as he was old enough.

What was left in the pantry was sent to Mrs. Larguier's, then Ma again closed the house and hurried back to the skiff and old Polyte, the rower. She was hailed from a gunboat and a warning shot was fired, but old Polyte was so scared that nothing short of death would have stopped his rowing. A yawl was sent in pursuit and very quickly overtook the heavy skiff. Polyte threw himself on his knees, closed his eyes and began to pray aloud. Ma was interrogated as to her business on the river. She answered truthfully and they examined her bundle of small children's clothes. Just then, Polyte, in his agony, screamed out, "O Lord, Mars Yankee, don't kill us!! We-ens got to go back to them chilluns what is missing at our bress."

That was too much for the officer. He fairly "roared" and said, "Well, begone quick before I can have a bullet fired at your old water-logged boat." And Polyte "begonned." He fairly "lay" on his oars, and he never crossed the river again till his young masters had returned after the close of the war. Let it be said here that Polyte (Hypolyte) and Ma'm Felice, his wife, were among those who stayed with the old home and old Miss Alzire.

Mother, of course, had brought over only one half of what she had expected to fetch, but those things helped us through the summer.

Very soon, a Confederate gunboat, the *Arkansas*, came down the river.[13] The Yankees, apprised of it, spread their boats on both sides. Two of them were opposite the house. Mr. Dubroca again thought there would be danger to the lives of the many in his care, so again he sent us off to the Duralds, this time without muffling feet or clanking chains. How I wished to stay, not for bravery this time, but to see a battle. From the great garret windows we could see miles of the river, and I had to go. I was a girl. I could not stay. Léon and Maurice stayed with Mr. Dubroca.

The firing began before we reached the Duralds' lane. We went on. Nearer and nearer came the sound and just as we reached the gate a tremendous boom, a tremble, a shock. The air over the river seemed black with smoke and debris, then nothing . . . not a shot. Of course, we *knew* the Confederate boat had been blown up. But how? By whom? Were the men all killed? Oh, to be there, to see, to hear, to know.

There was a crowd at Duralds', many refugees like ourselves, and there was much giving and getting of news of mutual friends. I crept back of some thick pittosporums and cried. Oh, how I cried out my anxiety and grief. Of course, *reasonably,* it could not be expected that one boat against six or eight could live, but I was not very reasonable. I felt the disaster. I wondered *why* it had come at all. I seemed to hear the cries of the wounded and see the dead floating on the greyish water. My pain was very real. I had never yet seen blood, real blood flow. Presently, Ma called for me and my solitary mourning was over, but the ache was left. It was about eight-thirty A.M. Later we saw Léon and Maurice galloping toward the house. They told us what they had seen and said the boat had been blown up by her commander. He landed all his men and took his chances. He set the magazine on fire and finally swam ashore where he was hauled up exhausted and sorrowful, but with his flag on his bosom. The *Arkansas* had been sent down on false reports that the fleet had left Baton Rouge and they, the Confederates, were to lend a hand to the land troops for some sort of transfer. Well, I was too young to know much and I am writing only our own experiences.

Léon and Maurice had picked up scraps of wood from the exploded ship. I wanted a piece, but the young ladies were ahead of me and wanted the keepsakes, so Léon said he knew where a piece had lodged in the garden hedge and he would get it for me in a few days when we got back, but, that for the present, orders were to get in the wagon and go out further back from the river, as the Yankees were tearing up things on the river front. It was warm and blackberries were ripe. A great cane wagon was made ready and all the children piled there-in on two mattresses. An old lady, Mrs. Janvier, sat near the driver but inside the wagon "to keep an eye on us." There were twenty or twenty-two of us. The old lady took quite a bundle in a red table cover and an umbrella. There were four of us Frémaux, four Pikes, some Duralds, and the old lady. [14] Our mothers and the little babies were in the carriages, the larger boys on horse back. We went out several miles and remained a few hours, then the elders decided they would risk the Yankees rather than a night in the woods, so we meandered back. As we reached the gate, either by accident or for mischief, the front hook of the wagon became undone, and we were all spilled out with the mattresses atop of us. Mrs. Janvier was screaming, "Murder. Help. I am dying. Help. Help." The driver was soon down at the back trying to help her. There were so many of us, more or less laughing or screaming, that it was some little time in the gathering gloom before we were sure that all were safe. Then came lamentations from the old lady. A personal utensil that she had fetched in her bundle had been broken in the fall and her recriminations were many and loud. Very much out of proportion with the loss, I thought at that time, but indeed, afterward lived to realize a broken vase is quite a loss when it cannot be replaced. She was surely over seventy-five years of age, and it was a sore loss to her.

We returned to Dubrocas' the next morning. Many fences were down, had been used for firewood. Calves and chickens had been killed and many depredations accomplished. Many of the niggers had followed the Yankees to freedom, etc., etc.

We were quiet only a few days when that impending battle did come off. [15] It may have been seven or eight A.M. when we heard the first shot and by eight-thirty Mr. Dubroca called out that all go to the garret windows where we could plainly see into the town. Opera glasses were in every hand. I got hold of a spy-glass of Father's. No one noticed me. No one took it from me. Kneeling on a trunk near an open ventilator, I saw my first battle, saw guns aim, saw the signal to fire, saw men fall and rise, or try to rise, and fall again, never to move again. In one street the Yankees seemed to be marching twelve or more abreast. The street was packed. All at once a cannon back somewhere shot and shot again, again, and again, I think five shots. Some said it was grape shot, others said round bullets. Be it as it may, it mowed men down at a terrible rate. The street was almost cleared but the sight was terrible. The wounded were carried to the levee to be embarked on gunboats. We could see them plainly. It was awful to see. It was blood, blood everywhere. I felt faint and I was sobbing. All at once musketry sounded very distinctly, but no more cannon from the Confederates. The boats were still shooting and the shells were heard bursting back of the town. The white smoke of the muskets hid the soldiers from our view. They were in every street opening on the landing space.

The Yankees were in full rout and came pell mell to their yawls. Many were left on shore. I suppose they were dead. The ships weighed anchor and left. I have never understood that move. Why did they leave? Yankees tho' they were, they could not *fear* anything of the land troops with light artillery which had made the attack. Nor did I understand the attack with nothing to gain, till I heard that the Confederates had gotten a great quantity of food stuff from the stores in the Garrison. All got quiet after a while and Mr. Dubroca and two negroes went over in a skiff. As I was folding up my spy-glass, I looked about me. All the grown people had gone down stairs. Lily and I were alone in the attic, both of us crying. Both of us knew that some of our own men must have been killed, but who? Later, we heard that only thirty-two of our men had been killed.

When the Yankees returned three days later there began a reign of terror for the people of the town. The dead Yankees were still unburied and were picked up in carts and dumped into the many pits that had been dug by the inhabitants. They were hardly three feet deep, and some were not as long as a man. As many were crammed in as the pit could hold. Then a blanket covered the so-called grave. A brick or two at each corner held it down to hide its gruesome load of filling. Such is war.

A short time before, a Mr. Favrot, a prisoner on parole, had come among us. The Favrots were also friends of ours and lived a short way up the river. It might have been further, but I think it was, or is, the third place above Dubrocas'. It turned out that Mr. Favrot was betrothed to Miss Titine and I saw my first pair of lovers. They were quite a novel thing to me. I was deeply interested in them. They seemed very picturesque to me walking in the gardens hand in hand. Lily and I met them at every turn, in the hot houses, on the mound, or reading under some tree, or in some "kiosk." Lily said Celestine was very happy because she had believed him dead at one time, and now he was running no risks, being a prisoner. He was not wearing his uniform. At that very moment we came upon the lovers. Titine was in tears. He was talking low but earnestly to her. We, Lily and I, vanished to our own special secret place within the limbs of a great petasporum and wondered what could have happened. A grown lady crying . . . that was dreadful enough, but that that lady should be Celestine, of all people. We were much exercised about it.

At supper time the mystery was cleared. In the battle of Baton Rouge, the Confederates had taken many prisoners. Now an exchange was to be made and Mr. Favrot was to be one of the exchanged men. So, he was going back to the army.

It was decided that they would marry before he went back, so one morning the house was decked with flowers, the piano was made into a temporary altar, and the marriage was celebrated. There was a sort of unrest over the whole thing, for he was now a free man, consequently in danger of being made a prisoner again. The bride hoped that no one would tell the Yankees of his whereabouts, but too many knew him and knew of the marriage. There were several exchanged boys of the vicinity, but the others had gone directly with the Confederate soldiers. Bride and groom repaired to the old Favrot place, and she was to be in the care of *his* people till the war closed. There had been a kind of dinner-lunch in their honor. People had yet enough to eat, not much wheat flour, but of other things, quite a plenty.

About ten P.M. that night the house was surrounded. The Yankees had come to take Mr. Favrot a prisoner again. He was not there, of course, but Mr. Dubroca would not say so. He told them to look for him, and such shooting at every shrub or dark object was quite dangerous to all living things. Maurice was sent to Favrots to warn them, but met a messenger from the bride saying the Yankees were there too, and he had gone to try to join his old regiment. More than half the night bullets flew around, window panes shattered and doors dented or perforated. We children were put on the floor behind a rampart of pillows and mattresses. Finally, the search passed beyond and died away in the woods.

In the morning, a delegation arrived and read to Mr. Dubroca an order to give up Mr. Favrot and one of his sons, under penalty of having his house shot to pieces in twelve hours if the men were not surrendered. To which the old gentleman said, "Do as you can. You are the strongest, but never be foolish enough again to ask a Southerner to give up his own. Now go!!" Mr. Dubroca's son, it seems, was on the place at the time. He had come with dispatches or something. No one knew of him but his father and Miss Alzire.

"Then the ruin of your house and the death of your children be on your head. In twelve hours the troops will be here." The officer turned on his heel and departed, got in his yawl and rowed to one of the ships. They said it was Farragut's flag ship, maybe it was. Farragut or any other Yankee was all the same in my estimation.

A little council was held between the elders and all was made ready for another migration in case the Yankees did come back. And at dusk, sure enough, two small gun boats were seen coming up from the body of the fleet. Again we got the vehicles and went inland fifteen miles to the house of a friend of the Favrots. I never knew their name.[16]

The entrance to the place was very grand. One came in a gate to the right, and drove on an avenue of poplars, then around a mound covered with verbenas of all colors to the foot of a short flight of steps to a wide gallery and next to a wide hall. There seemed to be quite a number of young boys on the gallery. The whole house was in darkness, only a taper burning back of a screen at the further end of the hall. An old lady came and made us welcome. She said Maurice and Léon had better sleep in the carriages (It was eleven P.M.), and that we must find place where we could as she had a few friends in already.

Ma gave Sister, Paul, and Eddy to my guidance. She and the baby vanished in a room to the left. Miss Julia Cade called softly to me to follow her. I felt lost and very uncomfortable. We groped our way into a room. Two beds were occupied by six people and on the floor were mattresses with children, more or less undressed, sleeping soundly.

I took off the children's top clothes and shoes and stockings. (We wore those luxuries then.) I made a bundle of them and wedged my little charges among the legs and arms that seemed to be everywhere. It all had to be done by feel. Then, I unhooked the belt of my dress and crept under one of the beds with my arm for a pillow. I more or less dozed till daylight, then I looked about me. There were three mattresses on the floor, and two big beds and a crib around the room. All the faces were strange to me but Miss Julia's, and I hardly knew her, so drawn was her face, half covered by a towel about her head. She was on the floor, and only her head rested on the edge of a mattress on which were five children, boys and girls, only half undressed. A lady was nursing an infant in one of the beds. She had long, wavy black hair and seemed very sad. Outside there seemed to be much bustle. About ten young boys were having coffee and dry grits in the yard. They seemed in high spirits. My little charges finally awoke. I dressed them and combed them as best I could with a hairpin. I saw no washstand. When we went out Léon took the little boys to a pump and washed their faces. I felt lost and desolate in that mass of strangers in the dimness of early dawn.

Finally the other children awoke and began to come out, and I recognized many. There were the Allain girls, Jeanne and Sydonie, and Phillipses from Baton Rouge about ten of their crowd, etc., etc. All had been driven from their homes by cannon or fire. We were all very hungry. The smaller children were crying. It was very late when Odille, our slave, came to get us for some sort of breakfast. The coffee, we found, was made of parched corn and sweetened, but there was no milk, the milk being reserved for the very little ones. Besides the "coffee," we each had three batter cakes. That was all we could get. The war was on in earnest and the resources of no single family could equal the call made upon them that day.

Later on, provisions came in from many neighboring plantations, and we ate in an irregular way outside on the grounds. In fact, we all kept outside till evening. I saw Ma at very short intervals when she came to call Odile to fetch the baby to be nursed. She looked flurried, and put her finger to her lips to enjoin silence if any of us tried to speak to her. Something terrible must have happened in that house that day. I never knew what it was. Was it a birth, or a death, or both? I have thought so since. Ma told me once, never to mention that night to her, and I never did. One thing sure, we did not see the mistress of the house at all, and the next morning the niggers belonging to the place wore white head handkerchiefs, a sign of mourning in slave niggers.

Toward dusk we returned to Dubrocas'. Everyone seemed to be leaving: every carriage and wagon was prepared and the drivers on their respective seats, but all seemed subdued and sad. The farewells were only nods, and, as Ma did not speak, we rode the many miles in absolute silence.

At Dubrocas' many of the slaves had joined the "contrabands," as the hordes of freed, starving, homeless negroes were called. Many of the cabins were closed. The still faithful slaves held their heads very high and mentioned their late companions as being "Low Livered Congo Niggers." Things looked indeed changed.

In the beginning of our stay at Dubrocas' there had been a "corn husking." They had them often on plantations and as this one is the last I saw I will say a few words about it. When we white folks walked into the quarters there was an immense pile of corn in the shuck at one end of the cabin row. There were barrels and barrels of it. Great fires burned here and there to give light. It was fine moonlight, besides. Little piccaninnies in white cotton shirts fed the fires. All in a row, facing each other, sat the niggers, men on one side, women facing them. Each had a large basket. The baskets held about one-half barrel. Before them, the men would shuck the corn and throw it over to the women opposite, who shelled vigorously. The shucks were carried by larger piccaninnies to the other end of the cabin row. The young negroes sang or joked awhile, then the oldest of the old women was called upon for a song. She was reputed to be a witch, and was feared a little, so could not be ignored on a festal occasion. She was respectfully led forth. She was one hundred and twenty-two years old and blind. She sat in the middle of the aisle and sang, if such an attempt can be called singing. There were fourteen verses to the song, and at the chorus all joined, clapping hands and patting feet. When she finished she asked if the white folks were present. Colo answered, "Oh, yes, all of us." In fact, there were only us children, Colo, and Mr. Dubroca.

Then the old crone asked Colo to sing. "Sing what I used to sing to rock yo Grandma to sleep, honey." Colo sang "La plainte du mousse," which, of course, the old nigger had never sung.[17]

The corn was by now all shucked and quite a lot shelled. Mr. Dubroca then said, "Mamie, get to bed. It is quite late. We are going back to the house. You people get your music and have a dance." So the baskets were piled around the mound of shucks, the triangle bones, banjoes and fiddles brought forth and the dancing began. Such dancing!! We looked on a moment then went up to the house and I went to sleep to the distant thrump of the negro melody.

But after the second exodus of niggers there seemed to be much less joy in the quarters. Many of the faithful, old and middle aged darkies were beginning to understand that their free children were forever lost to them. The men were embodied in the Yankee army to be sent in close columns against the Confederate forces. Regiments of negroes were always at the front of the Yankee forces, and thousands were minced as would have been the Yankees but for that shield of black flesh.

Ma never set foot in Baton Rouge after her trip in the skiff with old Polyte.

One day Mr. Dubroca came to Ma's room. He seemed excited. He sat down, then got up and walked on the gallery. Finally, he said, "Mrs. Frémaux, you would like to see your husband, would you not? There may be a way. It is only a may-be."

Pa had then been away fifteen or eighteen months. It seems that Father had been chosen from Gen. Beauregard's staff of engineers to determine the best spot to fortify the Mississippi river between Vicksburg and Baton Rouge. He started his investigation at Vicksburg and came on down. He decided on Port Hudson, and immediately the fortifications were begun.[18] He had been there several weeks, only thirty-two miles from us, yet no message had come, so secret was his mission and so closely were the roads and woods guarded by the Yankees. But at last an old country man had come through. He had been taken by the Yankees, questioned, imprisoned, searched, etc., but not a paper was found on him. He knew nothing, had seen no one, and looked so generally foolish and harmless that he was finally released. Then he began his pilgrimage of news giving. That was how Mr. Dubroca had been informed of Pa's whereabouts.

It was agreed that we should take the old carriage with a trusted driver, Léon would ride a meagre little pony, and that we should start next morning and go up the river bank until opposite Port Hudson, and try our luck at *seeing* father, if not of *speaking* to him, spend the night or longer at some plantation and return as soon as convenient. The trip proved very different—no calculations hold in war times. Our life over the river was ended. We never looked on Mr. Dubroca's kind face again.

❧ Port Hudson, 1862 ❧

IT WAS AFTER SUNSET when we got out of the carriages opposite what is now known as Port Hickey. We had several spy glasses and could see men going and coming. There was a picket guard near us and they advised us what to do. Ma waved a white cloth on the end of a stick. After a lot of "hailing" and waiting, Pa arrived on the shore. He was on horseback. We could just make him out. He took the trumpet and called out that no soldier could cross the river. Orders were very strict, as at any hour a Yankee gunboat was expected to attempt to pass Port Hudson, and a trial of the defenses would then be made. All this we learned later. Pa said there was a leaky boat that would be sent for messages.

Presently, a boat, the kind known as a "Flat," came to us. It was managed by an old white man and an old negro. Ma said she had no message. She wanted to go over. The old man objected a long while. Finally he consented, telling Ma that the boat leaked and children were sure to move and turn it over. Ma knew her children. She sat us each where she wanted us so the split plank would be fairly out of the water. The carriage had orders to wait till midday next day, then return to Mr. Dubroca's. It was quite dark while we crossed and once in a while a sheet of water came in at the crack and we felt ourselves sitting in the water. But Ma had ordered silence and no motion. We were motionless and silent. In the dark we had landed and soon were in Father's arms.

He had never imagined that Ma would cross over. Of course, he was glad to see us, but what he was going to do with us was quite a problem. Port Hudson and Port Hickey were soldier camps. In Port Hudson there were people and houses but where we had crossed there was just one house belonging to Mr. Gibbens, a thrice widower, who boarded all the officers of the Engineer Corps.[1] There seemed to be about twenty of them.

Up the bluff we walked, Pa carrying Henry whom he had never seen. Up to the house we went, our wet clothes dripping cold along our stockings. The scene to me was very impressive, or rather impressed itself deeply on my overexcited imagination. The night was dark. What light we had came from pine torches carried before us by two soldiers (couriers). Away off were fires here and there and great dark chasms between them and between us and them, and, now and then, cries or calls reverberated and echoed from all around. Back of us was the subdued rush of the river which we had just crossed at such risk. Léon, Sister, and I held hands and walked behind Ma who had Paul and Eddie by the hands, Pa a step ahead on a line with the torch bearers. All was awe inspiring to us. Something awful seemed to hover around and encompass us. I would have cried if I had dared. The walk was not long. On entering the house all was changed. The room into which we were ushered was well lighted. A number of officers were talking at once, it seemed to me. At Pa's entrance all turned questioningly. All these men, whose children were far away, kissed and cajoled us as a poor little makeshift of the yearnings of their sore paternal hearts. I was old enough to know that the petting was in reality for unattainable girls and boys in far away homes. The next room was one that Father and four others occupied. It was generously given up to us all—for that one night, we thought. We were all put to bed in our underclothes and Pa and Ma sat on the edge of a cot talking. I was almost asleep when Pa jumped up and said he thought he heard a shot. Ma had heard nothing. Pa went on the front gallery and listened, but heard nothing. Then it was that he told Ma that the Yankee boat, *Essex*, was expected to attempt to pass. That first shot must have been from a vedette a long way off and was very faint, but the next came full and distinct. At once the house buzzed and was full of commotion. Pa called out, "Put out the lights and lie on the floor. Good-bye. God guard us all."

It was perfectly dark out side. On the road could be heard the tramp of many feet in perfect rhythm as sounds of the march of a command. Then came a deafening roar, the house trembled and the smell of powder filled the air. It was the first shot of the thirty-two pounder battery about forty feet from us. Then the firing spread up and down the river front. The *Essex* threw very heavy shells. What we could see was an arc of fire which seemed to start from the water, pass far above us, and end in the darkness of the unknown distance. About half of them exploded out in the woods with a noise equal or greater than that of their start. All along its length the arc of fire seemed to carry with it the barking of immense packs of hounds. That's how the noise represented itself to me. We could distinctly hear the striking of our shot on the sides of the *Essex* and several times the cries as of a hurt multitude. Curses and cries seemed to mingle with the crash of broken iron or heavy timbers. Then the thirty-two pound battery ceased firing, then the next, and the next lower and lower down. That the *Essex* had been crippled was well seen. That she drifted down without steering gear was also seen, but that she had reached Algiers, a wreck, to stay mud bound on the bank a useless hulk was known only years later when the war ended.[2] We had one man wounded by a wood splinter. It was a slight wound. Father returned and we slept the remainder of the night.

With the sunrise came a revelation of beauty to me. Where the fires had been there were now seen rows and rows of white tents. The hilltops glistened with them. The awful "black chasms" were trees and bushes in the lowlands and gullies. Directly in front of the house was Profit's Island, generally called Prophet's island, and the mighty, swirling river going on its majestic course as if no strife or blood had lately disturbed its mighty roll.

Immediately around us all was unkempt and very disorderly. Men and only men ordered and lived in the house. At the back, quite near in the orchard, was the family's private burying ground. Three obelisks, exactly alike, gave token of Mr. Gibben's impartiality for his three defunct wives, and a smaller obelisk, beautifully carved, attested to his love for his only child, a little girl who had lived three years. Her rag doll, a little chair, a box, and a few broken toys were piled together in the hanging side of a large armoir in the room we occupied. Those little toys struck a tender chord in me every day of my stay. I walked over to the little enclosure and weeded, brushed and cleaned the little baby's grave.

During the fray of the night the "Flat" had disappeared. "Hailing" brought no response from our driver across the river. The night's events had been too much for his nerves. He had hitched up and gone at full gallop back to his master reporting that the soldiers, after drowning the whole family of us, had begun firing heavy guns at him, and he had saved the carriage and horses at the risk of his life. The pony, he declared, had to be left, and he supposed was shot to pieces by now.

All day passed without a boat being found. The next day a boy came along with a skiff. He consented to take Léon across. Ma's instructions were that Léon gather all we had at Mr. Dubroca's and fetch them up as soon as possible, also, that he bring with him a slave, Odile, and her child, Alice. Léon also carried letters to Mr. Dubroca telling that we would henceforth live as much as possible inside the Confederate lines so as to be in close touch with Father, and sending thanks, of course, and many messages from his sons whom Pa had recently left with the inland army.

Two days later Léon arrived at nightfall, opposite the fort, as we had. A storm was coming. He was hailed to, to get under shelter at the sugar house and await further orders. Obedience, it seems, deserted him that time. He sent the negroes to the sugar house with the mules and he himself, armed with a carbine stood guard over our unattached goods and chattels. When the rain came he crept under the wagon until daylight, having caught the drippings of a bag of sugar after that had passed through a large "carpet sack" of books. Such was Léon's idea of "packing carefully" as Ma had directed. Poor Léon, he seemed to love to heap coals of fire on his own unwise head.

Pa had managed to get a sort of pontoon upon which our goods and people crossed. I do not know where they were subsequently stored. For the first few days they lay scattered about in the sun on a hillside. We were all kept busy turning them from time to time. If that poor brother of ours had tried to destroy all he had been sent to get, he could not have done more damage. Clothes had been saturated by melted soap, salt, sugar, and a heavy paste of wet flour added its ugliness to the lot. Fine gilt-edge books and school books, and a box of paints with a lot of sticks of India ink had been pell-mell in that capacious carpet bag. Everything seemed to have been purposely put where it could hurt most. The loss, of course, was irreparable but yet I felt sorry for poor Léon's often recurring scoldings, cuffings, and ear pullings. We never *did* hear the end of the scoldings about that packing to this day. Léon has been dead many years. Ma still mutters, "That imbecile child," whenever she takes up one of her *fine* damaged books.[3] The clothes and sheets have, of course, become worn out and are past. The lost flour was the very last we had or rather did *not* have. Baby Henry had to come down to corn meal food like the rest of us.

I think we stayed in Mr. Gibbens' house three weeks, during which time the village of Port Hudson had been evacuated, not a single family being at this time inside the corporation. The officers had taken quarters in tents or deserted houses. It was rumored that a fourth Mrs. Gibbens was about to be fetched home. Father and seven of his engineer corps agreed to take a vacated house, throw their rations in together and with Ma as housekeeper, live together as long as the fortune of war allowed.

There were in the house, Ma and six children and Pa, Capt. L. J. Frémaux; Capt. or Major Dabney; a Mr. Woodside (not very educated but very kind); a Lieut. Reed (or Reid); very young, good looking; Mr. Ginder (after the war with Griswold jewelers); a tall old gentleman (rather cross), name forgotten; a Mr. Allain, courrier to Mr. Dabney; and two other young soldiers, courriers for Father.[4] It became necessary to have furniture, dishes, etc. It was also resolved that I should be sent for the things. Léon was not to be trusted alone. Mr. Gibbens was going to Baton Rouge on business. I was to go with him, and Léon, with two government wagons, was to meet me at our house the next day. It was reported that the Yankees had evacuated Baton Rouge for the time being. I was dressed in a muslin dress with figures. Just as I was about to leave, Ma said to me, "As soon as you reach town you will go to old Mr. Bonnecaze's, talk awhile with them and when the old gentleman goes in his office in the warehouse, you will follow him there. Then you will take a pin and rip the hem of your dress and give him what is sewed there, then you will baste it up again, and go back to the parlor and forget the incident."[5] A threaded needle was in my pocket book, also a note for the landlord, Mr. Pujol, and a letter to Mrs. R. G. De Laroderie to whom I was recommended.

Ostensibly, I was going to help Léon pack our belongings. I never knew what manner of papers I delivered to the old gentleman but they were closely written and the paper was watermarked in little squares as was used to write to Europe. Mr. Bonnecaze did not seem surprised and said not a word, only put his hand on my head and said I was a trustworthy child and the episode was closed. I went about my other business which was to pick out the things Ma needed and have them ready for the wagons.

They arrived in the early morning, entered Mrs. Larguier's back lane close to our fence and our work began in earnest. I found that the house had been used as a residence for Yankee officers. Things had been used but not abused but many had been carried away, all our toys, several paintings, and many curios of which we had quite a quantity. *I* regret those things yet. There were two, extra large, silver mounted alligator teeth, several carved cocoanut shells, a little urn made of Foam of the Dead Sea, large pieces of amber Mother had picked up herself on the shore of the Baltic sea sometime near 1826 or 1827, etc., etc. I suppose the things were sent as trophies and play-toys to some Yankee children who may be showing them yet to admiring friends, as tokens undeniable? of their father's bravery. Of course, they would not call it theft as I did then, and still do now.

We got quite a number of things in the wagons, beds, armoir, tables, chairs, the piano, a safe, a cooking stove, and case after case of crockery and glassware. I had time for very few ornaments and useless things when the drivers announced that rumors were afloat that the gunboats were coming up the river and they really could not delay their start, so I hurriedly threw in lots of bedding and unbreakable things and they went, and Léon with them. I was very anxious to close the house and pay up the landlord according to Mother's instructions.

A Mr. Eudes had had a new brick store built just before the war broke out. This store had never been used and stood vacant and closed all the time. Mr. Eudes came to me and advised me to take anything in his store, and only pay up to the occupation of the Yankees. He said he knew the house had not been taken by force but had been offered to them as a safeguard against its being burned or otherwise abused, so he took things in hand.

There happened to be some soldier trappings and things, Bayonets, cartridge boxes, belts, etc., in an out house. Mr. Eudes did not want those in his store, so he had two men dig a large hole on the grounds and bury all the soldiery equipment.

Then all was done: house closed, keys given up. When the Yankees poured into the yard the men all decamped, Mrs. Eudes remaining with me.

They questioned us. What were we doing there, who were we, etc., etc. Mrs. Eudes was French and claimed not to understand. I had nothing much to hide so I told a straight tale, leaving out that I had not gotten everything in the C.S. wagons. Then, about the hole, only but freshly filled. That, I told them was Confederate equipment. Where did I live? In Port Hudson, etc. They cursed around a while then began to dig. Mrs. Eudes and I slipped away over the back fence, she went home, I went to Mrs. De la Roderie's to await orders from Mother. I cannot now remember if I stayed 3 or 5 days before I was sent for. During those days I went about very little. It was not pleasant in Baton Rouge.

At the time of the bombardment many persons had dug pits, from 3 to 4 feet deep and from 7 to 10 feet long, and about as wide. In these they crouched in moments of danger and during the battle of Aug. 6th. These pits were now all filled with dead men in a more or less state of decomposition. When a pit was filled up an army blanket was stretched atop, the corners held down with bricks, and there ended the disposition of the dead. It was a cheap and lazy way but the Yankees escaped the offensive odors by getting on their boats and anchoring above or below the town— as the wind blew North or South. Swarms of large green flies covered the whole place. As one walked on the side-walks they were crushed or crept under one's clothing. People were often taken with nausea on the streets.

I saw most of these horrors on my way from Mr. Bonnecaze's to our house as I had to cross the heart of the city.

Near Mrs. De La Roderie's there were very few buried and the stench was only occasionally wafted her way.

One night a servant entered my room. However lightly she stepped I heard her. She went to the window and I heard a sort of smothered exclamation. I got up and went to the window also.

"Something is going on in the school yard," she said. "Look."

Several men were walking about with lanterns. They dug a long hole like a grave, but not the whole depth of their spades. Those with lanterns were officers, the gold braid showed bright now and then in the light. The others I could hardly distinguish. They carried a dead man to the edge of the hole, took off his coat and vest (evidently he was not a soldier), put him in the shallow grave, spread the vest across his face, put a brick on each side, and threw in the displaced earth. Then all was dark and when I looked around the servant had disappeared. My hair seemed to rise and hurt my head. I felt hot, and cold, by turns. I stayed rooted near the window and daylight found me there. My eyes smarted, my face was wet. I did not know that I had cried. I was still looking at that spot in the school house yard. The man's feet stuck out at least 3 inches and one arm lay flat out on the ground.

That is all I ever knew of the case. The next night I was given a room on the other side of the house, the two boys exchanging with me. They tried to tease me about being nervous, but next day "Teit" said neither of them had slept at all. They continually got up to *see* if anything was going on. That morning a Mr. Potts came for me, he had a note from Mother.[6] He only announced himself in the morning and said he would come for me after dark.

Mr. Potts was a small spare man. He was a sort of harmless cowardly man as was loudly proclaimed by the fact that he was there at all. He was middle aged and should have been in the army. It seems the Potts had lived in Baton Rouge for years, but we had never heard of them. They lived and moved in a different circle. But a War levels many ranks, and we knew much of the Potts' later on.

Long after dark, Mr. Potts came for me. I had no baggage at all. He carried a few parcels, I relieved him of one. We walked quite a long way skirting the Penitentiary walls. We saw no sentrys; all was as still as death. (Probably this was after the Yankees had turned loose the convicts.) Only our footsteps crushing small twigs, or moving the dry leaves could be heard in the stillness. I don't know how it was that a conviction came to me that Mr. Potts was scared. When he spoke his voice trembled. A sort of pity for him rose to my lips yet I despised him for his cowardice. I suggested that if we talked, it would seem less lonely.

"No," he said in a trembling whisper, "no, child, we might be shot at. Don't talk; we must be near the buggy now." And so it proved.

We were now on the big road and one could see one's way a little. We made as good time as the little old nag could make. We had 32 miles to travel. At times we took side roads, through the woods. Then Mr. Potts' breath came hard and jerky. At last we were nearing Port Hudson. When voices sounded Mr. Potts almost jumped out the buggy.

"Who goes there?" "Halt!" the voice said.

I knew it was the Confederate picket. Mr. Potts laid the whip to the horse and said, "G'long, Bob," and we rattled away. No shot followed and soon after we reached Mr. Gibbons' house.

In the morning I found that Mr. Gibbons had brought home another wife. She and two friends sat in the parlor, one knee over the arm of the rocking chair, each a little open mouth bottle in their hand, and rubbing their teeth with little soft looking sticks.

I was never so astounded in my life. I had seen a few brides, but this was a new kind. I afterward found out that they were "Dipping," a past time indulged in by many ladies in out of the way country places. Later I heard nice ladies speak of her quite as an equal. So it was only my narrow mindedness that made me at that time think that ladies were those who were like us, and our circle of friends.

That day we moved into a vacated house in the village of Port Hudson. It was a very nice house with many rooms and many out houses and an underground cistern not completed. Water had to be gotten in a near-by delapidated house.

There began for us an altogether new existence. To be sure, there were the evergoing, inevitable lessons, but beyond these, we had comparative freedom. Mother was very busy about her housekeeping and my work was to look after the little ones. That was not very difficult in a soldier town. In front of the house was a lawn. There the recruits were drilled several times a day. That occupied the young ones. Then the couriers would fly to and fro, take orders, carry messages, so there were always horses and men moving around. Then two or three times a day regiments or companies marched by with fifes and drums or maybe music.

We knew the commands and could drill like old troopers. The mistakes of the raw recruits were a source of great amusement to all of us. The boys would shout in glee, "That one don't know his right foot from his left; Look at this one presenting arms with his gun front behind;" and so on, as the mistakes were made.

On Sunday, Capt. Ginder would take sister and me to service in one camp or another. All this was such a novelty and such freedom from scoldings. It was war time, but we children were happy. There was an abundance of some things and a total lack of others. Candles and lamp oil were entirely missing. We went to bed when the Bugle sounded and Reveille brought us out of bed in the morning.

At this time I learned to ride horse back in a new way; it was without a habit and on a McLellan saddle. Long legged but ever kind Capt. Woodside would watch over me, and I often rode his horse to water a mile or so from the house, he riding or walking at my side. He was a wonderful walker, never seemed to use his knees, took steps 38 inches long (by measurement) all from his hips. At a distance, when he crossed a pasture he looked like a huge automatic compass. We were very fond of him.

His horse was a lean sunburned black beast that ate double rations and never showed it, but he was a long backed horse and four of us often sat on his back to look at some drill or passing troops.

Capt. Dabney was very friendly to me, particularly. He appeared to have been a wealthy man, all his belongings were fine. Many were silver mounted, and his horse's trapping were very fine. The horse was a most beautiful very dark bay. Mr. Dabney would tell me tales at odd times and always said they were true. I knew better, but if it pleased him, I was willing to appear convinced. He told me all about the girl he was going to marry and showed me her handwriting and picture. I believed it all, then one day he said, "You know my affianced is a Tar Heel." Then I did *not* believe. I did not know what a Tar Heel was. It sounded derogatory to my ears. Yet the tale was true. She did live in the Miss. Piney Woods, and was very nice, and he married her after the war.

I have in my papers a very graphic account written by himself of his horrible experiences in a Northern prison. He lived to a very old age in Crystals Springs, Miss.

Every evening we went the rounds of the fortifications with father. We learned many things about Redouts, Redans, Batteries, 12 Pounders, 15-

inch Columbiads, and many other things that children out of the army never hear of.

Once a fifteen inch columbiad had just been hoisted in place, and an officer asked me if I would like to crawl into it, just for the glory of having been inside a cannon, the largest in Port Hudson defences. No, I did not want to get in; that sort of fun did not appeal to me. I thought as a soldier he should have had more dignity than to put the word Glory to such a prank. I was beginning to have very exalted ideas. All soldiers to me were heroes, and if they proved not to be so, they fell below my notice. It is hard for a child to be perfectly fair in times such as those were.

Our supper table would astonish people of the present day. Ma used her porcelain and cut glass and silver. But the table linen was too small for such a long table as we had then, so table cloths had been made of two widths of unbleached cotton. As to lights, four small scoops filled with tallow, or suet, with a wick made out of a little piece of twisted rag sufficed. They smoked and smelt badly, but there were no tin-smiths to make candle molds, and we were satisifed as it was.

By this time our shoes gave out or nearly so. We were barefooted all week and put on shoes only to go about the camps on Sunday.

The weather was getting cold and Father had begun to be sick with the dread Army disease dysentery. Ma nursed him as best she could. There were good doctors and medicines, but the food-stuff was not of the right kind for a sick man. The doctor said Pa's food could be prepared only with goose grease, there was no fresh lard. With a great deal of trouble a goose was procured and the process of fattening it was begun. She was put in a very small cage and fed all she would eat, then that much again of soaked corn. The task of fattening that goose was given to brother. Brother forgot it at times and found it too hard to do at others. Ma scolded and punished, but goose did not fare well, and Father was getting worse all the time. I realized that Léon had to be helped or replaced. For a few days *he* helped, afterward at feeding time he had disappeared.

We had with us two of our women slaves. I often wondered why one of them had not been instructed to see to that stuffing process. Most probably Ma did not know that it was a *very* painful task. The coop was on the North East side of the house. The corn soaked all night and was in freezing water by morning. Our little fingers had as yet never been toughened. That goose just bit down on the hand that held her beak, and the other that fed the corn was all but frozen. Reader, you may smile, but the pain was intense. Standing bare footed in the frozen grass, with wet hands and fingers till they were blue. It was a torture from the second day. I could not well blame Léon for his backsliding. Yet, it had to be done and I did it, sister was too small. I did it, but I cried, not loud, but long at night. I would wrap my hands in towels to numb the pain, and I went to sleep.

It happened that just when Father was, so they thought, dying, Ma could not keep baby Henry in his room. So he was given to me for night weaning. Those nights were dreadful. I was so sleepy and my hands hurt so and the baby would wake and miss mother. I would take him in my arms and walk him up and down the room. Walk one way till I touched the wall and back in the darkness till I touched the bed. I was cold, sleepy, and tired. He was heavy and a year old.

We tried for four nights, but nursing in the day he could not forget. So we weaned him altogether and in three days he had entirely forgotten the breast. Unfortunately food for a young child was difficult to get. Ma did not dry her milk, and a week or so after, father being better, Henry was given the breast again.

In these few months my childhood had slipped from me, never to return. Necessity, humane obligations, glory's obligation, family pride, and patriotism had taken entire possession of my little undersized body, and my over developed mental being.

In these times of father's illness, he was taken to the fortifications in an ambulance and carried on a stretcher into every redout not completed. I always went with him, he was frequently faint several times during one round. If father could suffer and do his work, we could suffer and be silent about it. Ma never heard a word of plaint from Léon or I. Sister was young for her age and cried when she was cold, or hungry, or in the dark. The younger ones were never hungry because they had our share, never cold because we gave them all that was best. They were babies. But all of this suffering was in its very incipiency in Port Hudson and in 1862. December came in very cold. The fortifications were about all up. Father was better when an order was given that all women and children and non-combatants were to leave the town by the first of January as the Yankees were preparing to beseige the place.

I don't know if there were any non-combatants. Of women there were two: Mother and Mrs. Duquarny. Children there were six of us, one baby Duquarny, and one Ike Cox, 10 years old, and his little sister, five. I had never seen those till December 31st when we saw them pass our house with a little bundle. They were offered help and transportation with us on the morrow but the boy refused; said he knew where he was going: "Out in the country a piece."

I was in bed with fever that day, and also the next, but the time limit had come. General Garner, who was commander of the troops, lent us wagons and an ambulance, and on the 1st of January 1863 we moved to Jackson, La., to a house father had secured by correspondence.[7] It was bitterly cold and sleeted all morning. I suffered a great deal of pains in the head during the fifteen-mile drive. Army ambulances were very rough affairs, but they were curtained all around and we were well sheltered from the sleet.

❧ War Time ❧ in Jackson, La.

WE ARRIVED at dusk and found the house was not yet vacant. Several Jew merchants lived there upstairs over a closed store. After a little parley, they consented to let us have two rooms, one large and one small. These rooms both faced the north and were without a fire place. A mattress was put on the floor. All of us crowded on it and covered up with blankets. There were just eleven panes of glass missing from the casements.

Our belongings were piled up in a large hall down stairs. The two servants with the child Alice slept in the kitchen and had a fire, shared with the Jew's serving man.

Thus we spent our first and most miserable night. "Children," Ma said after prayers, "So long as we have Father we can not complain. You will never see me cry; I expect the same of you."

We never saw her cry. Léon and I never let her know any of our sufferings.

The next morning the snow and sleet had heaped up against the door so that we could not open it. The boys found exit through the small room window onto a side gallery. I was still with fever. The men in the next room had a big fire burning, we could see the glow through the transom. Ma sent the boys and the baby in the kitchen to get warm, but little girls, of course, could not go in that kitchen full of niggers.

104

Much of the food we brought from Port Hudson lasted quite a time, the meats being frozen, as the weather stayed for fifteen days the same. We were fifteen days in the same huddled condition. Only Ma had cut up the oil cloth rugs to close the broken panes.

When it thawed a little the Jew men moved out, and we fixed ourselves up in the house. There were five rooms in all upstairs, an attic, a large hall down stairs, a kitchen and an ironing room, a well with a windlass, and the yard was large and weedy with a big thorn tree in the middle.

My first knowledge of the outside world was of a funeral passing the house. We afterward heard that it was that of John Catlett, killed in a skirmish in Mississippi (I think).

Later some of the neighbors called—Mrs. Wiley, Mrs. Cross, Miss Perry, etc.[1] All were pretty women and were dressed in silk dresses protected by aprons, small, fancy aprons. Grown people's nice clothes lasted pretty well the four years. With children it was different, we grew out of them.

Just opposite us was a very nice place and on a shed Ma saw numbers of pumpkins. She sent Odile with Léon to buy two. The old lady to whom they belonged, it seems, had never sold her produce, so she called to a man and said, "What do you think these ought to sell for?"

To which he made answer, "Well, maybe 10 cts. apiece these yer wah' times."

She turned to Odile and said, "Well, you may take two for twenty cents a piece." Odile was surprised but proceeded to take 2 large ones, but the old lady said, "Now be fair woman, take one large and one small one." Léon paid the 40 cts. and bowing, retired, followed by the servant.

"Mother," he said, "that is a grasping stingy lady."

"Don't judge, son," said Ma. "We don't know her, and she need not have sold them at all; she does not keep a store."

And indeed, we learned to love old Mrs. Cary Fishburn. She was a highly cultured aristocratic old lady, who proved a friend and comfort to Mother in the dreary days that were fast coming.

Of course our lessons had hardly been interrupted. Wrapped in our blanket on our mattress we recited fables, and conjugated verbs, and parsed sentences. Ma wrote with soap on her mirror—our things were not unpacked for two weeks.

Léon was beginning to rebel at lessons, he kept himself out of calling. On pretext of getting news and foraging, he was much out of Ma's domination.

Just about that time too, he and sister began to disagree more and more, and they had very ugly squabbles. He did many forbidden things, such as chewing gum, or smoking porous vines. Sister would tell on him, Ma would punish him, and he would come back at sister and chastise her, in some way. She would go to Ma about it and there it was, right through till they were grown. If Mother gave Léon two slaps; sister would get four. She knew her risk when she went to tattle, but she was never deterred and so it went.

With Paul it was different, they seemed to belong to each other. Léon deprived himself of anything for Paul, and Paul was all devoted to Léon. Eddie and I were the same relation to each other. The baby Henry was our joint care.

We heard from Father often. Sometimes he was very sick, other times better. His usefulness was almost at an end in Port Hudson. He was awaiting orders for further work in some other place.

Occasionally, he sent us some of his spare rations, and always most of his pay. Confederate money was good then.

Once father rode out to see us. He was with a Mr. Miller—Mr. J. C. Miller, professor or President of Centenary College.[2] During the war, of course, every college boy was a soldier. Mr. Miller said that his brother, A. G. Miller, had a school a mile out and that we might find it best to go there to school.[3] The upshot of it was that I was enrolled the next day. Mine was a peculiar course of learning: these first years given entirely to French with very little English picked up here and there; now this totally inadequate American tuition.

The Miller school house occupied two rooms. One, a long one, contained pupils from the ABC class to girls 17 years old. The smaller room was supposed to be for higher classes. They all seemed to be grown women to me. In the large room a tiny, sweet-looking girl-woman presided over the little ones up to the third reader as payment for her own tuition in the other room. The larger classes of the big room were taught by Mrs. Miller (she was the third or fourth wife of Mr. Miller). The young teacher was Miss Clara Green.

My first day in the school found me very disappointed. I was made to follow the 3rd reader class. I read very badly, was probably more fit for second reader, but in other ways I was educated and wanted to follow geography and arithmetic with girls of my age. A girl, Annie Jones, said that I need not worry, no one learned anything from Mrs. Miller any way. The fact is that the arithmetic class had just entered into long division, and at the close of the term the page they were started on had not been worked to the end.

I listened a great deal, and in that way learned the pronunciation of many words. I soon saw that Miss Clara was a sort of martyr and was not allowed a moment to study or go and recite her lessons in the next room. Mrs. M. would be called off for hours for household cares or her babies, and the room would be left to Miss Clara. Then she would teach the bigger pupils and I was given the little classes. Such a school!! And Ma was paying tuition every month. A month or so later, I was sent into Mr. Miller's room for a dictionary. He was having a class in parsing. A young lady, Miss Bertha Taylor, was hesitating over a word. I whispered to her, "It is an active verb."

Surprised, she turned, Mr. Miller saw me and asked, "How do you know, little French lady?" Then I explained the position I was in, relatively to putting in English what I knew in French. Right away he took me into his room for History, Geography, and grammar. They used the large Bullion's *Grammar,* and there it was that I learned English grammar by comparing where the rules did, or did not, tally with those of

French. In French I was far more educated than Mr. Miller's young ladies; however, in arithmetic I had never been taught further than reduction of fractions.

I soon became quite a favorite with all the girls especially the big girls. I fairly worshiped some of those, first of all Blanche McCantz, then Cynthia Godbeau, Rhoda Worthey, Bertha Taylor, then Annie Jane, who was my age; and Miss Fuqua, also about my age.

I never cared for boys, but the boys had an immensely false idea of my capacities. They learned, or rather studied, Latin. I did not take Latin, and as I knew French they concluded that I knew Latin and Greek and for some reason would not say I did. No denials were of any avail. They *knew*. The oldest boy, I guess, was about 15 years old and he chose to fall in love with me, and he showered me with Latin letters, or was it Latin verses. They were put in my books, in my hat, on the roadside where I was sure to pass. He was a big fat boy who could never completely conceal himself in the neighboring bushes. I always saw him, so never picked up the notes (unintelligible to me anyway). Finally he tired [of] writing unread things and only indulged in Valentines every February.

Mrs. Miller had several boarding scholars. Blanche McCants was one of them. One day Mrs. Miller asked me if I would mind going up to Miss Blanche's room, as she was sick and no one was there to stay with her. I went gladly that day and the next five or six days. The doctor came while I was in charge. He mopped and burned her throat and remarked to me that she must gargle every twenty minutes. He added, "She has putrid sore throat and it is necessary to be regular with the medication." I only mention this to show what sort of schooling I was getting and what sort of care the boarders got. What luck there was no board of health then to scare me away from the contagion—which did not prove contagious.

Toward the end of April great preparations were made for a May festival. My life had not contained festivals as belonging to school or study. I was delighted. The queen was chosen by vote and B. McCants was chosen May Queen. It was quite an elaborate festival with recitations, odes, long marches, etc. We were all very prettily dressed. Our fancy clothes were not worn out or very much too short. Our "before the war" ribbons and sashes were bright and fresh. Ma had made me a nice pair of black velvet shoes for the occasion. A Mrs. Vigliny had woven my garland of rose buds and I was a happy child that day.

A pretty trait of Annie Jones's character was brought out at this time. There was in school a poor girl named Raby Mills who said she would not come to the May party as she had no proper clothes. Annie went home thoughtful and found her mother about to cut into some nice swiss to make her dress. She stopped her and asked if there was enough there to make two dresses. "No," her mother said, "Goods are too high to buy more than needed. There is just enough of this fine goods to make your dress, and of this common one for your under-dress." Then Annie persuaded Mrs. Jones to return the fine goods and get more of the common muslin and to make two dresses, one to give Raby. "But Annie," Mrs. Jones remarked, "it is very coarse and common. You will may-be feel sorry when you see the other girls." But Annie persisted; she knew she would feel quite happy enough in the thought that the other girl would be pleased.

So it was with Annie Jones ever: fair and truthful, generous and modest. She lived beloved of all who know her. She had many trials in life but she was never crushed. Her sphere of usefulness never grew less. As one beloved care was taken by the grim reaper she reached around for the most in need of help and ministered them.

Toward the end of the session Mrs. Miller's two youngest children had whooping cough and measles. Annie—four years old—died in a few days. To make her a coffin the boards of a Mahogany table were used. A negro carpenter did the job; it was badly done. The extension boards of the table were replaced by rough boards from a barn. I have seen Mr. Miller pass that table and almost tenderly, pass his hand on those boards. It would start the tears to my eyes every time for I knew how he had loved the little one, brought to mind by the defaced table.

The other baby Charlie, a year old, was saved. Annie had smothered in a coughing spell in the closed atmosphere necessitated by the measles. Old Mr. Miller and the Grandmother took the baby out for drives twice a day. He was entirely covered with a blanket having only a four inch slit fitted about baby's nose and mouth. And he recovered, later in manhood becoming a Methodist minister.

The school was closed. The class had yet a few examples of long division to work out; I had learned quite a great deal in spelling and in the pronunciation of words and construction of sentences that were not so "patently" translations of French thoughts. All the big girls were my friends and helped me in a great many ways. Girls my own age often laughed and would say, "Frenchy, you will always be French even in the next world, won't you?" But it was all in friendliness, and their teasing did not hurt. If they had known half as much in their own tongue as I knew in mine, they would have been formidable opponents during the following sessions. But they did not, and I left them far in the rear, excepting Annie Jones; we were together for arithmetic and later algebra.

At home things had settled into something like a home. The servants did the work, Ma did the teaching of those unfortunate little ones. I had had my time and I knew Léon had rebelled against anything like lessons. Ma held it against him and in many ways showed her displeasure but she feared that he would run off and join some guerilla troop, so did not push her point. Eatables were getting scarce, our life was getting harder everyday. It was ever: there is no more soap, no more brooms, no more meat, no more of this, that or the other.

No more communications with any place. During the vacations—the first I had ever known—I was busy making clothes for Henri. He was growing out of all the baby clothes. Ma's bed was a large four poster and the tester was made of Turkey-Red very thickly gathered. There were yards of it on a flat thin cotton foundation. I took all this cloth off and of it Henry was dressed until the 14th of August 1865. Shoes and stockings he never had, and did not seem to mind. His little feet were as hard as leather underneath. Shoes he also got on the 14th of August 1865.

Our woman, Mary-Jane, had made up her mind to taste the freedom offered by the North, and slipped away one night, together with alot of other niggers. That left us with only one servant. Mary-Jane stole nothing from us except a "night vase," quite an unusual thing to tempt a nigger. But she took off with her a number of articles belonging to Odile, the cook. Nice fine clothes—Sunday-go-to-meeting things.

Provisions were getting very scarce. There was a great *sameness* about the menu, and every meal bore a great resemblance to the one that preceded it.

With Port Hudson beseiged, greater hardships were encountered almost every week. Detachments of Yankees visited through the country, sometimes a whole regiment, sometimes only a score of men. They left in their tracks greater want, desolations, and losses.

Very few were the real nameless horrors or crimes committed on girls. For instance once the Yankees filled the town just about sun set, they had several companies of Mexicans and niggers among them.[4] Of course every one of the women stayed closely in doors. In a small house on the street that heads out toward the creek lived old Mrs. ———, and her granddaughter Carrie. She was a remarkably pretty girl with an abundance of light curly hair. Her father was in the Army. Carrie was beautiful of face, but not very bright. Her Grand-mother was sick in bed at the time, and hearing the tramp of troops, directed that the doors be closed, so also the windows. In some way, however, some of the Yankees saw the girl. They forced open the door, tied the old lady to her bed and carried off the girl. It was late the next morning when some one passing, heard Mrs. ——— groaning. They went in, and heard the appalling tale. Several persons joined in a search for poor Carrie. She was found nearly dead, and completely crazy in a jungle near a torrent, bathed in her own blood, disheveled and torn. Several months later her father's regiment being in the vicinity, he got a permit to run in and see his mother and his girl. What he found was worse than death: the beautiful babbling idiot for ever and ceaselessly begging for mercy; or laughing a frightful laugh at the bloody spots that she fancied were yet on her garment.

Another girl—a grown young lady—was also outraged. Her name was Ada ———— but I never knew the details of her case, only that she seemed to have grown much older all at once, and I never saw her laugh after that time.

As I said these very terrible sins were not numerous, but petty meannesses were many. During one "raid" the Yankees entered the only drug store and destroyed every bit of the contents. The community was left without an ounce of medicine.

Once they crossed Mrs. Green's plantation and killed every calf and pig they could find. They did not make use of the meat, just left it in the fields. Mrs. Green had a young baby, they took all its little clothes, and tore them to shreds. Just such sort of narrow, mean, unmanly, sort of acts, were perpetrated by every "raiding" gang. All our men were Gentlemen, and it did not appear as if any of theirs were so. A few officers behaved as soldiers should, but their men seemed—and were, in many regiments—the scum of immigrants and the out put of penitentiaries.

Shortly before Port Hudson was surrounded by the Yankees, Father, being again very low with "Army-flux," was sent out to try and get well, later to proceed to Mobile. He was home I think several weeks. He had been brought to Ma in a little wagon full of corn shucks, his horse had been left at Mr. Burton's near Bayou Sara. Léon was sent for it. As he came through town riding the fine bay, a lady asked him whose horse it was and how he came to be riding such a fine horse. Léon, knowing no better, told how it was that father was too sick to go off yet, but wanted the horse there near at hand.

Scarcely a quarter of an hour had passed, when a person dressed in a splendid riding habit and announcing herself as Miss Agnes Murdock wished to see Capt. Frémaux. On inquiry, it was found that she wanted to borrow Pa's horse for a ride, and so sure was she of getting it that she was prepared to mount immediately. Father sent word that a soldier's horse was not lendable; that even in a dying condition an order might come and he would have to ride off. She insisted to see father and plead with him. So Mother came down, in a very few words she made herself distinctly understood. The interview was ended; Miss Agnes Murdock left as she had come, a foot. She is the same woman who married a Capt. Jenks, known as Capt. Jenks of the "Horse Marines." During Reconstruction times she was notoriously prominent as the ——— of one of the most rascally republicans of La.

We children had been rather attracted by the "Lady's" looks, and were at a loss to account for our parent's evidently outraged feelings. We understood years later.

Once a lot of Yankees entered the town and came up to take father prisoner. Father was so ill that they could not take him off, so they consulted about it, and sent up a young Irish-peasant looking soldier to put him on parole, but Father looked so very ill that the man called down to his officers that it was no use parolling a man that was beyond speech, and was all but dead. Thus Pa escaped being parolled.

That night Father had himself strapped to his horse, and left for Mobile.[5] By a miracle he reached there alive a week later, and found that his brother and friend, Mr. Du Thillet, were stationed there. Mr. Du Thillet eventually cured Father, with some root infusion, the virtue of which he knew.

Until the 17th of August 1865 we never saw Father, and in all that time I think only four times did we hear from him.

The vacation being over, Mr. and Mrs. Miller did not reopen their school. A Miss Gayle had opened a school in one of the old preparatory buildings of Centenary College. A Mrs. Kanneer had for several years had a school for small children. Confederate money, or any other money for that matter was useless. Mother kept me home. The school had been opened two weeks when Miss Mollie Gayle came and asked Mother to allow me to come to her. Ma had not yet learned to accept things without pay. The next day Miss Mollie returned. She had gathered together many arguments. Her niece accompanied her; she was a music teacher, Miss Clara Faries. They argued with mother a long time. It was finally settled that I should go to school and be guided in music. In return, Miss Clara would use our piano to give several lessons, and her pupils would come to our house to practice. I was very much pleased. It had been so terrible, the staying home and seeing Ma teach the younger ones. The beatings and almost insane rages into which Ma's overwrought nervous system threw her against those poor children was even worse than to be beat myself. I caught a goodly number of stray licks myself, on any and every occasion. Ma seemed to have taken a spite against me because of the very flattering recommendation Mr. Miller had given when he told Miss Gayle of my existence and told her to ask me to her school. Sister had not been asked, in fact she was not known at all. She knew nothing of English and did not even desire to learn any thing in that language. It was not my fault, but Ma acted as if it was. Ma always spoke to me and about me as an unnatural sister who tried to rise and make friends to the detriment of my kindred. I wept many many bitter hours about Ma's manner to me. Léon was then my only friend at home. I think at that time sister fairly hated both Léon and me. The others were nil. Sister and Léon had a slapping match several times a day. I never slapped or otherwise hit any of Ma's children, but I often had to hold sister off till her anger was spent to keep from being hit or scratched by the jealous girl. Generally she screamed so that Ma would come give me a cuffing or a knock with anything that came handy. Once it happened to be a poker, and when she threw it from her it made such a noise on the floor that I think it recalled Ma to herself. I could not move my shoulder for a moment, and Ma mumbled something about not thinking it was iron. She took sister by the arm and went down stairs.

Léon was in the next room and had seen the whole affair. It had started by sister wanting a string of Chinkapins that I had. I had locked them in a little bureau drawer, the only thing I *ever* owned that could lock. The next day Ma ordered me to unlock the tiny drawer and never again to lock anything so long as I lived under her roof. She was obeyed of course. (I married in 1871 and have never turned a key on any of my belongings.)

As I said, Léon had heard the whole thing. He knew where my key was, he rushed to the drawer, opened it, took out the string of nuts, and relocked it. When I went to school next morning he gave them to me and advised me to eat them, but my desire for the ornament had passed. I divided them among the three little boys and never made another.

The pride of the girls at school was to see how long a string could be made in one day's gathering. My pride in little things of that kind died a hard but coercive death; in every effort that was not for the family's well-fare I was thwarted. My education was all I was allowed to have personally. Perhaps I would have grown romantic (who knows). But, if I came across a very touching piece of poetry or a very beautiful flower, Ma would criticize the poems line by line, and unpoetize it, and would say something derogatory of the uselessness of flowers or the triflingness of a big girl that might best be spinning rather than losing time as I always tried to do.

The war was on in its full devastation by then. I made, lengthened, mended, or patched all my clothes and Henry's. I went to school from eight A.M. to four P.M., gave the two boys a lesson in English reading every evening after school. I corded and spun all the yarn to knit all the covering that was knitable. Mine was the job of barking red oak and sweet gum, which Ma used to dye sheets and yarn for our dresses and the boys' clothes. My implements for the bark-taking work were a medium-size cold chisel and a small ax that had not been sharpened since the war began.

If soap was to be made, mine was the job to go out with the little boys and look for some dead animal, crack the bones and gather the marrow for the soap making. Kindling was always scarce, so I with the children would go and gather pine cones by the baby carriage load. Mr. Andrew Tomb had a thicket of young pine trees on his land. He told us we could get wood there if we could cut it. Léon and I had that work to do with the same little ax and the aid of a rip saw of father's. We did what we could, then tied a clothesline to the pieces and dragged them home, about a mile, up two hills, down one, across a branch of Black Creek, to the house. These, were the main things I had to do; and I was begrudged a flower or an ecstasy of any kind.

Once a lady said to me, "Your Mother is a Martinet, isn't she?"

I did not understand, I thought she meant a Martinican so I answered, "No madame, she is a Parisian." By the laugh that came, I knew I had made a mistake, so I looked it up in the dictionary later. I knew and felt very hurt that any one could have believed me capable of telling Ma's hard ways with us. I lived in fear that people would know, and since I have grown I have learned that people *did* know quite a lot of our home ways. I think they felt, however, that Ma was undergoing an ordeal herself. For a small, weak, highly cultured woman to do the hard work that she did, and under such constant strain of anxiety, and suffering with nervous sick head-aches at least twice a week—it was enough to make her do outrageous things.

When Ma slapped my hand up and down the edge of the schoolroom table—for having misspelled a word, or made a blot in a copy book, I cried and prayed that some day one of my fingers might break, so that Pa might know of it and maybe see to it that Ma be less vigorous. But my fingers never broke, and when I saw Ma inflict the same punishment on the little ones I felt desperate. No use praying for their poor little toughened fingers to break. Pa was far away and I was powerless.

I loved the school hours, I loved Miss Mollie, and I loved all my school mates. Miss Mollie herself was a brilliant woman and kind and just. She was a graduate of the Judson Institute of Alabama. All learned well, in her school and we progressed rapidly. I stayed at the head by reason of my previous French education. Calculation was never hard to me. We studied, however, under great difficulty. Books were scarce; for instance, four of us studied in one history. It belonged to Edith Jones. I borrowed it every Sunday and copied all we could learn in a week. The others lived near each other and studied from the book.

There were forty pupils and there were many different arithmetics used. Mine and Annie Jones were Greenleaf's. Others had Davies' of many editions, some big, some little, and so it was for every book. But we all learned.

Then again we were frequently interrupted for hours or a day or two.

If a band of Raiders swarmed over the town we got home as best we could, and it was understood that as soon as the town was free of enemies, school would reopen. Sometimes it was 10 o'clock and sometime only for an evening session. It was also understood that for every day that we stayed home, we studied up a reasonable lesson in each book and worked up a number of "Sums." And strange as it may seem, very few scholars failed to comply with these agreements. Children had become so reasonable in those troubled times.

Once we heard and felt the tramp of Cavalry. Nearer and nearer it came: shots we heard also. Miss Mollie ordered all to stoop to the floor, and not a moment too soon. The bullets came shattering the window panes, and quite a number pierced the thin weather-boards—there were no inner walls. Just then we heard a moan and a thud on the steps. We got out there just as the Yankees crowded up around a fallen Confederate soldier. It was the first time I had seen a man shot down and die just at my feet.

The man had fourteen holes through which his blood had run out. Seven bullets had gone through and through. He asked for water. The boys brought the pail. I handed him my gourd. He swallowed very little and whispered something to one of the big girls. Miss Mollie was putting compresses to the open wounds. I saw the big girl quietly steal away, go down the road a bit, pick up something, tuck it in her bosom, and come back. Meanwhile the Yankees searched the dead or dying man. They tore up his clothes, looked in his ragged shoes etc. The blood spurted all the time, their hands were red. Miss Mollie's dress and many others were blood smeared. Not a word was being uttered by any of us. Finally a Yankee came to the pail, took up my gourd, drank and hung it back on the edge by the crock. I lifted it off with my foot and stepped on it.

The man roundly cursed me and asked, "Why did you do that you ———— little Rebel?"

I only answered, "It was polluted," and I turned away.

Mrs. Kenneer had come upon the scene. She was an old lady, and had only one arm. She asked an officer if we could remove the dead man. He said, "Why, yes, old mammy, if you can do it with your one arm."

All these young arms are mine, she answered. "We are all one in this cause." She went in her house and got a sheet, the boys fetched a plank and all together we lifted the dead or dying man, and took him inside the building.

The Yankees had ridden on, the big girl, Miss Holdridge, brought forth her find: the man's cap with his name on it, and a paper to Gen. Ogden saying "Dispatches received, orders understood."[6] So the faithful messenger had delivered dispatches and was returning to his command, when overtaken and killed. His horse, a lame one, bled to death. Some of the boys had tried to ease him, but to no avail.

Mrs. Kenneer and a Mrs. Dyman took charge of the body. A little boy named Belden (I think) undertook to notify the soldier's people, and Sallie Decker saw his little sister home and notified his mother not to be uneasy about him. The boy, 11 years old, walked off on his twelve mile errand, and by daylight next morning two of the soldier's sisters arrived with a suit of clothes. Then the soldier was buried on the hill. This was a dreadful experience to me, I felt sick, and hurt like. I washed my hands over and over, yet they seemed to feel sticky, and the odor of blood seemed to be with me for days.

Next day, when we went to the school all had been washed up as well as possible and a heavy layer of sand spread on the floor. From my place I could see the flicker of the "tallow-dip" that burned in Mrs. Dymon's house. Between me and the blackboard that light and the man's pale face seemed to stand out pitifully.

All during the siege of Port Hudson there were skirmishes and fights in the vicinity. The Confederate scouts harassed the Yankee troops all they could. Then it was that Capt. John McKewen became famous for his daring acts, and his successful attacks on the Yankee Camps resulted frequently in the capture of commissary supplies much needed by our soldiers.[7] Eatables were extreme scarce. John McKewen and Scott McVea I looked upon as very little short of Demi-Gods. At times when a big lot of commissary was captured some of it was given to Old Squire Catlett to distribute among the people.

Once, among other things, were two barrels of flour. A small quantity was sent to each house. As soon as possible, it was converted into biscuits or "slap-jacks." We noticed that there was something yellowish in it, but thinking that some yellow meal had been spilled in it, we ate the bread. Léon and Mary Jane (a servant) ate more heartily than Ma and we younger ones, and about an hour later they were very sick with every evidence of poisoning. Ma was feeling badly too. I was sent for the doctor but found him and many of his household sick as our people were. It turned out that the whole town was sick the same way. Was it purposely done, or not? We never knew, but the top of each barrel of flour had the yellow specs in it. The fourth of each barrel was destroyed, and the rest was found pure and good.

Yankee Raids were made almost weekly, and every Raid meant a little more desolation, and the theft of some household article.

Then came the news of the fall of Vicksburg followed by the capitulation of Port Hudson (9 July 1863).

Never will I forget the bearer of the sad news. We saw a ragged, cadaverous looking, staggering man entering the town. He got as far as Mrs. Wileys gate, and let himself fall on the grass. Of course we crowded around. Could we do anything? Did he want anything? We thought he was a soldier, but he had no gun or pistols. We soon saw that the man was sobbing. Yes, that bearded man, lying full length on the grass, his face on his arms was sobbing. Without knowing why, we all began to cry. And there we sat four or five children, sorrowing with his sorrow, feeling that something horrible had happened, that a general disaster had overtaken some one.

Presently Mrs. Wiley, Mrs. Cross, and Mother, came out to us and the man told his tale. Port Hudson had capitulated. Its handful of heroes had been paroled by a more than surprised army of Yankees after the long seige that history will always recall as a most extraordinary event.

The soldier was prostrated by his long starvation, the disappointment of the surrender, and the walk to his home, found vacant. He continued to walk along anywhere, just so he was doing something, until the sight of a lot of children broke him up and unmanned him. He was tenderly cared for, but I never saw him again. To my dying day I will remember how he looked and hear the sound of those sobs. Then little by little, more news came, more skeleton-like men came to, or crossed the town. . . .

To be sure the Yankees had given food to the Confederate handful, but the first man we saw and a few others had not partaken of it. They chewed leaves and roots from the woods on their route to Jackson (14 miles).

During the seige of Port Hudson many of our friends had been killed or wounded while attacking the beseiger's works. One had had a wound in the head and a piece scooped out of his back by a piece of shell. Another was perforated through the lungs and shoulder blade, and so on and so on. Those two were Zack Lea and Scott Worthey. Willie Slaughter also was wounded on the 1st of May in a skirmish on Black creek. These I mention because they were more particularly our friends. John McKewen was wounded 13 times in all.

A Mr. ———, a private, was made a prisoner during a fight near Port

François Etienne Frémaux
(1787–1841), Céline's paternal
grandfather, ca. 1840.

Aimée Adelaïde Le Brun Frémaux
(1790–1842), Céline's paternal
grandmother.

Céline recounts the family legend of
how her grandfather received this
Legion of Honor medal from Napoleon
himself, but Etienne Frémaux actually
was awarded the medal by General
Bonnaire at the battle of Condé on 20
June 1815.

Marie Céline Marion de Montilly
Frémaux (1815–1848), the first wife of
Céline's father, Léon Joseph Frémaux.

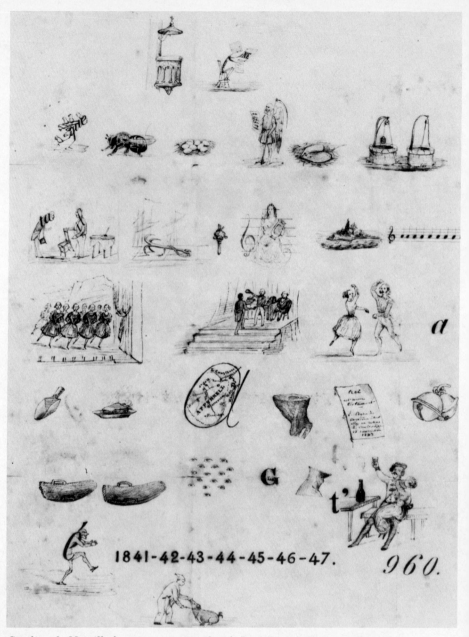

Caroline de Montilly became acquainted with Léon Joseph Frémaux when she visited him and her sister, Marie Céline, in 1847 after the birth of their son. Following that visit Léon sent Caroline a humorous letter in the form of a rebus, thanking her for a gift to the infant.

Camille Bercegeay, her childhood beau, comforted Céline with this fashion plate from a 1857 magazine after she was punished by her mother.

Camille's father, Jean François Aimi Bercegeay, composed this "Polka Mazurka" for Céline in 1858.

This photograph of Baton Rouge as seen from the river was taken in the 1860s. Céline's family lived less than a block from the State House, shown at the far right.

Old Centenary College figures prominently in Céline's memories of her life in Jackson, Louisiana, from 1863 to 1865. This view shows the college as it looked on the eve of the Civil War. (Print from the Louisiana State Library.)

Céline's memoir was written in a clear, strong hand on ten signatures of lined paper during the first years of this century.

Céline's father was among Confederate engineering officers stationed at Port Hudson when this photo was taken in 1862. The officer seated on the left closely resembles Captain Léon J. Frémaux, but the identification is problematic because he is wearing the uniform of a second lieutenant. Other officers pictured are (left to right): First Lieutenant (later Captain) W. B. Sewell, Lieutenant Colonel James P. Parker, Captain A. J. Lewis, and Frederic Y. Dabney. (Photograph courtesy of the Louisiana State University Department of Archives and Manuscripts.)

lore Caroline Marion de Montilly
rémaux (1818–1908), Céline's mother,
a. 1860.

Léon Joseph Frémaux (1821–1898),
Céline's father, ca. 1870.

Léon Victor Frémaux (1847–1890),
Céline's older brother, ca. 1870.

Joseph Garcia (1846–1920), 1876.

Céline's diary helped her to recall incidents which she discussed in great detail in her memoir.

Céline Frémaux Garcia
in 1917.

Hudson. The Yankees gave him over to the negro troops to do with as they pleased. They cut him to pieces and threw the severed members over the breast-works. His comrades gathered them under a heavy fire, and found they had all but one hand. Scott Worthey saw it lying on the slope of the redout and determined to get it, which he did, crawling back with his awful wound.

Scott Worthey was taken to his house for nursing. The dead soldier's remains were put into a uniform and into a rough coffin. All would have been well enough, had not his unfortunate mother in attempting to kiss him, raised his head. This head, severed as it was, from the trunk, told its own story. The horrid truth could no longer be concealed. I heard the aged mother exclaim, "Oh, my son, my son, I thought you had died on the battle field."

All these things, and privations, were more than ever in our lives after Port Hudson fell. School took in again. That is, not Mrs. Miller's, but Miss Gayle's. We had no news of Father, who was in the Engineer Corps in Mobile at Dauphin island and the forts.[8]

We more often saw wounded soldiers. After a bit, they would return to their commands or be exchanged if they had been paroled.

Once we were at Dr. Jones's and we saw through the thicket of pines, something white, moving.[9] We investigated and just then something turned into the lane. It was a white horse, with the rider lying back, his bloody head resting or rather rolling on the hind quarters, which was dark from dried blood. Joe Jones led the horse to the front steps. We called the Doctor, and with his wife, servants, and others, the apparently dead man was carried to a bed. As he was moved the mouth gave up great clots of blood.

Afterward I saw him often. He recovered finally, but for months he stayed at the Doctor's and for months could not speak. Any attempt at talking brought on coughing spells and bleeding. He must have been shot from above for the ball had entered through the mustache and come out at the back quite an inch below the collar band of his shirt.

I have forgotten his name. He was a tall handsome man. He loved children and when he was well enough kept some of us about him. He communicated with us by signs or by writing on a slate. He occupied his time braiding straw for hats and cutting rings for all of us from a black Gutta Percha stick. I have mine yet, a plain rounded ring. He had been wounded near Liberty, and was at a loss to know how he reached Jackson (40) miles, without having fallen off the horse, or having been stopped by anyone.

He came in the summer and left about Christmas. He was not quite well but feared to be made a prisoner.

We had of course becomed acquainted with the whole population. Ma never left the house, but we children went and really had to go "foraging," or visiting, in Ma's place to offer thanks for favors, or sympathy when distress visited one most particularly. Simple friendly visiting Ma allowed us very sparingly. However, when Rhoda or Sallie Worthey came for us in their carriage or asked me to walk out with them, Ma usually allowed it. Those were my halcyon hours. I loved all those people, the dear old lady, tall and straight with grief written on every wrinkle. Her five sons had gone to the army, one had been killed. How many would return? The question seemed branded on the dear old face. Mr. Worthey was tall but he stooped a little; he was always busy.[10] He had learned quite a bit of medicine and in default of drugs he gathered herbs, and roots, and barks, of medicinal value. These he cured and prepared or dried for the benefit of all who might need them. He took me about with him and taught me much about them. He talked much to me during these walks through the woods, always calling me "Frenchy" or "little one," never Céline.

Miss Sallie I tried to take for a model. She was quietly cheerful, devoted to her old parents, patriotic to her hearts core, but moderate in her expressions. She ministered to the wounded and seemed so motherly (she was ten years to the day my senior) that I loved her, but never presumed on her kindness to me to act otherwise than as a child to a superior. I met all the grown-up young ladies there and all of them liked me and talked all their business before me. None ever said, "Don't mention it, little girl." They seemed to know, as I did, that I would never repeat. Occasionally they teased me about my old-fashioned, quiet ways. A great deal of my quietness was timidity, and a part was respect for my elders. Ma was too strict, but she knew how to raise children.

Time wore on, and winter came, a bitterly cold one. The question of fuel was one that cruelly made itself felt both at home and at school. During vacation the Yankees had used our school room a day or two during a momentary occupancy in the town. In some way a hole about 5 feet by 3 had been burned in the flooring just in front of the fire place so that such fire as we had was nullified by the wind that came from below. Miss Gayle allowed us to warm a brick and put our feet on it, but even that way our short skirts and not new clothes kept us very uncomfortably cold. At home we were never quite without wood, but it was sent to us in great logs from seven to twelve feet long. With a good ax Léon might have cut some, but with our little dull one we never could start a single chip. We would all together drag and push one piece at a time up the stairs, put the ends of two of them on a pile of pine cones, and, in that way, burn them till they were short enough to get inside of the immense hearth. A constant watch had to be kept for fear of fire to the floors. All day Ma and the children remained in the kitchen, but by sundown we repaired to the Big Room, the only one with a fireplace. Oh how our arms and legs ached after fetching wood up stairs, our hands sore and skinned on the rough, heavy burden, our toes often mashed by some one missing his or her hold and dropping the weight on the overburdened others. Mother never complained, she too did unusual work; but we still had one servant, Odile, and her child 8 years or so old.

The months were passing, Christmas was near. We Frémaux children had never made much of Christmas. New Year was our Gift-day; Christmas, a Religious Feast Day. Christmas 1862 and New Year of 1863 had passed entirely ignored. Now this Christmas of 1863 we tried to celebrate. I knitted each of the boys heavy cotton mits. Paul knitted Ma a pair of garters. Léon and I carved and constructed a semblance of Toy Farm for baby Henry. We thought it would be fine to celebrate a day. It seemed so long since feast days, birthdays, or any notable occasion, that we anticipated some kind of joy. But all at once, when we gathered for the morning prayers we each and every one missed Father, and before we knew it Ma's voice was husky, and stopped, and we were all crying, and our little Christmas tree appeared like a sort of sacrilege to me. I got up and took the things, and silently Léon and I put them near each one. Then I grabbed my hat and flew to Mass. The day was spoiled, as every day was that we attempted to make gay, in those terrible years.

A week later Miss Ada Perry asked Ma if I could go for a walk with her. Ma said yes. We walked out toward the college, then between the buildings to the pine thicket beyond. It was getting dark, and I so remarked to Miss Ada. She said it did not matter, she would go up to Dr. Jones's and he would see us back if it was dark. At the Jones's, they all chatted, and there I was reminded that this was New Year's eve. Then we had supper. I was feeling uneasy, wondering if Ma had included a visit and supper in the permission for a walk, but I said nothing. After supper they began to guess charades, then they talked of acting some. I *knew* it was time for me to go, and said so.

"Why, child, you are with me, your Mother will not expect you till I fetch you back." Mr. and Mrs. Jones were of the same opinion. I waited one more charade, then said I *must* go. I was told it was too late for a little girl in the woods alone. I was urged to "make myself easy," that it was raining and we would go back in the morning. I did not want to make Ma appear too strict, but the enormity of the act—staying out all night—completely overwhelmed me. I confessed that I was afraid to be punished, as it was; and beat, if I stayed on. They seemed very much surprised, and the Doctor told his son Joe to saddle his pony and take me home. I almost enjoyed the next charade on the word Bal-ti-more, which they played as Ball-tea-moor. But Joe was very long about the pony. I thought maybe he could not catch it in the dark and rain. I was mortified to have had to put him to that much trouble.

Finally he came in pretty wet and announced, "Mrs. Frémaux says it is all right; Céline can stay all night and come back when she pleases." They were then perfectly at ease. I was not. Joe, in his eagerness for me to "stay and have fun," had stolen off on the pony. He found all abed, but clamored till Ma came to the window, and gave permission. A more miserable child than I was never played charades. The last words of the permit, "She can come back when she pleases," had settled me. I knew what to expect but I was too proud to show it—proud for Ma's reputation, be it well understood.

Presently the old year was out, the new one in. There was general kissing and good wishes. Then we all went to bed. Annie tried to talk some, but I did not encourage her. I wanted her to go to sleep so I could get up and run away. I dressed and groped around, but it was a large and strange house. I got in a hall down stairs, but I was all "turned around." It was so dark I could not find the door. The doctor moved in his room. I was afraid to be caught there, so I finally found the stairs and went up again. I crouched on the floor near a window to await the first glimmer of daylight. I must have gone to sleep there on the cold floor, for Annie, waking early, called out that I should have called her when I got up, but she hoped breakfast should soon be ready, etc., etc.

As soon as Mr. and Mrs. Jones were visible I made my adieux and left. Miss Ada was not yet up. I walked off decorously to the turn of the lane. then I broke into a run. I ran to the college campus, then I slowed down. My fine resolution to face Ma and have it over, began to desert me. I wanted to see some one first to see what humor Ma was in: Léon or sister, or one of the little ones. Mass bells were ringing. I thought, I had better go there, Ma would of course have sent the children. Besides, that was the best way to begin the year, and it put off meeting Ma.

Mass had begun, the children were not there, they might come later. . . . I waited . . . prayed? No, I did not pray, I was scared and every minute my fright was worse. Ma would think I had to stay to break-fast, or to enjoyment of some sort. I could not prove my say. I would not summon witnesses, strangers, and none of the home folks were at church. After the sermon I could stand it no longer. I left the church and went home. I saw Paul at a window and beckoned to him, he shook his head and did not come. I saw sister in the yard but at sight of me she ran in. My heart was beating so it pained me. I turned the knob and pushed the door. Ma was just behind it. She did not beat me—I wish she had. She cut my feelings, she hurt my pride, called me a heartless gad-about who preferred her pleasure and a supper to staying with her sorrowing family. The others had employed their evening writing a joint letter to Father, to be sent at the first opportunity. That opportunity may not come for months, and the letter was kept open, but I was not allowed to send my wishes of long life and happiness as the others had. More over, Ma informed me that my unnatural conduct had been mentioned so Father would know that his apparently dutiful child was an ingrate, a selfish, pleasure-loving run-about.

That was the last straw. I was crushed. I never tried to think whether I was right or wrong after that. I was a passive tool. I never asked Ma a permission, I never accepted one, only took *orders* from Ma and at that I often was punished for not using my judgment. I was truly between two fires and I began earnestly to wish I was a boy so I could look to going to the army as a deliverance from home. I would have gladly died those days, yet I was useful. I knew Léon was thinking of running off to the army. He was only waiting to be partly equipped—a horse he wanted as the first thing. I was glad that I saw no chance of his getting one and thus all the spring passed and summer came on.

At school we were doing well; we had ransacked the college garret for books and a few had been secured. We had gone into algebra. Mine had the name of Clark Miller on the cover. Mr. Clark Miller was in the army, a man perhaps 24 or 25.

The Yankees came in the early summer and drove us out of the school room in a hurry. I took all my belongings, but several of the pupils left books and slates. The Yankees burned them and used our desks to feed their horses—as troughs—or as tables where on to cut their meat. After they left we had a lot of cleaning to do; all their offals were just below the hole in the floor. Then school closed and vacation began. I really needed time for spinning and knitting. Our clothes were so thin and poor.

The third of August 1864 was sister's 11th birthday. It was rumored that there would be an attack made on the Yankees who had been in full possession of the town for several days.[11] A little Jew boy, David Openhimer, told mother of it. Ma thought that if everybody knew it, even children, there was little chance of its being a surprise to the Yankees. David was very full of his tale. He said he had been with the Confederate soldiers, that they had no cannons because of coming by way of the sandy creek bed. "But that makes no difference," he added. "We will jump on them all of a sudden, take their cannons, and shoot them down with their own guns." David was eight years old.

"You need not believe me, Mrs. Frémaux, but you will hear in a few minutes. We were all ready, most, when I left." It was then deep dusk: and even as he spoke we heard the Pop Pop of musketry, toward the college. Léon darted off before Ma thought of stopping him and we began to pray downstairs in the hall. Then we stepped out on the side walk. The booming of cannon mixed with the lighter shot and a sort of roar like many voices and trampling of feet and hoofs. The fighting came nearer and nearer. We could see the fire and the dim forms at the end of both streets. Ma had not yet missed Léon. I felt that he was in the midst of it all and was very disturbed. Presently the noise neared, balls struck here and there at the corners and at the end of the street. Soldiers were coming at full gallop, all pell mell, and from their midst came Léon leading a fine horse. Paul opened the bars (gate) and he went straight into the cellar with his horse.

Ma soon made us go in, as the fighting was all around our house. We all went in the cellar with our dog Fingal. There Léon explained he had gone toward the college and got there after the battle had passed that spot. He saw five Yankee officers dead on the campus. Then it occurred to him that he might secure a horse from the next man he saw fall. He rushed among the combatants. A soldier ordered him away. He took momentary refuge on the steps of the Campbelite Church.[12] The steps came up on both sides of the porch and were protected by a brick wall. Leaning his head against that wall, he was thinking and watching. All at once something hurt him on the side of the head. It was a bullet that had nipped a piece out of the brick. He had only felt the counter knock. At the same moment he saw a Yankee Major fall from his horse in the midst of a bayonet charge. Léon made one rush, caught the bridle, and pell mell with the men reached the corner and safety.

The fighting passed toward the bed of the branch and the asylum road. Up on the Asylum Hill the Yankees formed a battery. The ground formed a natural breast works. It had become evident to our officers that the Yankees had mistaken the Asylum road for the Port Hudson road. Ours knew that the battery once taken, the fight would be over, as it would degenerate into a disbanded rout. The order was given to charge, and up hill they charged. All the cannons were taken and the fugitives were pursued through the woods, where they had to leave their caissons full of ammunition.

When the cannons stopped booming Ma let us out of the cellar. It was a very large cellar and we were all in there with a horse and a dog in pitchy darkness. We were glad to get out. We could see nothing even then, but could feel under our feet a layer of chopped leaves which had been shot from the trees in the yard. We also counted forty indentations of bullets in two sides of the house—these of course we saw only the next morning after the sunrise.

Ma took us all upstairs and we prayed for the dead, the wounded and those who loved them. The Yankees lost 7 white men, 82 niggers. Some 25 or 30 were taken prisoners.[13] On our side there were ten wounded.

none of whom died. Ma sent us to bed. Léon crept under his sheets without undressing. When all was still he came into our room and from our window-sill got into a tree, then to the street. He came back before day break and, not being able to come up as he went down, he sat on the kitchen steps. At 5 A.M. Ma got up and so did we, and to my immense surprise she walked out with us all to the bed of the branch where the longest fighting had been done.

The sand, so smooth and white usually, was trampled and dug into deep uneven ruts. A broken caisson with three horses dead and one dying seemed the center of the confusion. Here and there a dead horse, and great spots of wet dotted the field. I felt a little sick and backed toward a fallen log overgrown with brambles. Just then from the clump came feeble groans. I called Léon. He spoke a few words to Ma and she took us home. Some men were coming our way searching for the wounded. Léon stayed. Decidedly Léon was getting out of Ma's jurisdiction. He came home in the evening looking worn and sad. He told me not to ask him questions, as he would not, or could not answer me. This was the first little line of severance to our childhood's chumminess.

Léon looked up a number of unexploded shells, unscrewed the caps and emptied the powder into dozens of quart jars (preserving jars). A few days later he gave it all over to our soldiers. They told him to keep one pint for his own use. He had an old gun all patched up. The barrel was perforated in several places. I can not think how it was that the old thing did not kill him and Paul when they shot it off. It was never shot off more than twice without needing a fix-up or an extra wire consolidation. It had been a musket for years before and the barrel had been shortened for some child. Léon found it in a field.

We also had Pa's little model carabine Morse gun. I used that for bird hunting. I was very careful with it, as our caps were running low and no others could be gotten. Léon and I would reload the shells (they were metal). We had learned to make shot of different sizes. Our implements were crude, but the shot were nice and round. We never passed by a bullet, we looked for and picked them up always and everywhere. In fact looking for things on the ground had become a habit of the time.

We had been out of shoes for a long while. The battle furnished us with nice leather for shoe soles. We found many cartridge boxes and belts. One top or flap made a pair of soles for any of us but Léon. We had small feet. With Pa's razor Ma shaped them and dented them. From a velvet hunting suit we made shoes till the war ended. We had a spool of fine copper wire that I used to sew my shoes to the soles. It lasted seven or eight wearings, our home spun thread only *one* wearing.

Of course we wore them only for church. Then for visiting or school I went bare footed and put on my shoes and stockings on reaching the steps; same thing to return. We always carried a cloth to cleanse our feet; the soil being sandy we could do that easily enough.

One of my hardships was studying in short days. We had no lights. Even little tallow lamps were not always procurable—that is, the tallow was missing. What few mules or horses died from exhaustion in our district had not a spoonful of tallow about them. Cows were all but extinct and never killed. Hog fat was used for food. All that remained in the way of lights were pine torches for out door use and a fire for indoor illumination. To study by a fire is a poor help. I have had the top of my head so hot that I would put on a hat to sit and work out problems at night. The flicker and heat were very bad for my eyes and inflamed them very much. Some nights after one or two hours of study, I would go to bed but not to sleep for the smart and pain in my eyes.

You who read this try some of these experiments just for a few minutes, then judge what we suffered during four dreadful years.

I had become quite brave as to danger and hurt, but the Dark was still a sore point with me. Once we were all at prayer, I was on the threshold of my room, my back to it. There was very little light even in the living room. All at once I felt a weight on my collar bone. I gave a low moan and crouched to the floor and turned. "Danny! Danny!" was all I could say, and there stood Danny, the idiot of the town, grinning and seemingly enjoying the scene before him. He was an immense man, more like an overgrown boy. Perfectly harmless, everyone said, but I was so startled that for years, and even now, I have a decided objection to sitting with my back to an open door. Danny was given a piece of bread and gently led to the street. The street door was locked. He must have been asleep somewhere about the rooms before we locked up.

During the winter of 63–64 Ma had taken a fleecy bed spread and dyed it grey, then made us coats and cloaks as far as it went. Léon had a good coat; sister, a sizeable talma; and the baby a little sacque. Those garments looked comfortable but were more heavy than warm, as are cotton goods of the canton flannel order. I was not at all cold blooded and well it was, for my cashmere winter dress was getting as thin as barige at the back and at the elbows, and under that I wore a high neck and long sleeved under waist, *that* too was getting very small and thin. I could not spin enough to supply myself with an under garment, my time was too limited or crowded too full.

That coat of Léon's caused me another fright. I had occasion to go down to the kitchen with one of the children. We had a few splinters of burning pine to light our way. That hall must have at one time been divided, but only a portion of that division was up when we occupied the house. As we were returning the little sticks nearly burned out. I held them up for the little ones to reach the 1st step, then I put the light out. As I did so I was caught in great wooly feeling arms, and groans were about my ears. I was so frightened that I fainted. Then it was Léon's turn to be frightened, for he it was, with his big coat on. Ma heard the racket; Léon thought I was dead. There was no more pine so of course no more light. I got over it, of course, but that partition in the hall was an object of dread. I was brave in the face of a visible enemy, but darkness and surprise were a tax on all my energies, but I was soon to have overcome even that.

After the little battle in Jackson quite a number of niggers had become separated from their command. They knew the law: All slaves taken armed against the whites were hung or shot. So they wandered about the woods for some days. Some of them, no doubt, found their way back to Port Hudson. Others were caught by the soldiers and summarily executed. I knew this was done but of course I never saw an execution. I knew they took place in the woods. The vagueness of the spot made all the woods a place of dread after dark.

It happened that one of the children was quite sick, and Ma sent me with one of the little ones for Dr. Jones. It was not exactly night, but deep dusk, a November day. Léon was away from home. To cut short we went through the college campus to the pine thicket behind the main building. I saw something moving and nearly lost my strength! Just before me, a little to one side, two niggers were hung to a tree limb, their feet just clear of the ground. I hid the sight from Paul with my skirt, tried to run, then tried to speak, but my tongue was frozen and my legs like cotton. Only the fear of Paul seeing gave me strength to move on. The horror—to me—was having them at my back. Cold chills ran up and down my spine. I thought I heard them moan, then laugh, then shriek. When fairly in sight of the doctor's house I had to stop and collect myself. I had almost forgotten what I came to ask. When I became composed I went on, got the doctor's instructions and started off by way of the big road. Doctor called out to take the short cut but I told him no, I preferred the long way, as it was lighter. The next day he remarked to Ma that he was glad I had taken the long way, for he had come the short cut and, seeing the hung men, knew I would have been frightened. Ma told him I had seen them going, and he could not get over it, that I had not asked some one to see us home. Thus I got a reputation for bravery, very little deserved, but which kept me ever striving to retain it. I was frightened many times after that, but no one ever knew it. I thought I owed it to Father and Grandfather to be as brave as a soldier.

Children saw fearsome sights during that awful time. Then again there were at times funny little episodes: There lived in Jackson an old lady very prim and prudish. At the time of the battle of Bull-run, she became very excited, as her kindred, she knew, were in the army there. Wishing to get all the information she could, she stood on her door steps and inquired of every one if they had heard anything of the last battle. Getting no news, in desperation she went to Dr. Jones's and said "Doctor, have you heard any thing since the battle?"

"Which battle, Madame?"

"The one lately fought at . . . at . . . er . . . Gentleman cow's Run, Doctor."

The Doctor and bystanders exploded, and she remarked that there is always a way of chastening words if one is very refined!

Her daughter Luella was not quite so prim, and once at Mr. Worthey's the girls had just finished knitting some shirts for the soldiers. Luella put one on. It was grey with blue trimmings. She stuck a pipe in the breast pocket, put on a belt and sabre and a cap, and asked us what sort of soldier we thought she would make. We laughed (she was ugly), but her mother got up and left the room declaring that she would leave the house and go home if her daughter remained in that masculine outfit one minute longer. Mrs. Campbell was a great source of amusement to the young people, though she was a lady, kind and helpful in the community.

Léon had secured a very fine horse from the battle field, but we had not the space for a horse to graze. Feed, of course was out of the question. Mr. Worthey told him he could put the horse in his pasture, which he did. A few days later, several C.S. officers needing horses, Léon's horse and 2 or 3 of Mr. Worthey's less broken down horses were pressed in the service. They left there an old black mare and colt, nearly starved, lame, and with a sore back. For some reason or other, these were given to Léon. We worked with that old mare for weeks. The colt died; we cured the mare's back and diminished her lameness. I never worked so hard for a beast, cutting grass and tender cane and fetching it for miles for her. One day Léon swapped her off for a small bay filly and a pair of medium size shoes. The shoes he gave to Paul. The filly did well enough, but did not do for a "War horse" and Léon was cherishing the idea of getting off to the army at the first opportunity. A while later he went to Liberty on an errand for Mr. Delle Pianne. While there he swapped the filly for a "calico" horse and several pounds of tobacco. The tobacco he gave to the soldiers. "Calico" was considered as fit for a war-horse so on the 1st of September, 1864, Ma let Léon start for the Army. He was nearly 17. The C.S. law took the boys at 17, and Ma was willing he should obey the law but would have reproached herself if any thing should happen before the law claimed him. She made him promise not to join scouts or guerrillas but to go on to Mobile, meet Father, and follow his advice as to which corps to join. He was to be 17 on the 14th of September.

It was quite a business to fit him out for the trip. He left with one suit of unbleached under-clothing on and one in his bundle, his pair of college blankets, the top shirt he had on (made of mattress ticking), pants of Pa's surveying suit, and a coat of cotton wool bed spread (grey). He was also in possession of: three pairs of home-spun and knit socks, some lint, some old linen bandages, 3 needles, 6 bone buttons, and about one third of a spool of good thread; an old but sharp pocket knife, an old flint-lock musket, some powder, and balls that he and I had molded from an old black tin syringe and a piece of lead pipe; and spent bullets that we found in tree bark, sides of houses, or on the ground. At every place where a fight had taken place, we had been gathering them since the first days of the War. He also had a little cracked skillet. Léon was considered well equipped for a volunteer of 1864.

With Léon's departure went the last ray of gladness left to my "cut off" childhood. My grief was awful, but no one saw me in my agony; the pines back of Mr. Tomb's old house were my only witnesses. Women were sending their sons and husbands off with a smile. I could be as brave, but my bravery left me the moment I was alone in the woods.

With Léon gone the work was harder. He was stronger (though very small) than any three of those left to struggle with the coming winter. The winters were so hard.

At different times Léon had possessed a horse, more or less broken down. Now we would have to go on foot everywhere. Our corn, for meal or grits, we got from Mr. Tom Fishburn. He gave it to us, shared what he had. At times it was mouldy, at times full of weevels, but his was no better. Mr. Fishburn lived some two or three miles out of town. With a horse Paul could go for the corn in a sack, but after Léon left we had to go two together and fetch it in the baby carriage. It was all such work, and I was beginning to have headaches very often. I was growing very slowly. I was glad of that, as my skirts were then lengthened to their full possibility.

In the fall of 1864 food became more and more scarce. Negro workers had all left. The fields were open. All the fences had been burned for fuel by the soldiers of both armies. A few turnips were occasionally found in some old field. These gave a little taste to our weevily meal. At one time we were four months with nothing but corn and a little salt for food. My stomach rebelled against it. Once I tried to eat it at breakfast, but it stuck in my throat and I had to give it up. I well knew that later I would be so very starved that I would eat again, so I put a chunk of the bread in my basket and started to school. The grass was stiff with frost. My feet ached, they seemed made of lead. I was cold and hungry and miserable. Léon had been gone several weeks. I dragged on till I reached the school house. I was early so I fixed the fire and went over to Mrs. Kaneer's to get a coal of fire. Matches, of course, had been exhausted long ago, and try as I may, I could not bring a spark with a Flint and Steel knife as some people did. Mrs. Kaneer had some tea on the stove and seeing how cold I was and what an internal tremble I was in, poured me a cupful of tea and made me drink it. To be sure, it was an infusion of tender blackberry leaves and we had no sugar, but that tea was good to me that day . . . . When I was well warmed, I took a fire brand and went back to school and lit the fire there. At recess I ate my cold corn bread and swallowed it, such was my necessity for food.

After taking a few music lessons I knew that Miss Clara could not teach me anything. She could not play my easiest pieces. She sang rather agreeably and she took up the time of these two lessons trying to teach me to sing Annie Laurie, so I had stopped music lessons. I practiced two hours a day, one in the early morning. The other, at night, I spent on scales, as it was too dark to read music.

The Christmas of 1864 passed all but unnoticed. There was no Priest in the town. On New Years day, January 1st, 1865, an old hen had been given to Ma. She had stewed it whole and we were happy in the anticipation of some sort of gravy to accompany our bread. The meal at that particular time was *very* mouldy. I went out, maybe to school, if it happened on a week day, but at any rate, I left home early. Henry and Eddie were in the height of joy at the prospects of such a dinner! The bread was to be moulded in waffle irons and eaten with chicken and gravy! They were shouting "Hurrah for New Year, Hurrah for chicken!" One even remarked "Oh, if Pa and Léon were only here to eat some of this fine dinner." Just at dinner time, which was late—that chicken very tough— the Yankees swarmed all over the place. They were on a hunt for young boys to "press" into their army. A searching party came into our house. They helped themselves to any and everything that took their fancy. Two of them came into the kitchen. "What have you there, old woman? Smells all right." With his bayonet he impaled the chicken and was off laughing. His companion, noticing Eddie crying, tried to make the man return his "trophy," but he would not do so. In his kindness of heart he took a handful of crackers from his haversack, and threw them on the grass to Eddie.

The child's tears dried instantly. "We are not beggars, mister. We want our own things, but we ain't asking for yours!" screamed the angered child as he ran to the grass and flung the crackers out in the road. When I came in the crowd was sobered down considerably but all tears had dried. We ate the waffle shaped corn bread with chicken gravy. Such were our days of great festivity.

In early January we heard from Father and Léon. The letter had been two-half-months coming. I had also a letter of my own from Léon. It was a cheerful letter. He was in high spirits. He was in the cavalry, still on Calico, but hoping to get a better horse soon. Uncle Justin had been frightfully wounded, but was doing better, etc., etc. They were well, cheerful, and hopeful. That is, Léon was. But I was neither.

When I started to school in Jackson in 1863 it was my intention *not* to love these new people, as I had my friends of Baton Rouge and of over the river. My heart was sore from the many separations. I felt that we really were homeless exiles. "Rufugees" was the word that applied to us and several other families in the town. I did not want to love anyone, as I knew there would some day be another parting and more heartache. But these people made us welcome. They shared with us their food, their joys, and their sorrows. We lived together, starved together, froze together, feared and hoped together. It was a life different from the life in times of peace. One became more intimate these war times than one would have been in five years of ordinary visiting friendship. All around they became my friends, then Ma's and sister's. How could I help loving them? It was not two or three friends; it was having for friends every family in Jackson and for several miles around. Some called me "Frenchy"—old, old people. Some big girls called me "Celynie" and others of my own age "Céline." But no matter how the naming was done, one felt good will behind the lips and it warmed my heart to live among them.

Principally among the many were Sallie Worthey, Rhoda Worthey, Felicia McVea, Emma Miller, Edith Jones, Sallie Decker, Annie Jones, Nora Magruder, Annie and Mary Ward, Pet Ripley, Bertha Taylor, Blanche McCantz, Melina Openheimer, and Isabelle Fuqua. There were many others, all very friendly and all the old ladies. They all made a pet or a confidant of me. Many read their son's letters to me and many would have me read to them from packets of letters that would never be more numerous, little packets, tied with crepe, or some sort of black ribbon. Many cried with me, or, rather, I cried with them and prayed with them for the absent ones. There was abroad a spirit of confidence, of kindly feeling, of hopes and fears shared by all that drew me in its magical network and left me for the rest of my lifetime one of them at heart. They, their children, and their friends, will always be welcome to the little or much that it may be my lot to have in the years that are to come.

Because of these new loves I forgot none of the old ones, but news of them became very scarce. The Bercegeais' we knew had refugeed out of Baton Rouge. The son was reported to have been "pressed" into the Yankee army. *That* worried me exceedingly. Callie and the Larguiers were still in Baton Rouge. The two Ratnowsky boys had been killed at the siege of Port Hudson, both commanding negro regiments for the Yankees, one of them in a tree looking with a spy-glass into the Confederate lines. Of many of our friends we had no knowledge. Mrs. Garlinski, my music teacher, was, we heard, in Washington, D.C. She was a good and noble woman and suffered intensely from the desertion and treason of the men of her family. We loved her very much. Helena and Willie and the twins were nice people but the men were bad. Mr. Garlinski was a gambler. That is why his wife taught music. His salary was often gambled months ahead. We knew this through Father. She, Mrs. Garlinski, would never have said it.

I often wondered at what would happen if the War ever ended, with Father living, or maybe without Father at all. So many around me had lost their father. Edith's father had died. Many more died every day. I was applying myself all I could to my studies. I wanted to be as ready as possible for earning a living when the time would come.

In the spring of 1865 an old negro on the George H. Jones place made me a pair of calfskin shoes. They were coarse and heavy to be sure, but such a comfort not to have to sew them up every walk I took! Sister was very anxious to have some too, but somehow "Uncle Tom" did not like her. He did not say that he would not make them but the time passed and they were never made.

Years later my husband made "Uncle" Tom a fine present as a return for those shoes. The old man died a year later and left the gift as a legacy to his heretofore young master Mr. Ventress Jones.

There was no May party in our school in 1865. Miss Mollie's betrothed had been killed. The war news was of the most saddening character. Festivating had never seemed very festive at best, but one felt that it would be sacrilegious at that time.

The year before, the May party was held at Cool Springs near Thompson Creek. Emma Miller was Queen and a number of younger girls were flower girls. Everyone of them were bare footed, but their dresses were of the finest swiss muslin. Even the sashes of fine ribbon were fresh looking. People cared well for these fineries and they were worn very seldom. The underclothing was coarse, or really all patches, and shoes had disappeared so long ago as to be hardly remembered. I can see Sister yet, as she was that day, her long thick hair plaited in two braids, a fine white swiss dress, a scotch plaid sash and ribbon to match, a gold chain with coral pendants on her neck, and a long garland of flowers over her arms—barefoot, of course, like the others. Sister was pretty even then.

The party broke up suddenly. Some vedette announced that a regiment of Yankees was approaching from the cross roads. In great hurry we picked up our diverse belongings and scattered. I took off the little jewelry I had on and put it in the ticking bag each and everyone of us wore under our skirts for the purpose of hiding things from the Yankee raiders. I tried to take off Sister's things, but she would have none of my advice. She fought and struggled and ran off. When we reached home just pell-mell with the vanguard of the Yankees, her chain and pendants had disappeared. The whole regiment passed at full gallop. If the chain was in the dust it must have been ground to pieces by the horse's hoof.

Even to the youngest of us, we wore a strap with a well made ticking bag under our clothes. In any moment of danger the silver spoons and forks and jewelry were thus distributed so as to be a burden to none. It did not clink and Yankees were not apt to search little children. Our house was searched several times and we hung around looking on but were never suspected. Ladies wore hoopskirts in those days and could hide much beneath them, and they were personally searched. Ma was little and thin and wore no "hoop"; she was never searched.

Once a ludicrous scene was enacted on one of the streets. Miss Jane Pond had her silverware and valuables attached in some way to her hoopskirt. The Yankees came suddenly; she ran for her home. In some way her things began to drop and tinkle on the hard earth of the sidewalks. Three Yankee officers dismounted and helped her pick them up. They were laughing but she was crying with vexation. They were gentlemen and kept nothing. Poor Miss Jane never heard the last of the affair.

Once, I do not remember the date, the Yankees came into the town quite unexpectedly. Several Confederate scouts were about. They tried to get away but with their underfed horses soon saw they would be captured, so two of them, Bob McLelland and another, whipped up their horses, caught the low limbs of a pine tree, and gained the topmost branches, which concealed them from view from below. We, from our school room, saw them very plainly, but we had seen them start up. The horses continued to gallop through the woods. They were pursued a moment and we saw the Yankees come back, tether their horses under that very pine and begin preparations for a meal. This was a sort of post on that side of town. It was getting dark. We were so interested that we stayed on and on in the schoolhouse, maybe fifty yards from the pine trees. Presently the Yankees lay back with their hats over their faces and presumably went to sleep. There were five of them. Indistinctly in the gathering darkness we saw our boys lower themselves, take each one a horse and gallop away. The Yankees shot at them, of course, but did not attempt to pursue them. Miss Mollie filed us out of the school room and we went home.

Once the Yankees went in at Mr. Worthey's to look for soldiers, they said, but they opened the most tiny chests and workboxes and took everything that struck their fancy. Old Mrs. Worthey was sick in bed. A Yankee approached her and said, "Old woman, you must get out of that. This bed must be searched."

Another, a young Irish looking man said, "She need not move. I'll do that." So saying, he took the top mattress by one edge and turned it quite over leaving the old lady half smothered between the two. Sallie was so enraged that she caught her bedstick and fell to beating the man. The others did not help him, and, in a moment, he was routed and ran out the gate, got up on his horse and did not come in any more.

There was at that time a wounded C.S. in the house. As soon as the tramp of cavalry was heard, Mr. Vincent, the soldier, was made to get into a hogshead, in a garret. A dusty piece of sacking was put over him and a lot of old hand-irons, pokers, tongs, etc., were put atop of him. The Yankees went into the garret and one even took a poker from the heap, but he soon let it go, remarking that it took a War to shake the dust from Southern people's overplus. All day and all night Mr. Vincent remained in his cramped prison. I was present when he was helped out. His wound, not dressed for so long, was very painful. He was half starved and he was dirty, oh, so dirty. Sallie gave him food then proceeded to dress his wound. "Come Frenchy," she said, "you must help me. I have no one else." She put a lot of bandages in order over one of my arms and as she took the soiled ones off put them over my other arm. All went well for awhile till she came down to the bloody ones. I began to feel weak in the knees. Then the head was bared. The hole was the size of a silver dollar and diminished to the size of a twenty-five cent piece where the brain showed; moving or pulsing it seemed to me. Then I opened my eyes. I was lying on the floor. Sallie was pinning on the last bandages. She turned to me. "Well," she said, "for a soldier's daughter you do not do well." I felt very mortified. She washed my face in cold water, made me drink, and told me to lie on the bench a moment. Mr. Vincent was on the lounge. He seemed to be in great pain.

That evening Sallie called me again to help her. When she came to the blood, I closed my eyes but stayed erect. Afterward I often helped her with that, and other wounds. We had to learn many things.

In one of the Yankee raids on Mr. Worthey's place they wiped all the crockery from the pantry shelves with their swords and threw the spoons, forks and knives broadcast in the neighboring fields. They remained in the vicinity five days, then it rained two days. When we went in search of the things, we found three knives, four spoons more or less disfigured by the horses feet, and also four forks, one whole, one with two prongs and two with only one prong a piece. With these few table utensils the family had to be content from the spring of 1864 to end the war. The day we searched for the things, Sallie sent word for Sister and I to come and spend the day, also for each of us to fetch along our own plate, knife and fork. We wondered why, and when we got there were informed of their loss. We insisted that some of the family use our silver forks and nice knives but they refused. The old lady, however, finished her dinner with my fork. There were around the table nine persons and there was not a whole dish or plate. Mr. Worthey had a large piece of a turkey dish, his wife had a portion of a deep dish, other nicked or half plates. It seemed perfectly ridiculous and we all laughed very much during that meal, but it was not a laughing matter.

In a few days friends had divided their own and they were a little better off but no one had many to spare. Breakage went on during those four years and nothing could be replaced. Ma had barrels of crockery all packed up, but somehow, to my great chagrin, she did not send any. Afterward, when I went there I fetched nothing but ate as they did with a wooden paddle, a sharp stick or a roughly carved fork. As drinking vessels we used gourds. The pail stood on a chair near the table and whoever sat nearest it handed the water around.

No one seemed to mind in the least excepting old Mrs. Worthey. Month by month she seemed to sadden after her youngest son received the fearful wound in picking up the scattered remains of his friend. The old lady seemed to give up. Her distress was visible at all times and in every act. Such a dear old lady that she was, tall and erect with her white muslin caps, the ties of which she no longer tied under her chin because it wore them out quicker than to let them hang. I loved her dearly. Mother had a number of caps, each more beautiful than the other, which had been Grandma's. Once after seeing Mrs. Worthey trying to darn an already very darned-up cap, I asked Ma if she would send Mrs. Worthey some of the beautiful caps. She gave me three. Timid as I was, it was an awful task to offer them. I showed them to Sallie first. She approved of them. Then I made my offer. Mrs. Worthey refused them. I insisted and she finally took one saying she would only wear it when the war was over, if she had a son left to welcome home, or if she died, she might be buried in it. The fact is, they did look out of place with the rest of the old lady's attire. Alas, when the war ended, the way of its ending was so sad that no one dressed up or made any show of joy, for next to the few that came home, hovered the shadow of those who would never return, and through the tears that veiled all those sad mothers' eyes, the forms of the dear departed seemed to be more distinct than the wretched living, sobbing men, who silently crept to their ruined fireside.

With the need of clothing, food, lights, medicines, etc., the patriotism of several women succumbed in a degree. The law required all cotton not used to be burned rather than let the enemy get possession of it. Yet some reconciled their conscience to driving to some point occupied by the Yankees and selling cotton then buying goods of all kinds with the proceeds. In order to *leave* the Yankee lines those persons were required to take "the Oath." It was an oath of allegiance to the U.S., then represented by those who were our enemies. Many times Ma was approached on the subject of selling cotton for one or the other. To Ma this appeared treason. Treason to her duty, treason to the law, treason to her heart— treason ever and always. How could she, with husband and son in the C.S. Army, take that oath? She always indignantly refused. She was a refugee among them. They could withdraw their friendship and their help, but they never would have to withdraw their respect. If her children starved or froze till they died, she would, with her diminished band, meet her equals as an equal when this awful time was passed.

Once, a Jew made very generous offers to Ma, if she would go with a load of cotton to Baton Rouge. She would not have to take the oath, he said, as his wife had taken it and Ma would have the certificate with her. Ma, of course, refused. Several days later this same Jew offered Ma some provisions as a mark of esteem, he said. Ma would not take them. The next day we found in the hall ten yards of calico and a small bag of salt. Ma kept them and sent thanks to Mr. Cerf, the Jew. He denied any knowledge of the gift. After the war we found they came from a most treasonable, conscienceless old reprobate of a deserter, who though unworthy, admired Ma's conception of duty.

And the months passed, as the years passed. I was well advanced in school. We had passed most of the algebra. The older girls would have taken up geometry, but only two books could be found in the parish. The boys, one after the other, had gone into the army. The oldest one left was fifteen years old. One was older but quite a cripple. Every day some one gave up another son. Mrs. Fluker was about to give up her seventh. The others were all dead, husband and six sons. His name was Joe. In two days he was to be seventeen years old. His mother was working on his kit and homespun uniform. He announced to Edith and me that he had enlisted. He was proud and gay and rode about telling everyone that he was a soldier now and would carry dispatches on the morrow as his uniform would be finished.

On the morrow he was in town again trying to get buttons to finish that dear uniform; but buttons were a luxury. The little band of new soldiers and a few officers to drill them were stopping across the gully on the south of town. Nightfall would see them on their way to camp. We met him on our way to school. An hour later we were dismissed as word came that the Yankees were at the cross road on their way to town. It was understood with Mrs. Jones that in any emergency Edith and Lola stopped with us, so home we three went. Joe Fluker was on a pony at our corner. Edith spoke to him and asked him what he was waiting for. He said he was to notify "the boys" if the Yankees came across the branch. Being as yet without a uniform he ran little risk, he thought, of being shot. Someone had to act as vedette, why not he?

When the Yankees got on the top of the graveyard hill, it was plain they were not going to stop. They started their horses at full gallop. Joe started at a lope to warn his friends. The Yankees were firing as they came. Joe's horse began to limp. Joe shot over his shoulder at his nearest pursuer. Joe was gaining. We held our breath. We saw his arm drop and his pistol fall to the ground. He was going straight toward a bridge over a gully. We could no longer see him but we could see that the Yankees were crowding up. Something had happened. Edith was deathly pale.

"He is killed," she moaned, and so it proved. He went up the incline of the bridge, then discovered that only that portion was standing. He tried to leap the distance but it was very wide and the pony hurt, they fell into the debris, a fall of some twelve feet. The horse's neck was broken. Joe's head was split wide on the very top. The Yankees crowded around. Some went down and pulled him upon the bluff. There they searched his pockets and his cap. Disappointed at finding nothing of dispatches or sign that he was a soldier, they struck him several blows over the head with the butt of their guns and threw him back in the gully. This time his face was in the water.

Some women, the Murdock girls who lived at the gully, saw the whole awful event. They ran down to the water, got Joe up, and carried him into their house. His eyes opened and shut many times but he did not speak. At this moment Ma, Edith, and I reached there. Edith was frantic and on her account we went. He opened his eyes and evidently recognized Edith. He sighed and that was all. Mrs. Fluker's seventh son was dead. A little boy was sent through the woods to tell her. He found her sewing. The uniform lay on her bed, finished all but for two buttons. In the stillness of the night he was put in a cart, drawn, they told me, by boys, and taken to his home seven miles.[14] They took him to his last resting place in the uniform without the two buttons. I surmised a good deal from Edith's appearance, but she said nothing then and I asked nothing. Ventress came for her next morning. It was more than a week before I saw her again.

Barely an hour after Joe's death we heard loud talking right under the window. It was Dr. Barkdull, doctor and manager of the insane asylum.[15] He had taken the oath, of necessity. He had to feed and keep the insane. He was telling as much to three or four Yankee soldiers and was in the act of pulling his papers from his pocket when a corporal came up and cursing, said, "What is up? Kill him and be done." So saying he leaned far into the buggy and shot twice. The horse started, Mr. Barkdull fell out, his papers still in his hand. Ma, Mrs. Fay, and another lady ran to him. They asked the Yankees to help lift him into a house. Ours was too high, Mrs. Fay's was low and next to ours. The men refused saying, "Many are buried in a trench, leave him in the gutter, and pile trash over him. He is dead all right." So the three ladies dragged him to Mrs. Fay's, up four or five steps and into the parlor on the floor. He was a large and fine man. All three of the ladies happened to be very diminutive women. It took them nearly one hour to get him to that parlor. Not before night could a doctor come. Mr. Barkdull was not dead. He lingered exactly one month, to the hour.

It happened that as they were burying him the Yankees again came. They came into the graveyard, and hearing of who was being buried, the murderer was called up by his superior officer and then, and there, congratulated on his zeal and patriotism. I was standing touching the officer, in the crowded enclosure, and Mrs. B. and five children were immediately next to me. That day of horror ended with the town full of Yankees. Many slept in our yard that night. Edith pushed me and said, "Look." I looked, and saw two Yankees in a mulberry tree just out of the window. They were looking toward our bed. I crept against the wall and let down the sash. With the window open they could have come in easily but with the sash down the ledge was too narrow and rotten to hold a man. We two, Edith and I, slept no more that night. I don't think she had slept any before. Joe's body being slowly taken home was too present and too painful to her. Ma was not sleeping either. Probably very few rested at all that night.

In the morning Ma had a sick headache and I had to go down into the kitchen with the children. Ma did not know the yard was full of Yankees and I did not want to tell for fear she would get up. I gathered up all I needed for the day and sent it up by the children and lastly having attended to baby Henry's necessities, I picked him up to get upstairs quickly. Two men emerged from a lumber room and one of them ordered, "Here, girl, draw me some water and be quick about it."

"Sir," I answered, "I never draw water. I am not strong enough." On that he began to curse me as a ——— rebel, etc., etc. His companions dipped some water from a barrel near by and moved back a few steps. Number one still insisted that I draw him water from the well. The fact was that, alone, I could not draw it and I would not call on one of the others to help me draw water for a big man, and a Yankee at that. The Yankee got exasperated and said he would make me do it. All the while I was backing toward the steps. When I felt them at my heels, I stopped. I could not go up backward with the heavy child who was stride on my back. My arms were not strong enough.

Once more the man called out, "D—— you, are you going to come here?"

"No," I said. "Positively no."

So he put the barrel of his gun in the angle of the shed support and called out, "Well, then you are going to die, for I will kill you or get that water." I could see into the gun barrel. It seemed to be an inch wide and looked bright and smooth. I wondered if the ball would come straight or whirl in its flight. I told the baby to slip off my back and run up to Ma. I heard his little feet pattering down the hall, then the exploding of the gun. Before the smoke had cleared, I was up the five steps, flung the door shut, and then turned my back to the enemy and ran upstairs. The shot had startled Ma. She met me at the upper landing. We looked out the window. Mrs. Wiley's cow was dying some forty feet to the right of the steps, and the Yankees both together were drawing water.

The Yankee could not have meant to shoot me and missed that much, but when that gun went off it was pretty real to me. I had not noticed the deviation of the gun barrel in my anxiety to save the baby from my impending fate. All I cared for just then was not to be shot in the back, running.

They remained in the villages three days. There must have been several regiments as they had Negro, Mexican, and White troops. It was during this occupancy that poor Carrie was taken to the woods and several other more or less atrocious things were done, with or without the officers' sanction. After that shooting incident we remained upstairs until they left.

A strange example of what fright can make a nigger do, was that of a young negro soldier. The day of the skirmish in Jackson he became so frightened at the first volley near the college that he got under the building and stayed there quiet until late in the third day when hunger made him call to some one passing for food. The passer-by happened to be a boy who ran to some scouts and told of the nigger. They came around and ordered him out but he could not pass through the broken iron ventilator through which he claimed to have entered. And in fact no other opening was found. They threatened to shoot him under there and he tried in vain to get through the ventilator which had to be removed, enlarging the hole before he could get out.

Months were passing. Spring was almost merging into summer when the news of the surrender reached us. . . . The War was done. But what next? We were not hearing from Father or Léon. Then soldiers began to come home. Even after all these years I can not write about it. My heart beats to suffocation and my eyes fill up at the memory of those home comings. Coming home where no home remained. Many never found their families. Many were years finding them. . . .

We stayed on waiting for news. One day a young soldier passed and said he had seen Father a few weeks back. Another day I was returning from school. A soldier had just reached our gate. He got off his horse and spoke from behind the pony. He asked if this was where the Frémauxs lived. I said "Yes" and asked if he knew Father or Brother. He said he knew them some. His voice was hoarse and cracking as young men's voices are at times. I thought it strange that he spoke always from the other side of his horse so I stepped around to see his face. I had a moment of doubt, then knew it was Léon. In those nine months he had changed very much, had quite a visible mustache, was much taller, more sun burned and more slender. Oh, how glad I was to see him, to have him back, to have been first to meet him. He said he lingered on the hill till he saw me come and had calculated his time to meet me at the gate.

Léon had been mustered out of service, or paroled, or whatever they called it, in the vicinity of Mobile, April 9th, 1865. Pa was well he knew, but was away somewhere forty or fifty miles from Mobile at the time. Léon got no instructions from him with regard to us, as he would have if they had been together at the surrender.

We tried to be patient about this waiting. Ma was especially nervous and irritable. This uncertainty about our next move was very hard to bear, I suppose. I was still going to school. Ma had a class of French. She had quite a number of scholars. During the French class I was supposed to teach the younger ones English. There were three of them. They knew that Ma was not to be disturbed during that hour and they took advantage of the fact to behave outrageously to me. Sister would lie on the bed and claimed she could do just as well that way. She was only two-and-a-half years younger than me so would not obey me at all. Paul, two years *her* junior, followed Sister's cue and Eddy, two years Paul's junior. did likewise. So they really learned nothing at all and it was a very irksome task. Once or twice our voices rose above their due. Ma came to the door, ordered silence, and afterward scolded me roundly for the interruption, always bringing up that Father would be informed of my feelingless behavior. I was being well educated and I refused to teach the little ones. I was an ungrateful little girl. But what could be expected of a girl who could galivant the country and spend nights out, etc., etc., all of which referred to the unfortunate episode of that New Year's night.

Léon had learned some sort of independence in the army. He seemed to fear Ma much less than before and he once or twice came into the schoolroom, *made* Paul and Eddy stand correctly for their lesson, and threatened Sister with dire punishment if she ever caused Ma to beat or punish me again. At last he went to Ma herself about it. I do not know what he said, but from that day there were no more English lessons. Ma's silent treatment of me was very hard to bear. However, with Léon back my life was less bitter. After school we often went on long walks with Edith and Lula Jones, sometimes going all the way to Monk's corner with them. Sister came with us sometimes but she and Léon generally managed to fuss on the way back so the pleasure was spoiled.

Quite a number of horses had reappeared in the country with the return of many of the soldiers. We often gathered quite a little crowd for evening rides. As sad as we were at the disastrous ending of the war, it was ended and Pa was living. With the buoyancy of youth we felt that all would be well. He would get another home and we would fare as before the war. Alas, we did not yet know that homes, once broken, are never well mended. We did not then dream of the horrors of Reconstruction.

Eddy was still the self-hurting child. He had at least seven scars on his head and numberless ones all over his limbs. I can not recall a time when he was not wearing a rag on a finger or a toe, if not both. He once tried to break a bottle with his bare foot. He succeeded and almost cut his heel off. While yet bandaged and hopping about he followed Ma up in the garret. The stairs were narrow and in coming down he fell and his chin caught the top corner of an open door on the floor below, and there he hung. We were all too short to lift him off and we were dragging a table under him when a Confederate soldier, a Dr. Ryleigh, walked in. He was the bearer of a letter from Father. He grasped the situation, lifted Eddy down, and sewed up his chin which was badly cut. The letter was an old one, about two or three months old. Eddie, as I was saying, was still hurting himself. Ma sent him on an errand. He was a little longer about it than he might but no one noticed it at the time. That night after going to bed he began to cry, complaining of pains in the abdomen. Ma tried all she could to relieve him. There was no mark on him, but he said that in going from the house that evening he carried an old chair rung in his hand, and while running, one end struck a tree, the other end striking him in the abdomen.

The next morning Léon and I started out to Bayou Sara for horse feed. We were in a small wagon and were away all day and night. It rained in the night and the creek was up on our return. We just did escape drowning and got home with our feed all wet. We found Ma very worried. Eddy was very ill. Three doctors had come in and agreed that there was little to be done and that the child had very little chance of recovery. Oh those vigils without light. Ma had saved out her stores in 1861, a half dozen sperm candles, saved them for an emergency, but this emergency threatened to be so long that we dared not let them lit. We kept a little fire in the next room and when necessity demanded it we lit the candle and put it out again as soon as the remedies were given or applied. In the darkness then we waited until the next urgent moment. He suffered intensely all the time and was delirious for hours at a time. The blow had closed the intestines very low down and all excrements came up through the mouth. He was about eight and one half years old and understood his disease, and disliked having strangers around, but we had to have them. It took two persons at one time to give him the necessary cares, and we were obliged to accept the services of a few of the many who offered their help.

Mr. Worthey came in every day to look at the child and speak a few words of cheer. One evening there came a lady who introduced herself as Eddy's friend. Eddy was a favorite with old and young. This person was elderly. She lived in the old Bank building with a family of refugees. We had never met any of them but Eddy had done so, evidently. I never could remember her name. I will designate her as Miss Z. Well, Miss Z. sat up every other night, I every third night, Léon every third night, and Ma every night with little intervals of sleep when she could sleep. Whenever Miss Z. and I nursed we spoke little and very serious that little was. When she sat up with Léon they would play Muggins near the window as long as the moon allowed them to see. They seemed almost to enjoy the nights. The child grew steadily worse. At last, one evening, the doctors gave him up [and] told Ma that one of them, Dr. Perry, would be at Wyley's all night. If the child died before morning she could send for him. We were appalled. . . . Mr. Worthey came in late and asked Ma to give him light to look at the boy once more. He gazed long, then said, "That child's eyes do not speak death. If there was a knowing doctor here, something could be done. But without help he may go, he may go."

Léon had outgrown saying his prayers with us. He even claimed that men did not say prayers in camp; they prayed only Sundays, etc. I was distressed about it. That night as I crept out on the gallery to pray in sight of the stars (I loved to pray with the stars above me) I found Léon kneeling on the dark gallery. He was looking at the stars and praying out loud. I knelt beside him and our souls were well lifted to the Almighty when some one ran up the stairs. It was Mr. Delle Pianne who had met an army doctor returning to his home, Dr. Marsh. Mr. Delle Pianne asked him to call on the child, and though his family was only two blocks away and he had not seen them for two years, he stopped and came in. He looked at Eddy, shook his head and after feeling him, asking questions, etc., finally said that if nothing at all had been done to him, he would never have come to his sorry pass. The last thing the doctors had done was to give Eddy a dose of Croton oil, and they had left one to give him after midnight if he was still living. Dr. Marsh said that for the present he would simply not give him the dose and that later in the night he would return and bring some drugs. When he returned he carried two bottles, one white, the other black. A spoonful was given alternately every two hours and so it went for days and days. Eddy suffered six weeks and was left a sort of living skeleton.

During that time the explosion of the powder magazine of Mobile had taken place.[16] When the news reached Ma she silently slid to the floor in a faint and it was a long time before she could be revived. A week later her hair was all streaked with grey. Some time later still we heard from Father who gave a graphic description of the explosion. This time, after Ma read the letter, she got on her knees and with her face in the bed-clothes, sobbed aloud.

The next letter from Father told Ma to come to him in Mobile by way of Bayou Sara and New Orleans. A comrade would wait for her there and see us safely to Mobile. However, getting away just then was out of the question. Eddy was not yet out of danger and there was no way of letting Father know. We stayed on and on.

Finally Eddy was saved and I broke down. Mr. Worthey insisted on taking me to his house for a rest which I really needed. I stayed with them five days. They should have been very happy days if I had not been haunted by the thought that soon we would have to leave these friends, the Baton Rouge friends, the New Orleans kindred and friends, the old Donaldsonville friends and memories, all and everything I had ever loved and seen—leave Louisiana! Léon liked Mobile well enough, but his reasons for liking the place were just what I knew would prevent my love for the place. His girl friends, I knew, could not be mine. He did not even suggest it. One of them had sent me a pretty Saint's picture accompanied by a letter. Such a letter—ill worded and ill spelt to an amazing degree. The girl, Tudy Murry, claimed to be sixteen. Léon said she was eighteen. I certainly longed to see Father but I felt that the happiness of the reunion was to be dearly bought. My attachments always caused me pain; they were so deep and lasting.

I wondered much at Father not *coming* for us. We found out later that he had not been paroled, as he had been on a mission at the time the Engineer Corps surrendered, and was on his way back when the other corps in its turn was paroled. For this reason he did not want to make himself conspicuous by asking for a pass or out-going papers.

Then he had chosen to stay in Mobile because the explosion had caused so much disaster that he knew one of his talents (architecture) would be needed, and it offered an immediate means of livelihood. Of course having to begin again, in a ruined country without friends or influence or money, he could not well pass by any opportunity. My last twelve weeks in Jackson were like weeks of farewell. As Eddy got well and Ma began to think of ways and means to go meet Father, the worry and nervousness of the thoughts made her very irritable and my life was pretty hard, all but for the hope of seeing Father in the near future.

About this time a dance was given in the McNeely's sugar house as a welcome to the returning boys. I have often wondered how they could give that dance and how anyone could go to it. Yet, as I was asked and Ma said I could go, I went, as a child goes to grown people's affairs, in care of the Worthey family. I went in a buggy with Pet Ripley and Will Slaughter and returned in the Worthey's conveyance. I had never been to a dance and I really enjoyed it in a quiet way. Sallie introduced me to her nephew, Ned Worthey, telling me that I looked so sweet and demure that she was sure Ned would fall in love with me and that she would be glad of it. That settled Ned for me. I became so timid that I hardly spoke to him. I had not intended to dance but as he led me out I was too timid to say no. Then his brother, Willie, came up. Willie was younger. not sixteen. I was not ashamed of him so we got along famously. There I saw Mr. Bud Bryant dance with a peg-leg which had been made for him by his body servant. It was quite neat and answered the purpose so well that he danced all evening. I also met a number of young men, brothers and cousins of the girls I knew.

That night I wore a new dress. Ma had the cloth, English Barège, since 1861. It was a double plaid, pink and white with hair lines of black. It was piped with three cords, one black silk and two pink ones of cambric. The dress was pretty and long enough, and I wore a petticoat hand embroidered that had been Grandma's. My hair was braided in a coronet and two long plaits in the back. Three or four natural pink rosebuds were twined in the coronet like a half wreath and Ma gave me a pair of gold earrings, little doves with a ring in their bill, which my Godfather had given me at my christening, but which I had never really possessed before. Of course, my shoes were not in keeping. I wore the shoes old "Uncle" Tom had made for me.

No other balls or parties were given for the "boys'" return. I think everybody felt sadder after the dance than before. Even the boys who had come home felt keenly the loss of their brothers and friends and it was a fact that those absent or who would never return were almost more present than those who were renewing their intercourse with their families.

In August 1865, Wilson Miller, one of Sallie's cousins returned from a northern prison. He was a wreck. Harsh treatment, disease and humiliation had brought him to the brink of the grave. He had been "forgotten" as many prisoners were for nearly four months. He was in a prison where the prisoners were "viewed" for pay. To be on exhibit in an enclosure was deep humiliation to southern gentlemen. He took it very hard. He was not twenty when he came home. I met him frequently. Mr. Worthey, always a tease, made me very miserable one day in particular. At the dinner table he noticed that I had very little appetite.

"Frenchy," he said, "If I had known that sitting next to Wilson would disturb your appetite, he would have been seated elsewhere." I blushed furiously and I suppose looked embarrassed. Then he made it worse by having Wilson change his seat and put him directly across the table from me. Then he made a few other remarks that completely "undone" me, and I had to hold down my head to hide the tears that were fast gathering. (Alas, when they gather they overflow.)

Sister was not timid. She laughed and said, "Céline cries if boys look at her. They can look at me all they want, I don't care." Presently, Wilson Miller left the table, and after a while the meal came to an end. Mr. Worthey was teasing still and I thought best to leave early, so before sundown Sister and I started home. When we had gone a quarter of a mile we came upon Wilson sitting by the roadside. At our approach he got up and began to walk with us. Sister chatted like a magpie, but he did not answer her. He began to talk to me and was sorry for what I had gone through on his account. He spoke rather low so that Sister would be out of the conversation. But she would none of that. She told him Ma would not approve of his whispering to me on the road, that she was going to tell Ma that Mr. Worthey said he (Wilson Miller) was in love with me and so on and so on. I was very much ashamed of Sister and so generally confused that I ran into a tree, broke my bonnet slats and hurt the side of my face. I sat down and Wilson removed my bonnet and fanned me with his hat. This enraged Sister and she started running ahead to tell Ma that Wilson Miller was making love to me, and I had stopped with him.

I was very much frightened so we hurried all we could, but he was sick and could not walk very fast. I begged him to go back but he would not. He had an idea that he could help me if Sister told the tale. Fortunately, at the branch Sister met some little girls and we found her playing in the pebbles and we got in quickly.

A few days later I had reason to think that sister had told her tale. Ma called me up and asked me many pointed questions about several of the young men. Fortunately, by answering to the letter, if not to the spirit of her inquiries, I got out fairly well. In the morning Léon had come to me and said that if any of the boys were in love with me and if they had even told me so, I was in no way obliged to tell *anybody* of it unless I had made promises to any of them. Then, of course, Ma would have a right to be told. Léon was decidedly getting independent and I wondered at his advice, but it helped me with my answers to Ma. Really, I had made no promises. How could I when I did not exactly know how we stood, Camille and I, and our parents.[17]

Ma was preparing to sell a part of our belongings to have means of removing the rest and ourselves to Mobile. Mr. Delle Pianne was of great help to Ma in this business. Many placards were written and tacked by Léon on trees or fences at every road crossing for miles around. The day of the sale Ma sent Sister and me to Sallie's to spend the day. She did not like to have us among all the people who might be there. Then arrangements were made for wagons to take us to Bayou Sara.

To many persons Ma gave handsome presents. To Mr. Delle Pianne she gave a clock and candelabras (our parlor set) of guilt bronze. To Miss Mollie Gayle she gave a box of painting and drawing implements and fine water colors and two paintings of the discovery of the Mississippi River. They had adorned our library in Baton Rouge. Dr. Marsh would accept nothing but the curious sword of a monster sword fish, just as a keepsake. To the Fishburns she gave a very fine Chinese vase that had been Grandma's; to many others, many little tokens. We gave our roller skates to Kemp and Willie Cattlett. I gave a doll to Miss Louise Delle Pianne. She was a grown young lady but asked for it. I had to give it. I gave Edith a pair of bisque angels and to others many little trinkets of the few the Yankees had left me.

Soon after the surrender, Sallie had been quietly married to Mr. Zack Lea. He humorously said it did not take much to get married: he owned the clothes he had on, a sore back horse, and a confederate fifty cents bill. For her marriage Sallie wore a calico dress and a tatting collar and cuffs; Mr. Lea, his same and only uniform of rusty grey with a patch on the shoulder where a piece of shell had scooped a hole in his flesh just as if it had been dipped out with a spoon.

Sallie continued to dwell at her father's. He would not hear of her moving away to the half ruined Lea place.

Somewhere between the 12th and the 14th of August 1865, with our belongings packed in wagons belonging to Mr. McKewen we left. Mr.

Tom Fishburn drove Ma and the baby, Henry, now four years old, in an antiquated and delapidated buggy. We children went on in one of the wagons. We started before daylight and after going a few miles realized that our dear dog Fingal was not with us. Léon had to ride back on one of the wagon mules to get him. He found him in the house locked in. When they rejoined us we again proceeded. We had a wait of only one hour in Bayou Sara for the steamboat we took.

✑ Reunion in Alabama ✑

I N JUMPING OUT of the wagon my dress caught on a splinter and was badly torn.[1] It was a black silk of Grandma's trimmed in narrow strips of blue, the leavings of the blue stripes which had been inserted in the Creole Guard's flag to change it after the secession. The old dress had done its time and more, but I felt very sore on walking down the cabin of the boat with my clothes in tatters.

There were on board several ladies and a young girl of my age. They were all very well dressed. I felt awfully poor and "backwood" in their presence. Although we had never thought of our attire in Jackson where everybody looked the worse for wear it came on me like a thousand stings; the figure we must have cut to people who had not suffered want or had had time and opportunity to recuperate. As we walked in that boat here is our picture or description. Ma wore a grey, glazed cambric dress with trimming bands of Persian design calico and a new bonnet she had just had sent from Baton Rouge. The bonnet was green straw trimmed in green moire ribbon. She had on a beautiful lace mantle fastened on the shoulders with gold pins. Those kind of garments, not being worn during the war, were nice and fresh as when she wore them last in 1861. Her shoes fitted her well. They were of brown velvet with leather soles of the top of a Yankee knapsack.

Sister and I had on those black and blue silk dresses, at least four or five inches too short, and mine in tatters. Sister had no shoes on at all. Mine were heavy ones "Uncle" Tom had made. My stockings were home-

159

spun, home knitted ones, more or less soiled by the dust and grime of our fifteen mile drive. Our hats? Well, they had been of pearl grey straw at Easter of 1861 and had had dainty pink sprays of arbutus as decorations, but the rims had become so nipped. They had gotten so sunburned that they were of a mottled, faded, orange hue. I had cut the rim down and bound them with faded Scotch plaid ribbon and an apology of a rosette of the same ribbon ornamented the crown. They were simply better then being bare headed, that was all. The two little boys had trousers of mattress ticking, narrow white and blue stripes, and whitened, unbleached cotton shirts—barefooted.

The little one, Henry, had a kilt skirt of turkey red testering calico and a fine cambric hand embroidered waist with his gold and ruby shirt front buttons and cuff bottons—barefooted. All the boys had homemade soldier caps or head gear.

We girls immediately went into our cabin. As the boat stopped at Baton Rouge one hour, Ma gave Léon money to get the boys shoes and hats and shoes for Sister. When we emerged from our room later we were freshly combed with clean stockings and a nice French cambric dress, white ground with little lavender vines all through, a nice lace collar with a pretty breastpin. That dress was our only one long enough and rather new, also made of one of Grandma's ample skirts.

I felt very shy of the other girl passenger until I found out that she was a Yankee girl coming down the river to see the "conquered country." (That we heard from the chamber maid.) It was sufficient. My head went up, my steps were firmer, I spoke to our crowd as if no one was there but us. She simply did not exist to us.

Eddy was yet such an invalid that he could not walk unsupported. For that reason he attracted attention. An old lady passenger spoke to us about him. She seemed a very nice well-bred and aristocratic old lady. I answered her with much reserve fearing that she also might be visiting the "Conquered Country." I was not happy during that trip. I had not seen the landscape since 1861. Everytime I looked out, only ruin, unkept roads, unplanted land and general devastation met my eye. I did not recognize the places. All seemed so silent, so dead, so sorrowful.

We reached New Orleans on the 15th of August, 1865. My uncle Justin Frémaux and Pa's friend, Captain Gallimard, met us at the levee. We were taken to Uncle's house at the corner of Esplanade and Galvez streets. We went there in the Esplanade mule cars. I had never seen streetcars. When I had been in New Orleans before we traveled in omnibuses or carriages. Ma left us at Aunt's and she and Aunt went out on a shopping tour. We needed so very many things. They got us hats. They were called Gunboat hats and were white. The brim was very narrow and like a cap's visor. Front and back, from the visors, hung a fringe (an inch wide) of white beads. White ribbon and blue flowers were the trimmings. The boys were dressed completely in nice little fashionable suits. Léon also left off his old soiled uniform and had a good suite of citizen's clothes. We had no lessons at all for four days.

We found our cousins very nice and friendly. Our Aunt too was lovely to us. Aimée and Hortense were beauties, so also was the little boy, but the two little girls Blanche and Regina were not at all pretty, or well behaved. Alas! That it was so, the first night there arose a dispute as to how we should sleep. Aimée and I had one bed, Hortense and Sister another, and the two little girls were to sleep on a pallet. Aunt's house was small and of course we crowded her. Well, both the little ones decided they wanted to get in our bed. That was too many, so Mémé said she would take Blanche, who was her God-daughter, but Nana must go with the others, and there it began. The fuss was great. The elders were sitting on the front steps with Mr. Gallimard. The two little girls from fussing had gone to fighting. Then Sister, ever ready for a fray, joined in. I was shamed and frightened at her action.

I said, "Francine, for God's sake, don't join in. Ma will come in and we will be scolded."

I don't know why my remark so angered her but she screamed out in a loud voice, "Oh, Ma, Ma, you are always afraid of Ma. She never does me anything and you know it. You are just scared for yourself," etc., etc. She was talking yet and the two little ones fighting yet when Ma and Aunt appeared.

Aunt took in the tableau and laughed, then said, "You little cats, what is the matter?" Ma was pale to the lips.

The little ones began to explain and in their not very polished manner of speech said what they had to say and wound up with saying, "Francine mixed up because Céline told her to shut her jaw," she began to holler. I was so dumbfounded at this translation of what had been said that I was speechless. Ma told me to get up and stand before her. Then she gave me four slaps on the cheeks as hard as she could, then told me to explain. I could not well talk, crying as I was.

Aimée explained and Ma wound up saying, "Very well Miss, it all amounts to your having meddled and tried to make me out a mean mother. Your father will hear of this, and we will start our life with a straight understanding of your worth." Then Léon, who was in the hall reading, said he had heard the whole affair and he would tell Pa what he thought if Ma said anything at all. So Ma turned on him and the last I heard was Uncle calling to Léon to come and see Mr. Gallimard to his hotel.

Mr. Gallimard had been a captain in the French army. He had come over to take sides with the South and was with Father in the Engineer Corps of Beauregard's army. He had been taken prisoner and had been kept in a prison ship (the treatment there was horrible). It had shattered his health. He was going back to Mobile to get some papers of importance to him before returning to France.

That night my little cousin Blanche had a frightful nightmare. I calmed her as best I could. Aunt came in and sat on the bed a long time. She said Blanche, who was nearly seven years old, had poor health and she would like the child to have a little trip by sea. If *I* would promise to look after the child, so Ma would have no trouble about it, she would ask Ma to take Blanche to Mobile. We were going by sea (there was no other way then), and she would leave her till an opportunity presented itself for her return. I wondered greatly at Aunt's daring but she said I would do my part, and so it came about that Blanche came with us. All day Aunt and her Mother prepared the child's clothes, cut out new ones and packed her little trunk. In the evening we repaired to Milneburg where we took the boat for Mobile. Events and trips were crowding so that I felt dazed.

Mobile, 1865

WE HAD hardly gotten fairly started when the wind took Eddy's hat and carried it out in the lake. He was very distressed and wondered why the boat could not turn back for it. He had to end the trip with a handkerchief knotted at the four corners as a head covering. His hair had all fallen out during his fever and his head was as slick as a billiard ball. I was not seasick. Neither were any of us but Sister and Blanche. They were in the midst of the most deadly feelings when we passed the forts at the mouth of Mobile Bay. The war was so fresh upon us and cannon meant death to us. I looked out to see what the shooting was about and soon realized that the fighting being over, it was some sort of signal, and I saw a small boat leave the fort and come toward us. The scare had cut Sister's and Blanche's sea sickness short, and then we were entering quiet waters. They saw the Yankee boat approach and almost had hysterics, finally they were quieted and dressed as we neared the city.

Presently, the boat was moored and at last we went ashore. Léon had pointed Father out to the little ones. I was shocked to see him with glasses (he was 44 years old then). I was glad to see him, yet I began to speculate about Ma's telling him those horrible things about me. I felt pretty sure I could get one kiss, one big old hug as in the days of yore before anything could be told, yet my arrival was spoiled by the fear of how long a respite I could count on.

On board the boat Mr. Gallimard had been very nice and friendly to me. I felt that he knew little of me but that he had heard Ma scold me and had heard the slaps I received. I was very timid in his presence, always feeling those resonant slaps and blushing for shame every time my eyes caught his. He helped me with my little charges. Ma had Eddy as her care; I had the others. Léon had almost forsaken us. He talked to the captain, the pilot, the sailors, etc. He did keep Paul by him most of the time.

In Mobile

AT LAST we were in Father's arms. The war must really be over. We were all there. No grave had been made for any of our blood—we were very happy. Pa took us to a boarding-house hotel for supper at Mrs. Murry's. I met there: Mrs. Cuyler, a recently widowed daughter; Miss Sara Griffith, a daughter by a first marriage; and Tudy Murry. She was very gushing and called me "my dear friend" and seemed to be going to take me under her protecting wing from then on.

After supper we went to the home Father had lovingly provided for us. It was a nice two story house on ———. He rented it and had bought the furnishings as they stood. It certainly was not furnished as our old home had been but it was tasty and comfortable and we started life anew there. Pa was doing quite well in the rebuilding business. His partner was a Col. Shelia, a Prussian. Mr. Gallimard was to live with us till he recuperated, but he did not do so. Day by day he became more feeble. Our first evening in our new home brought a visitor, Miss Florence Higley. She was very pretty and a lady. Léon introduced her with high recommendations. I found that she knew Tudy Murry but I could see by her reserved comments that she did not approve of her entirely. I was not surprised.

When Miss Higley left she took Sister with her to show her the way, that we might call on the morrow. It was only four blocks away, still much time passed and Sister had not returned. When Léon and Pa came home Ma sent the former to Mrs. Higley's for Sister but Sister was not there. She had insisted on returning alone hours before, Léon reported. Pa and Léon set out to find her. At eleven P.M. a gentleman and Miss Sara Griffith walked in with the lost one. She, it seems, had turned the wrong corner, then another and another till it became dark, then she began to look around for someone to inquire of. She chose an old gentleman and told him her name but she did not know the name of the street we lived on. She bethought herself the name of Murry. Did he know the Murry's? Yes, he had known them years ago so he took her where they had lived before the War. After that he proposed supper; Sister knew better than to accept. She was a lady. They therefore walked up one street and down another till it happened that they passed Mrs. Murry's just as the house was being closed. Miss Sara knew the child and called out to her. Mutual recognitions took place and the two brought Sister home.

For two or three nights Blanche had nightmare[s] so I started in to cure her. I gave her a light supper before dark then took a short walk with her and at eight sharp put her to bed. She never had nightmare[s] after that. The child gave me very little trouble but she was ever at odds with Sister. I kept them separated all I could and in this Mr. Gallimard helped me.

He was getting worse sick all the time. Mrs. Shelia came very often to see him and bring him flowers and jellies and things. Miss Sara Griffith also came but she seemed to work on the poor man's nerves. He could often be excused from seeing her; later he never saw her at all.

At last it was evident that he could not live long. Once Mrs. Shelia was there, sitting by his bed. I came in to bring his milk. He tried to raise himself but fell back in a spasm. Mrs. Shelia was a cripple and walked with two silver mounted ebony crutches. She was always beautifully dressed. This day her dress was blue silk with white lace in plenty. She gave one look at the distorted face then began walking up and down, up and down the hall. I could hear her clot, clot of crutches and the swish of her silk dress.

All through the hours that the doctor and the priest were there, she was moaning and crying and saying wild things like, "What will life be now? When he is gone what will come? He is going God, going, etc., etc." Finally Ma persuaded her to go home.

He lived several days longer. The day before his death he called for all of us to say good-bye. Ma suggested Mrs. Shelia. No, he did not wish her. It was raining and he said he was only recently acquainted with her and she seemed very hysterical. No, he would rather only see the children and Father. I was sent to the school for the two boys. It was raining and blowing so that I could not open my umbrella but I reached the school. I was sent to Brother Ben's room and got the boys. The Brother was young and dark haired with a kindly face. He came to the door, opened the umbrella and said he would pray for the dying man.

Next day Mr. Gallimard died quietly. I had always a sort of fear of dead people. It was different with dead soldiers in the open air, but a dead in a room with tapers awed me.

We had never had a dead in our own house. Mr. Gallimard was laid out, as was the custom then, on a table draped in black, the candelabras tied with crape. Father was in the dining room and he sent me for a piece of crape which was on the table at Mr. Gallimard's head. I had to pass in a narrow place between the draped table and a row of chairs. Not for worlds would I have said I was afraid, yet my hair seemed to rise on my head. I went up, took the crape which partly covered his face, then I went a few steps backward and forced myself to turn and walk off steadily. I wanted to run. Strange, that after that day I never felt the least fear of laid out dead.

Mr. Gallimard was buried in the Cuyler's plot in a cemented vault so that his body might be taken up and sent home, if his people so desired. But they never sent for it. He had a father and two brothers, all in the French army. Father sent them all he found belonging to his friend. They acknowledged receipt and there it ended. We never heard from them after that.

Ma had stood all the strain possible to her constitution. The next day she was in bed and was sick many weeks. Mr. Gallimard's sickness had lasted six weeks. We were now at the end of September.

Ma had been very anxious to see me at school and it had been resolved that I should go to the Judson Institute in Marion, Alabama. Mrs. Higley was taking Florence there. My trousseau could not be made in such short time, with Ma in bed, but all that the pamphlet called for was bought and by the 6th of October all was packed in a large black leather trunk.

During my seven weeks stay in Mobile I had made very few acquaintances, had had no time. Brother's girl friends were not at all to my taste excepting Florence and her cousin, Miss Theilman.

Two young men came occasionally. One was Mr. Turner and one Mr. Chilton Gifney. I liked Mr. Gifney best. He seemed more like the young men I had seen at home in Louisiana five years before. Mr. Gifney brought me flowers once or twice from his mother's garden. He said he hoped I would come to see his mother some day when we were out of trouble and well settled. Léon went there often and volunteered that Mrs. Gifney was a lovely lady but had no garden and that Chiltie bought or begged the flowers that he brought. The day I left for the Judson, Chilton Gifney sent me candies. Not from his mother's pantry, Léon said.

Blanche was improving every day. She was getting plump and her complexion was very good. Her manner of speech had improved most of all. I was very loth to leave her. I really hoped Aunt would send for her before I left as she and Sister were always wrangling, but it was not to be. She stayed on till the day after Christmas. After I left home she preferred to go to school which she did. She was a great favorite with Father. She followed him around much after the fashion I had myself.

Two days after our arrival in Mobile Father took us to see the center of the explosion scene. From a mound of brick and mortar debris there still issued thick smoke and occasionally a low explosion as of a gun underground. This was five months after the explosion of the powder magazine. Eight square blocks were perfectly bare and levelled. Over 10,000 niggers, "contrabands" they were called, were herded into those annihilated cotton presses. Not even a piece of recognizable flesh was ever found of them. We also visited less gruesome places, pretty churches, the bay shore, and the tiny little park.[2]

The custom, then, seemed to be that, after the almost universal two P.M. dinner, everything younger than twenty-five or thirty donned its hat and coat and took to the street toward Government St. There, boys and girls met and paired off or went in bunches, as it seemed to me, whither fancy pushed them. From after dinner to nine P.M., no mother could possibly *know* in what part of the town her daughters might be enjoying themselves. Florence, being an only daughter, was very much more restrained. She had to say where and with whom she expected to spend her time and also had to be in by eight P.M. Her mother was considered a cranky, Frenchified, old despot.

Of course, it was just as well that I could not go at all. With that wild young set one could not have done things by halves or in my case by sixteenths without being counted a curiosity or a crank. Elder people seemed to think that the war was responsible for the unconventional behavior of the younger sets. Be it as it may, it was an impossible pace for me to take up and I was losing no fun by going off to boarding school, but I was filled with a sort of dread at this renewed separation from Léon and Father. Ma had made good her threat to report my shortcomings to Pa. I knew it by some queer looks I caught him bestowing on me at odd times. They were sort of sorrowful, speculative looks that brought a resentful blush to my face and lump in my throat. I wanted to talk it out with him but I feared he would look upon it as a disrespect to Ma. I would lie awake at night and plan and form my sentences as to how I would approach the subject the next time we would be on the street alone, and as many times my courage failed me. I never spoke.

After things were ready for the trip to Marion, Pa once put his hand on my head and said, "My little girl will be happier at school."

"Oh, Father," I began.

But he said again, "I have thought it all over, my girl. It is best for you."

At five-thirty P.M. I left Mobile. Ma was in bed. Father took me to the boat, the *Grey Eagle*. Mrs. Higley, Florence, and her brother, Mr. Horace Higley, were aboard before us. I was duly put in their care and the boat got under way.

The Journey to Marion

THE Alabama River looked to *me* like a pretty bayou with my mind full of the mighty Mississippi of my earliest acquaintance. The Alabama River seemed like a joke. The water was very low at that time and in many turnings the boat grazed the bushes. It was a pretty river, but so narrow. We progressed very slowly. There were very few passengers, maybe eight or ten ladies. Mr. Higley, who was about thirty or thirty-two, I think, was very kind to his sister and treated me with protective amiability.

The second evening just after supper there was a very considerable jar felt. It threw me against a column and Florence half across the cabin. Mr. Higley, half carrying his mother, hurried us both up to the hurricane deck before we knew what had happened. In no time he had our three trunks up there too, then told us that the boat had struck a snag and that he thought she would sink. In the meantime the employees were taking mattresses from the beds to close the awful hole in the hull. We could feel that the boat was *stuck* and the water was rising slowly. Then the boat rocked from side to side and there was a crash of crockery, glass and woodwork, and an awful sizzling as the water reached the fires, but the boiler did not burst. The freight, boxes, barrels and whatall began to float down stream. The boat listed a little to one side and all was still. Every human being was on the hurricane deck. The deck hands had grappling hooks and many boat torches. They are great iron baskets swung on an iron pole and filled with resinous, fat, pine. When we had settled, the water on one side lapped within six inches of the deck. On the other it was about two feet from reaching the deck. The captain said we were in no danger at all so long as the wind did not freshen. If it did, he feared that the weight of the chimneys would carry us over. At many spots of the river chimneys becoming horizontal would have formed a bridge to the shore but at this place, abreast of the Cobawba Bluffs, the river is wide and on either side the slippery yellow clay bluff rises perpendicularly from eighty to ninety feet. We had to wait for relief. After two hours we saw the light of a coming boat. The lights seemed to be stationary, as they were. The *Joab-Lawrence* was aground around the nearest bend. Six hours later she was alongside and took us all aboard.

Among us was an Irish woman who was on her way to St. Louis to do the cooking for a family. As she expressed it, "I'm a lady of birth ye all must know, but a woman I know in St. Louis wants me to cook for her so I am going to her." As we got on the upper deck of our sunken boat a box was seen to float off. She screamed and wrung her hands till a deck hand had caught it with a hook. It was her Saratoga trunk she had been very boastful of. I know it cost her a pang of pride to have it seen that her effects were nailed in a dry-goods box. She found it necessary to explain that she had sent her Saratogy by express and finding a few more dribbles had in her hurry had them put in the common old box.

Aboard the *Joab-Lawrence* was a Miss Atkinson, also going to the Judson. She had been there before and explained many things about the school. We found her very pleasant and entertaining. She also said that in Selma we would meet sixteen other scholars so that we would be nineteen entering together.

Our amusement on board was the Irish woman. She had her box opened and taking a clothes-line from it proceeded to tie it around the parlor cabin and hang up her belongings to dry. The chambermaid remonstrated. The woman was obdurate. The captain was called in. The woman was in tears. Her reasons for drying her things were good enough, only she put them in such a ridiculous way. Finally her grief was so loud that the other guests said if it bring peace they were willing to have her expose her properties, as one and all were tired and wanted to retire. We three stayed up a long while to watch the woman. The most comical dialogues took place between her and the boat's chambermaid. We watching girls enjoyed it as long as we could keep our eyes open.

We reached Selma six hours late. The train was about to start. A messenger was dispatched to beg the railroad to wait for us. Mrs. Higley could not walk. Four men carried her. There was not a carriage or hack to hire in the town. Nothing like a livery stable had been established or reestablished since the fighting had ceased. Mrs. Higley had been almost completely paralyzed for fifteen years. Halfway to the train her carriers were almost spent when a doctor in his buggy had the kindness to take her in and drive her the rest of the way. We young people had been hanging back not to be ahead of Mrs. Higley. Now we had to run to keep up with the buggy.

The train was slowly moving when we climbed in, we easily enough and Mrs. Higley pulled up and pushed up by a number of people. We got in our seats and thought that at last we were safe and would reach Marion in good time to enter the school at once. But we were counting on better travel than we had. The train was a few minutes late at a crossing. One half of our coaches had passed when a locomotive cut us in two. One coach was demolished and the train divided. As soon as possible, they backed up, hooked on the rear section and proceeded. It was impossible to "make time." The road bed and coaches were too old and all was very rickety. We arrived in Marion two or three hours late.

At the depot we met the sixteen girls mentioned by Ella Atkinson. We had plenty of time for introductions as the "bus" had given us up and gone to stable. It was sent for and came full of the town boys. I wondered how they would get back. After we had completely filled the "bus" and Mr. Horace Higley had found a seat with the driver, all the boys who could do so climbed on the rounded top of the vehicle. The planks began

172 / My Life As I Remember It

to groan and crack ominously. The driver tried to induce some of his forced passengers to get off, but in vain. All at once with a jolt of the "bus" the top split and a man's leg came through. Then the other boys jumped off and the bent wood rebounded. The poor young man's leg was terribly lacerated, the ragged ends of the broken wood entering the flesh and causing the blood to spurt freely. His agony was so great that he screamed aloud. Every step increased his pain so that the driver ordered the boys to get on again to try to reopen the fissure to relieve his horrible agony. When we arrived in the town opposite the hotel the men were all there and he had finally fainted. We all were bespattered with blood, our faces, hats, dresses, etc. I was feeling very faint myself. Many of the girls were crying. That leg, up to the thigh, dangling, bloody and swollen, spraying us with that red blood, the screams or groans of the sufferer, the poor words of encouragement of his friends, all buzzed and surged in my brain and left an indelible picture.

Three months later we saw a young man at church. He had crutches beside him. We were told that it was our young man of the bus. I never knew if his leg had been amputated or not but he had a suffering look on his pallid features even then.

Of course, it was too late to enter the school. Most of the girls went for the night with friends in the village. I did not follow the movements of any of them. We had our own troubles. There were no bedrooms on the ground floor. There was a large one with two beds up one flight of stairs but said stairs were so old and delapidated that men carrying Mrs. Higley would not trust that weight on them. She was put in a chair and hoisted, her son and one man guiding her ascension. All the light was furnished by small pine torches burning in the vestibule below. On the upper landing was a "tallow dip." Finally we reached that room.

It was beginning to be less dark as the moon was rising but the room's windows were to the west. We tried to reconnoitre but we could only see the outline of one bed and two windows. Mrs. Higley got on the bed and Mr. Horace called Florence and me to come to supper. I had travelled very little, had once been in the St. Charles Hotel parlor in New Orleans and several times in the beautiful old St. Louis Hotel on Royal Street, also in New Orleans. But that was before the war. I had no idea of a country town hotel in good or bad times. I was horrified, afraid, intimidated, all this, and I had not gone through the worst.

We went down into the dining room!! Save the name. The room was very long and very low. A very narrow table made of boards laid on trestles occupied the length at the center. There were three tallow candles stuck in a heap of tallow the size of a man's fist, to light the whole room. No table cloth, of course. Dirty or used dishes covered every place. Supper seemed to be over. Some thirty or forty men were in there talking excitedly, not hostilely, but low. Most of them had their hats on, hats as men had then, remnants of old army hats, caps, or nondescript head coverings. Their clothes were on the same order, old uniforms, old hunting suits of corduroy, old velvet trousers and smoking jackets by way of a coat. It was quite cool. I would have given worlds not to go into that room. Nearly every man was smoking. I thought of the cavern of Ali Baba and the forty thieves. That was the worst thing I had ever seen a picture of.

I pulled Mr. Higley's sleeve and whispered, "I am not hungry. Please let me go back upstairs to Mrs. Higley." He did not seem to hear. I looked up at Florence. The candle at the end of the table lit her beautiful aristocratic face. Her red-gold hair clustered in curls about her face and neck. She looked no more like one belonging to that den than I felt in sympathy with it. We entered. Some of the men removed their hats. Many, maybe all, were gentlemen, impoverished, ruined, southern gentlemen. Thus country gentlemen looked just after the war, six months after the surrender. On a coarse plate we were served a lavish portion of fermenting molasses and a "hunk" of plain cornbread. We were hungry but I could only take a few small mouthfuls of the supper.

"Anything else?" Mr. Higley asked. No, there was nothing more. Then it was that we heard that supper was served in the early evening to the guests but that, tomorrow being a mass meeting day, all these old soldiers had come into town and eaten everything available.

Florence and I went upstairs very quickly and sat on the edge of Mrs. Higley's bed, her son having promised to fetch up one of the candles as soon as the dining room should be vacated. We were in the midst of a speculation as to what sort of floor covering we were stepping on when a motion, or groan, or snore startled us. It seemed to be coming from the other end of the room where the other bed should be. The voice resolved itself into shrieks and half-laughter of a being fighting with the bedclothes, some imaginary foe.

The voice laughed, "Look at them. They are swimming, swimming. Look, the shrimps are all over them. Ha. Ha." Then it shrieked, "Get off me. Murder. Murder. Monkeys and shrimp, get from me, etc., etc." We were as crystallized with fear.

"Florence, call your brother, call somebody. There is somebody in that bed and they seem to be crazy. Go, Florence, go, dear," said Mrs. Higley. But neither Florence nor I would go. To go meant to pass quite close to the *person*. We had passed there once when all was silent, but now, with the voice saying terrible things and the bedclothes being tossed about we could see nothing but we could hear it all. The shrieks became so frightful that they were heard by the landlord.

He came in haste and asked, "Why, ladies, what is the matter? Is one of your party sick?" We did not answer. We girls left it to Mrs. Higley to explain but for some reason she remained silent. He then called for help and a light. Several persons came up, Mr. Higley among them. Then something was done to drown the voice, something was carried out, and silence comparative reigned. The someone carried out was taken to a distant room and all night we heard those diminished cries.

There were no other bedclothes to change so Florence and I both crept into Mrs. Higley's big bed. There was not a latch, hook or bolt to the door and only one pane of glass to the two windows but no gallery ran on that side. Mr. Horace took an armchair and declared he would stay at our door till daylight. I do not know if he stayed there but in the very early morning Florence and I were sent in search of a maid or of someone who would find many necessary adjuncts to a sleeping apartment besides a bed and one chair. We walked around and met no one. We started down a back stairway where many stairs were missing, as many as four in one place. We climbed down and finally found what we needed but could never come up that way again. The only wash-basin we could get was a very battered tin one. We used it very gingerly and did not stay for breakfast. As soon as Mrs. Higley could be gotten in a carriage we drove to the Institute. All arrangements were quickly made. Mrs. Higley obtained board in the school provided she occupied an ordinary room like a scholar. Florence and I were assigned to a room for two, five rooms from that of Mrs. Higley.

Having to unpack, this first day we saw very little of the scholars but we met all the residing teachers. Our real studies began the next day. I was the only Louisianian and the only French descent girl there. Florence and I were the only Catholic girls at the Institute. I determined then and there that I owed it to myself, my state, and my religion, to get all the honors possible and I went hard at it. It was hard to *learn* all the rules but I never found a rule hard to obey. It was fortunate for me that Miss Mollie Gayle had been a graduate of the Judson as it made little change in the general manner of instruction.

At the Judson

THE PROFESSOR of mathematics and chemistry was Colonel S[amuel] Lockett, one of Father's late war companions. His wife taught music and singing. She was very pretty and he seemed immensely proud of her. They were both very much thought of in the Institute. There were also Mr. Rev. and Mrs. Thomas W. Tob[e]y. Mr. Toby had been ten years a missionary in China and was very pleasant to converse with. He taught

Grammar, Literature, Reading, and History. Mrs. Toby did not teach or perhaps she taught a class of very young day scholars. I saw her only at meals or when she "visited" in Mrs. Higley's room.

The second week of our stay many more pupils came in. We were a little crowded so Florence went to room with her mother and a Miss Smith came into my room.[3] I was informed that it was only for that one night as the next day we could rearrange ourselves to suit all parties best. The information was an indication that Miss Smith was judged not to be very suitable to or for me. Miss Smith was an inoffensive, ordinary looking American girl. Her manner was gentle but it was to me a great hardship to have a total stranger thrust into not only my room, but my bed. I had never thought of a strange bedfellow and it embarrassed me very much. I let Miss Smith undress and get ready for bed, making very little progress that way myself. When she was quite ready she produced a large white ball the size of a baby's head and rubbed it all over her face and hands and arms. I could not imagine what it was. She then put it back in its flannel bag, hung the bag to the back of a chair, then got into bed. At that moment the curfew bell sounded. I put out the light and hastily undressed, said my prayers and got on the narrowest possible edge of the bed. However, I knew what Miss Smith's white ball was. It was suet, mutton suet. The smell worried me till I got asleep and her pillow next morning proclaimed the fact at sight.

I had hardly gotten in bed, feeling lonely and homesick, oh, so homesick, when I heard the door open and Miss Marianne Hentz came in. She was the French teacher. She came to the bedside and said she came from Mrs. Higley's room and that Mrs. Higley had sent me a piece of white nougat. I should have laughed at the idea of getting candy as a consolation, like a baby. Instead, I acted like a baby. I burst into tears. Miss Hentz then spoke to me quite a while in French, telling me that other girls would be in in two days and that she thought one of them would just suit me. Anyway, she would give me the first choice of rooms on her hall in the change that had to take place. I had expressed no word about change but she knew and felt for me in my loneliness.

Two days later Miss Laura Gaultney arrived also the two Misses Montevelt and Miss Marietta Steel. There was on our hall only *one* room to be occupied by three girls. It had a big old-fashioned fireplace instead of a stove and for that reason there was no room for two double beds. There was one double and one single bed. Miss Hentz told me of the room and I immediately jumped at it, for the single bed. Then she asked if I had any preferences about the new girl. Miss Gaultney suited me at sight and Miss Marietta Steel, but Miss Steel and Miss Vista Welsh had elected to go together leaving Miss Mattie Goodloe out. She and Miss Foster went together and Miss Claudia Herron asked that we take her in so we did and to the end of the term we were together. At first, for a month or more, I had the single bed, but Later Miss Gaultney and I occupied the double bed and Claudia, the single one. Claudia was a "case," just a queer girl, kind generous, quiet, but so effusively grateful for the least little token of friendship that it was at times very embarrassing. I helped her with the French translations. It was a nothing to me and not even worth thanks. Yet she wrote home about it and her mother wrote me quite a nice letter and every time Claudia got things from home she claimed that her mother meant half of them for me.

At the same time, in a stage whisper, she would say, "We will divide in three parts, Miss Frémaux. *I* don't mind having less and Miss Gaultney would feel badly maybe. *You* don't mind giving a part of your share, do you?" That was Claudia's queer way instead of opening her package and offering some to both of us. No, each must have a share to do with as she pleased. Once or twice she had some trouble. That, too, she insisted on sharing. "Girls," she called out once, "cry with me. Mother has lost five bales of cotton." And indeed she was in such distress that we did share her grief. Another time it was some other bad news and several times through the night she called out, "Girls, please don't sleep sound. I am in such trouble."

Miss Gaultney was several years older than Claudia and I. She had been two years at "Nazareth," a convent near her home. She was very intelligent, a good French scholar and altogether a lovely woman. Her father remained in Marion one week and at dinner recess he took her into the town every day. Through her we got several articles of comfort for our room. One was a small armoir, a small cooking pot, a large curtain, and a set of fluting irons. We hung the curtain so as to divide the washstand corner. In that way we could take our bath privately, and to have some warm water for it the kettle came in very handy. We also made chocolate in our pot and once a week thin starch to flute our ruffles. The school laundry only ironed them flat. Many girls sent their ruffles home for fluting. We lived too far away. We were almost always four in the room except in sleeping time for Florence was as my sister then and ever after in our married life.

When Christmas came had I written home for a box I would have had one, and a nice fine one, but my people knew nothing of college girls' boxes. I would have had to ask for each thing and I had never asked for anything so I did not ask or mention Christmas at all. However, it happened that Pa met Mr. Higley as he was preparing to send Florence and his mother quite an elaborate box or boxes.

So Father told him that if such was the custom, "Why, go ahead, make it enough for my little girl, too, and we will divide expenses," and so it happened that we gave the teacher and our most intimate classmates quite a supper Christmas Eve.

The supper was early as college suppers are. Afterwards several of us and Mrs. Higley went to Colonel Lockett's home for a dance and a midnight supper and fireworks. There I met several young men. One, a Mr. Reed asked to see us home. Home that night was at a Mrs. Crow's, a friend of the Higleys. Mrs. Higley went in a buggy and we walked, Florence and Mr. Pony Lockett, Mr. Reed and I. The night was cold and misty. It was the first time a boy had seen me home from anywhere. He gave me his arm and I very lightly rested the tip of my fingers on it. The clay walks were rather slippery. He said, "Don't be afraid to lean on me. I am not a broken Reed." Just then his feet slipped up and he slid on his back down the enbankment. There was a pale moonlight and he looked very comical picking himself up again. I felt very much like laughing but refrained. Florence and her escort roared. I can see her yet looking back over her shoulder, all her face aglow with youth and joy, her curls peeping out here and there from her white head covering. She was really lovely.

Mr. Reed asked, "Why did you not laugh like your friend? Look how pretty her laughter is. I would like to see you let yourself go once, even in laughing at me." He was certainly not overly sensitive or overly timid either. I said I would never look like Florence, never.

"No, he remarked, "you are a dear, timid little wren. She is a bright butterfly."

"Now, draw in your horses, Reed. You forget our bargain." This came from Mr. Lockett. He *drew in* and we proceeded quietly to Mrs. Crow's.

Mr. and Mrs. Crow lived in a pretty little cottage on the very edge of the woods. It was a pretty little house and pretty woods even in winter. Mrs. Crow had a fine baby boy a few months old. She told us that her maiden name was Green but she could not really afflict her boy by calling him Green Crow so she had named him Jim. I thought it was about the same. To carry as a name Jim Crow would have been a burden to me.

We were not due back to the Institute before dark of Christmas day. So, after breakfast, we went for a stroll in the woods. Behind the first big tree we found our escorts of the night before. They said they had been there two hours watching the house to see when we would come out. I was very much worried at this meeting. I knew Ma would not have approved. Florence was joyous and unconcerned. She was used to boys' company. This time the escorts were reversed, Mr. Reed to Florence, Mr. Lockett to me. He insisted that we should go back to his home to visit its beautiful garden which we had not been able to see the night before.

I said, "No." Florence also thought no. After arguing a long time he finally produced a note the Colonel had received from Father permitting me to go to dinner with them on Christmas, so we went to see the place, which must have been beautiful indeed before the soldiery had all but destroyed its fountains, grottos, and other embellishments. There was a pretty walk of hazelnut trees, the first and only ones I have ever seen. My escort showed me some unexploded fireworks on the lawn and I noticed that they formed the letters C E L I N E. "Who is named Céline in your family?" I asked.

"Why no one . . . that is no one . . . yet. I thought it would be nice to light them as you came in last night but all of you came together and . . . and . . . and brother Colonel would not let me fire them." That was a speech!! I was very much embarrassed and wished I had not come.

However, his young sister and little brother or nephew made much of us and the little boy said, "Uncle Pony wanted you to be queen of the party last night but Uncle Colonel said you would be too timid to feel happy about it, so we could not shoot off the name. Uncle Colonel is so mean some times."

I would not stay to dinner. Mrs. Crow had made preparations and it would have been ill-bred of us not to be there. We had quite a fine time and little Jim Crow was seated on my lap most of the time. The evening was spent conversing in the parlor, from the windows of which we could see Mr. Reed and Mr. Lockett seated on a log at a little distance. Every now and then they would walk past the gate and then go back to their log. Mr. Crow offered to go out and invite them in but I protested vigorously, for me, and Mrs. Higley thought also that it was unnecessary. When the carriage came to the gate for us they advanced, helped put Mrs. Higley in, said a few polite words, and that ended it. I saw Pony Lockett many times after that but I never made it convenient to speak to him.

On returning to school I found a small package from home marked to open on New Year's day. And on New Year's day I found it contained a ring, clasped hands of turquoise in a bed of little diamond roses. It was a piece of antique jewelry. I had seen it in Ma's box several times. I was very proud of it and it was much admired especially by teachers who understood its artistic value.

On the first of the year we passed our semi-annual examination, a public one. I was very much frightened. It was my first experience of that kind. My voice left me almost completely and many of my answers were repeated louder by the obliging Claudia. I got on much better at the blackboard as my back was turned on the public. My examination marks were perfect. So were Florence's and Miss Gaultney's and others also. The girls afterward said that Pony Lockett was in the audience. Maybe he was but I saw no further of the audience than the first row, all old men, preachers, I suppose. They seemed to glare at us and tried to propound the most difficult questions. I can see that row of old men yet.

The stocking hanging at the Institute was done Christmas night instead of Christmas eve. It was quite an affair. Many of us had little tokens for many of our companions and we had much difficulty in obtaining permission to go into the other halls to leave them in the different stockings. The teachers also hung their stockings at their own doors. Miss Tallbird was the exception.[4] Miss Tallbird was always the exception. Miss Tallbird was very much opposed to the stocking hanging in every way.

Mollie Lowry was the most mischievous girl in the school. Having found that there would be no stocking on Miss Tallbert's door, she hung her own there and told it about to the girls saying that as most of her friends were in the "old" building she had made it convenient to them by putting her stocking at the end of the hall. After curfew the teachers gathered in Mrs. Higley's room for a chat and on leaving it saw this stocking at Miss Tallbird's door. She had reconsidered, they told each other, and straightaway they fetched their presents and put them in or near. None of the girls were giving Miss Tallbird anything but many gave to Mollie Lowry. Very early in the morning Mollie came and carried everything to her room. Everyone greeted everyone else with a smile of good fellowship the next day but Miss Tallbird had a cold, sour stare for all, teachers and girls alike. We were rather used to her "vinegar" ways but the teachers were surprised. They exhibited their presents and thanked each donor. Miss Tallbird said not a word. At breakfast Mollie looked queerly into the cups of coffee. Around the table she did it so noticeable that Miss Talbird rapped smartly on the board and asked what she saw so strange about the beverage.

Mollie put on a face of perfectly idiotic astonishment and answered, "Miss Tallbird, if you will believe it, the milk has not curdled in these cups."

The girls all understood and most of them repeated, "Well, it really has not." We at Miss Tallbird's table did not laugh but all the other tables did so and the teachers' table took it up. Miss Tallbird was pale with rage. She announced that each and everyone would report five points lost at the calling of the roll.

"Miss Tallbert," said Mollie in her sweetest voice, "you deserve a present for the luck your door knob gave me. My stocking never contained so many fine things. If you will please accept this purse, I will gladly give it to you." The purse was one that Mrs. Toby had put near the door. Miss Tallbird exploded; the teachers began to explain. There was quite a lot of explaining and readjusting. Mollie, with the look of an innocent cherub, fetched everything she had received, was profuse in excuses and peace finally reigned but both the Lowry girls were informed to "keep themselves well to the mark" or it would be worse for them. It was an unfortunate remark. I saw a look pass between the two and I knew something else was coming.

Hardly had the study hour begun when one girl asked to go nearer to the stove. She felt cold. Miss Talbird denied her saying that she never went near the stove and was even the furthest from it. A very few minutes later, a dreadful odor and smoke seemed to issue from Miss T[albird]'s footstool. It was not bearable. The curtain which surrounded her desk was raised by an investigating porter and behold a great heater had filled all the space and on that heater crumbs and crusts of cheese were melting and smelling. How the Lowry girls had found out about that heater and how they had put the cheese there, I never knew, but the study hour was broken up, the room aired and reheated and I never knew Miss Tallbird to refuse to let a girl go to the stove after that.

Miss Talbert, in her youth, had ruined her hair trying concoctions to make it curl. At the time I knew her, she was an inveterate hater of curls. Poor Florence got many rebukes about her rebellious curls. She had *orders* once never to be seen with curls again. Mrs. Higley appealed to the principal, Mr. A. J. Battle, about it and it was decided that, provided the girls were never seen in curl-papers, they could dress their hair as they chose. I had often wondered at the rarity of curls in this school. It was simply due to their obedience. No one had thought of appealing to a higher court. Miss Talbird had been the Law. In a very few days, however, the schoolroom was quite changed. Lovely black, brown, and golden curls were seen at many desks and Miss Tallbird sought other ways to make us miserable.

About this time there began to be rumors of the thefts about the old building. Two girls, the Misses Ellen and Betty Shields and a Miss Mattie Grant seemed to be the most frequent victims. We were all feeling very blue about it when the thief was caught. When she was sent to her piano practice was the time she chose for pilfering. She had keys to several rooms and to several trunks. She was expelled, of course. I will never forget the face of her father when he came for her. I do not know where she was kept pending her father's arrival. None of us saw her. When he arrived I happened to be in Mr. Battle's study. The porter flung open the door. "Mr. M——," he announced.

"Go, go quickly," Mr. Battle told me and I fled, but I had seen him, the unhappy, mortified, desperate man. Tall and handsome, his black hair and eyes showed such a contrast to the deadly pallor of his skin. I can not describe what I felt. I wanted to help him, to cry out that we would try not to remember. I had such a longing that someone would go to him and comfort him before he met his wayward child. A half hour or so later a carriage drove up to the back steps, quite close, then from the side door of the study came forth the girl and her father. He looked even worse than before. His lips twitched and his chin trembled. Great tears fell unnoticed on his shirt front. The girl was bareheaded and carried her hat in her hand. The father almost pushed her into the carriage and hastily entered after her. The stares were let down and it was quite a moment before Mr. Battle moved from the steps. I was sobbing. When class hour came and we were all assembled, Mr. Battle made a short speech and asked if we were willing to hush this matter and never mention it among ourselves or outside by letter or word.

Many of us said, "Yes. Yes."

"Let me be sure about this thing," he said. "Let everyone who is willing to hush this thing hold up their right hand before God." It was an oath as I understood it, but Mr. Battle added, "This promise, young ladies binds you for as long as you hear nothing more of this young girl's fault from outside sources." So many held up their hands that it seemed to me that all had done so. He then asked if anyone objected to the promise, please to rise. No one arose.

A few days later a young lady remarked to a number of us that Miss M—— could never again hold up her head in her town. "Why?" we asked.

"Why, because I wrote the whole thing to a rather gossipy friend there and she will get her desserts."

"Miss Ida Collins," I exclaimed, "you have taken an oath!"

"Not I," she said. "I held up my left hand." I do not know what the others thought or said. I left the group and never felt at ease when Miss Collins was around. In the world I never met her and hope never to do so.

Our oath bound us about seven years until in a New York paper we saw that Miss Emma M—— of such a town had been arrested with a public character and sent to prison for theft. They seemed to have pockets and false sleeves to their garments and in them concealed their booty, etc., etc., but even then I have never spoken her name. When I think of her the agonizing features of her father arise before my mental vision. I pity that father.

We were quite sobered for a few days, then Miss Lowry thought it time to rouse our drooping spirits. She came down to the study hour with her hair in three lovely rows of curls. It looked tidy and lovely. As she passed Miss Talbird's desk a thundering "Miss Lowry" made us all look up.

"M-a-a-m," she answered in the mildest tone.

"I will not stand your hair buckled up in that manner, Miss. Go and comb it out this instant."

Mollie bowed, winked at us and went up-stairs. Presently, she returned. Her hair was not over nine inches long. Every hair stood to itself. Her head was the size of a water bucket. She was perfectly composed and was again about to pass Miss Talbird on her way to her desk. With a sort of roar Miss Talbird was on her feet. We were all *silently* choking Miss Lowry.

"What *do* you mean?"

"I did my best to obliterate the curls, Madame."

"Don't dare to Madame me, Miss. I am a Miss and you know it." Mollie had reached her desk.

"Go and reduce your hair. Do something. Tie it down, cut it, wet it, but reduce it instantly."

Mollie again crossed the big room with her bristling head. This time we were less silent, a sort of groan rippled all over the room. I felt my neck squeezed and felt my chain and coral cross being drawn off. Miss Ella Atkinson, my desk mate, was the culprit. I dared not ask even with my eyes why she had taken it. The rule read: Communicating thought entails the loss of two good points. I did not want to lose points.

Then Mollie returned. She had been out quite a time. Her hair was so wet, so slicked and smooth, so glued to her head with water, that it looked as if she had to a dozen strands. She was a sight. Little drops of water dripped and rolled down her wool waist to her skirt. "Will this do, Miss Talbird?"

"It will do, Miss."

Presently she chirped up, "Miss Talbird, can I go to the stove? I feel chilled although I did my best. I had Dr. Shivers order me hot water for my head but I feel mighty cold."[5] She was allowed to go to the stove, and indeed her head was all but freezing. Then she wrapped a shawl about it. That would have been all right but she chose to use a bright tartan, very large, and fixed it like a huge oriental turban with a fringed part hanging to one side. Nothing but seeing the slender girl with that turban would give an idea of the ridiculousness of her appearance. She was docked ten good marks. She appealed by letter to the Board of Directors. The whole faculty assembled, she stated her case quietly in a dignified manner, proved that she had broken no role, given no saucy replies and obeyed the letter. It was all true. Her marks were returned. From that day every girls whose hair could curl, was arrayed in the glory of curling locks. Not a voice was raised against it. Mollie's hair was the stiff, straight kind and had on that memorable day been done on a hot poker.

We were soon again to be shocked by an event more dreadful than theft. In the fifth month of the session a baby was born in the Judson to a very young girl who had not the slightest idea of what was happening to her, so that the two other occupants of the room came very near to being witnesses of the advent. Being uneasy at the evident pain of their friend, they both left the room, one to call Mrs. Daniels, the other to go for Dr. Shivers. I saw the little one a few days later. I was sent to ask something of Mrs. Daniels and she had the infant in her arms. It was a girl and resembled its mother excepting that she had a very retreating forehead. Her eyes were blue, like a piece of the summer sky. Poor little babe. I learned the whole history of its existence many years after I was married.

The day that baby came Miss Atkinson returned my chain, cross, and medal. She had never wanted to tell me why she took it, saying she would tell me when "it had proved itself." On returning it she explained that she had seen the medal for the first time when I tried not to laugh that day and took it to wear for "good luck" but it had proven itself worthless and as she had been at the Judson seven years and it had never happened that the school had been so disgraced, so the medal was "no good." She was a funny girl, doing such things all the time, yet a number one scholar and a perfect lady.

We had always been allowed an hour and a half's leisure on Saturday evening. We played the piano, sang, talked, danced or visited the different teachers in their own rooms. It was a social time. It happened that some girls had lately entered school who had been to dancing school and they knew many fancy dances. One Saturday they danced them for us and a number of the younger teachers. Old Mr. Toby was also there telling us how these dances compared with those of the Chinese, etc., when in came Miss Tallbird. We did not stop as dancing was allowed but she stopped us. Mr. Toby made himself small behind the girls. She had the retiring bell rung and to bed we all had to go. We were not allowed the "social hour" after that.

It snowed one Saturday and Sunday. In fun, Mrs. Higley threw a snowball from her window sill into the midst of a lot of us in the yard below. We immediately returned it with many others. Several teachers were in the room throwing back at us. As soon as Miss Tallbird heard the laughter she had the bell rung and kept us in our rooms till supper, then immediately after to bed.

These tyrannical acts seemed to pass unchallenged yet they must have been reckoned in high quarters for at the end of that session she was dismissed and the Judson knew her no more. At times however, Miss Talbird had to rescind many of her despotic announcements.

Fifty marks lost in a session caused expulsion from the school. Even the giddiest girl kept tally on her marks and was careful to lose less than the dreaded fifty, so that to some girls an unexpected "ten off" put them in a dreadful plight.

One Saturday evening six of us had obtained permission to visit Miss

Fanny Chilton's room. Miss Fanny was one of the music teachers. She was our idol—petite, pretty, bright, with black eyes and short black curly hair. We lavished on her all the pent up love of our souls. It was with her the same as happens in every school. I had discovered her perfections and offered my incense. I let Florence into the secret of my find. She told others and in no time she was the idol of our hall. She seemed to love us all, I, because I was one of my kind in the school, Florence because she had such a lovely old mother, Nannie because she had no mother at all, and so on and so on. There was no jealousy. We were perfectly happy when she was with us and almost delirious when she invited us to her room.

This Saturday we had permission to stay with her from supper till retiring bell. We were in the midst of acting charades when we distinctly heard the supper bell. At the Judson every bell had a different sound. We knew and obeyed by their sound. The dining room bell was cracked and there was no mistaking its sound. We had had supper so we supposed that it was some sort of extra supper of good things for the teachers. We spoke to Miss Fannie about it. She had heard of no extra feasting. We urged her to leave us and go but she said she was not hungry and was having a pleasant time, so we thought no more of it and remained in her room until the retiring bells sounded.

The next morning Miss Tallbird was very angry and very harsh and as she called the roll, announced that all the girls who had not come down to the study hall the night before were quietly losing ten from their maximum. That ten off sounded to me like one hundred. Florence and another girl began to cry. I could not believe my ears. Miss Mary Battle, who had been with us, asked if we would be allowed to know why. She was told that several of the "faculty," two of them ministers, had visited us and had a speech or two, then prayers, and that we had been grossly impolite by refusing to appear. Miss Battle then said that the study bell had not been rung; that, she and her companions knew; and that in the name of all the absentees she entered a protest. There was a scene, all but blows. Miss B[attle] was ordered from the room. Miss Tallbird threatened to double our lost mark. About twenty girls were to suffer.

Miss B[attle] went straight to her father and laid the matter before him. All twenty of us were summoned one after the other. Each gave her reason. Miss Fannie was also summoned. It turned out that the study hall bell had been misplaced so the dining room bell had been rung instead. The more curious of the girls had gone to see why the bell was rung, others to know who was invited to a second supper, and others had remained in their rooms thinking the second supper was none of their concern. Then there were we six in Miss Fanny's room. Of course our marks were returned, but Miss Tallbird was cross for weeks at not having been sustained by the board.

Several of the girls decided that she should be punished fittingly but nothing happened for a while. One evening Miss Tallbird was dressed in a grass green silk, very fine, trimmed in lace. She seemed to be going to some entertainment. She hurried us through study hour and hurried us to supper. "Haste, young ladies, haste. I want this supper over quickly," she said. There was immediately a lot of whispering, the two Lowrys, Eudora and Mary; Miss Florence Bender; Miss Ida Collins; and others. "Order," Miss Tallbird thundered, "order and haste." Order was immediate, but haste seemed to "lag." Every table was filled and waiting before the one at which presided Miss T[albird]. Finally, just as she took her seat at the head, the table seemed to waver and rise at the foot. Twenty-two glasses of water and twenty-two cups of tea poured down the length of that table. Six syrup pitchers also spilled their contents. On an oil cloth surface liquid runs fast. Miss T[albird] received a good half dozen teas and water in her lap where reposed her gloves, her handkerchief, and scarf. It was awful. Twenty-one girls jumped up to protect themselves. The secret of that "trick" was never disclosed but Miss T[albird] was punished. She did not go out, nor do I suppose she ever wore that green silk again. Women with tempers and without tact should never attempt to make a living in a boarding school.

Back to Mobile

WELL, things had not quite settled after the baby had come and later its mother and itself had been removed from the school when Janie Foster, a lovely girl, was taken with the smallpox. Immediately, we were all vaccinated or revaccinated. It was rumored that Janie got very poor care. Mrs. Higley offered to sit with her all day but was refused. The matron, Mrs. Harrold J. V. Harrell, was very pockmarked yet was afraid to approach Janie. An old nigger, a field hand, was secured as a nurse. There seemed to have been quite an epidemic of smallpox all over Alabama. I had heard that my mother was in bed with it. Selma seemed to have been a very infested place. All the day scholars quit coming and finally one day it was announced that the school was closed. We were all to go to our own homes. In the commotion of the many departures a window that I had never seen opened was left so. As I passed I saw Janie in her bed. The window next to her bed was curtainless and the sun shown down across her bed. Her hands were over her eyes to keep out the glare. I got over the low sill and walked in and almost fell over the sleeping old nigger. I passed on into the second room, Janie's, and spoke to her. She was an awful sight. She asked why the bells had not been rung these two days. I explained, then I asked if I could do anything for her. Yes, if we were going by boat we would pass ——— landing. Would we please have a note ready and deliver it to Dr. Foster, her uncle. He lived there and would probably be at the landing. *He* would know what to do for her. Yes, that was all. She would feel better now that she knew help would soon come. We left Marion an hour later. No one had seen me go in or out of Janie's room. I had pulled her bed around out of the light. The nigger still slept.

We got to Selma without trouble and found a boat just leaving. Then, under Mrs. Higley's direction, I wrote the note for Dr. Foster. It was not sunset yet when we reached ———— landing. The Clerk of the boat delivered the note to a gentleman who was on horseback. He read the note, bowed to Florence and I, put spurs to his horse, gave the note to a darky and pointed to a dwelling we could just see through the trees. I felt greatly relieved when I saw him start to Janie's relief.

We came on down the river without accident and reached Mobile in the early morning. Our people were not apprized of our coming so we took a carriage and drove to the Murry's to breakfast. I knew the family had moved after I went to school but did not know where they then resided. It was Sunday. I had not been in a Catholic church since October, so immediately after breakfast, Florence and I started for Mass. I was fairly sure to see some of my people there and they would take me home but no one was there. After much coaxing, Tudy Murry consented to take me near the place, point out the house and leave me. The fact that Ma had the smallpox accounted for her fear of approaching the house. So, I went to the door alone, rang the bell, then knocked. Finally, a muffled voice called for me to go round by the gate and in by the back way. Ma was up, but still confined to her room. She was alone just then and I explained the situation.

Presently, there was a knock at the parlor door. I had not removed my hat or gloves. At the door stood a young man. He enquired for Léon. I had just heard from Ma that Léon was at Black River on business and would not be back for several days. I told the young man so and, as he bowed himself out, blood began to spurt from his nose. Before he could get his handkerchief, five or six great drops were on the carpet. He seemed very confused, so was I. I rushed for a wet towel but I really did not know the house nor where to get water or towel. Ma's room was not to be thought of.

Ma called out, "Take him upstairs to your brother's room." I could see the stairs, so thither we directed our steps. He seemed to be familiar with the place and passed me running up. Just then Paul came in and I told him to go up; there was a young man in trouble up there. Then Sister and the other two little boys came in and I went into Sister's room to remove my things.

After a bit, Paul came in and said, "That was not a young man upstairs. It was Joe." Then I learned that "Joe" was Mr. Joe Garcia, a very intimate friend of Léon's and a very frequent visitor at the house. I do not know when he left Brother's room. It was about a week later when I met him again and was duly introduced.

On our way down the river from Selma we had had quite a pleasant time. Several of the Judson girls were on the same boat. One, Miss Suzan Marshall, had her brother and cousin with her. The cousin was dark and very handsome, the brother light and boyish and gay. The boat boasted of a caliope, but the present pilot was not a performer, so, for the last few trips, the music had not been heard at the landings. Mr. Marshall found this out and took us up to the pilot house. All of us played fairly well and the echoes of the river bank reverberated to the tune of the operas, dances, sacred music, jigs, and all sorts. We played at landings, between landings and had quite an enjoyable time.

I liked the Marshall boys quite well but it had not occurred to me that they would call. I had never had a caller and great was my surprise when on the very first evening, Mr. Marshall, the dark one, called. Pa was in the parlor with me. When he came he made a short call and he said he and his cousins and Florence would come next evening to get me for a walk. Pa was very nice to the young man but as soon as he was gone, Ma called me to her room and told me that ladies do not introduce people to their family, that she and Father would choose my company when they saw fit, etc., etc., that I must manage to keep the others from coming next day or she would make it plain to them that uninvited guests were not welcome in her house. So I went to bed crying on this my first night home.

If only Léon had been home, but he was not, and the next day was a day of anguish. I was quite busy, however, unpacking my trunk and esconsing my things in Sister's little room. Really, the room was very small, but it hurt me to see how I was considered an interloper in that room. It was never our room. It was Sister's room in which I crowded her. There was a large room upstairs but even before I returned Father was contemplating moving back to Louisiana. That was perhaps why no provision was made to room me.

In the early evening a boy brought flowers and a note from Mr. Marshall regretting that the walk would have to be postponed till Wednesday. To anyone else the incident would have been nothing at all. *I* was frightened nearly out of my wits. I threw the beautiful flowers under the kitchen and was about to destroy the note when Sister was on me. She had not seen the flowers but I had to acknowledge the note. She went straight to Ma about it and I got another scolding for the "impudent persistency" of Mr. Marshall.

That night Léon came home and I got him to tell Florence that I could not go with them for the walk as Ma was sick and needed me near her. However, after the walk Wednesday they stopped at the house to inquire about Ma. Fortunately, Léon was home with his friend, Joe, so the crowd came. We stayed on the front gallery and Sister was pleased at the company. Really, if Ma knew of their being there, she said nothing and after that, Léon took me out often. We went to the Higley's, met the Marshalls and had quite a nice time. Mr. Marshall's flowers, however, always adorned Léon's room and no one knew they were mine. Thus it was that I was forced to practice deception because I was too timid to tell the Marshalls not to come to see me. Florence's brother married Miss Lily Marshall.

Preparations were now being made for leaving Mobile. I was glad. I was raised too differently from the Mobile girls. I knew I could never be happy there and Louisiana was home. Mobile had never been but a stopping place.

My little cousin, Blanche, had returned to New Orleans on the first of January, 1866. She had greatly improved in health and wrote me nice letters every now and then.

While I was at the Judson, Miss Sallie Worthey had written to me twice. She being ten years my senior, I was very much pleased at this token of her remembrance, and I answered her letters with affection. At school my letters had been very much less looked over than were those of other girls. Mine were always written in French and Miss Hantz was the one to see that they were o.k. and to the right persons. Many times she took them from me and without even reading the address on them would seal them and drop them in the mail bag.

Once we were packing some crockery in a box, Léon, Paul, "Joe," and I. Some sort of discussion came up about a mouse. Anyway, Léon said, "Well, of course, Joe will side with you. I saw that coming some time. Why can't a girl know a boy a week without his being in love with her?" I fled and I managed to keep out of Mr. Joe's sight till the morning that we left Mobile.

Sister had been preparing for her first communion but Ma found that we would be leaving before the class was ready. Sister was examined privately by the Bishop and on the thirtieth of March at the five A.M. Mass took communion and was confirmed. There was a grown young man who, for some reason, was going through the same as Sister. When he got the Host in his mouth, I do not know where it lodged, but the contortions of his face to swallow it were so ludicrous that I came near laughing in church.

On the first of April we went on board the ship which was to take us back to Louisiana. Florence had bid us good-bye the evening before and Mr. Joe came aboard to see us off. I was in high spirits. "Do you regret nothing, leaving Mobile?" Mr. Joe Garcia asked.

"No, sir," I said. "Just think, we are going home where the people are like us. We have not known home life since Father left for the war." I was sorry after I said it. He flushed so and looked so distressed. He made a dive at Léon's pocket, snatched his handkerchief and ran off the ship as the bridges were being drawn in.

With his face buried in the handkerchief he came very near to falling overboard and Léon exclaimed, "Confound that boy. If he had drowned I ought to cry and I couldn't. He took off my handkerchief." We laughed over it and the ship started. Two days later we were in New Orleans.

Take it all in all, our stay in Alabama was not a very pleasurable one. In less than a year, we had had Mr. Gallimard sick six weeks, then died; Ma with nervous prostration three months; Henry with typhoid fever; Ma with smallpox; and I had been away from my loved ones nearly the whole time. I thought the Judson a good school and as my aim was to learn I never made a complaint in my letters. Yet, we were wretchedly fed. Breakfast consisted of biscuits and rolls of such inferior quality as to be heavy and dark, darker than buckwheat; molasses; and a cup of something. We never knew if it was meant for coffee or tea. Dinner was thick slices of beef, boiled, but still not tender, corn pones and rolls, molasses and stewed peaches or apples, dried. Supper was the same as breakfast, never any variation, excepting once. The day of a great baptizing feast we had stewed chicken and it was good and well done.

After a while it was discovered that the washwomen in cahoot with the cook put quantities of alum in the tea or coffee. Mrs. Higley then instructed Florence and me never to touch the liquid food at all, even after quite a rumpus had been made about the alum.

When sick, we had, so to speak, no care at all. Mrs. Harrold was matron in the infirmary and Dr. Shivers was the physician. There were few girls sick. For my part, I was subject to nervous sick headaches and went to the infirmary only once with a bad headache and fever. Dr. Shivers gave me some blue mass pills which I did not take. After being in bed twenty-four hours without anything to eat or drink, three other girls who were also sick, about like myself, clamored and stomped and pounded on the door with the heel of a shoe until Mrs. Harrold finally made an appearance.

She was asked, "What about eating, Mrs. Harrold?"

"Well," she answered, "there is no rule about food. Before the war the sick girls called for whatever they wanted and this session you are the first girls sick. What do you want to eat?" I said nothing. My fever was gone. I felt very weak. The girls clamored for ham and eggs. An hour later word came that no eggs or ham could be gotten. So they said they wanted chicken, a big fat hen cooked in rice and plenty of gravy. That succulent dish made its appearance at sundown. I had not tasted food for thirty-five hours. Miss Fanny Chilton came in and brought us some crackers and we five had a grand supper. Next morning we went back to our classes. It did not hurt us but it was certainly poor care for girls who paid $2.00 extra per day for the care in the infirmary. *My* bill for medical attention and drugs was $12.00. I was never in the infirmary but that one time and I did not take the pills because there were no conveniences in the building. With fever on I should have had to go down two stairs and out in the yard. If there was any provisions made for any other course, I was not told of it.

Florence went back to the Judson the next year and graduated. The school had been much improved as to food and medical attention. Miss Tallbird had been dismissed and quite an able, lovable lady put in her place.

The few weeks that I spent in Mobile, from my return home to our departure for New Orleans, were not especially comfortable ones. I foresaw that I was and would be as it were, in Sister's way. Sister was growing very pretty and Ma certainly meant her to shine all she could regardless of who had to stand back. Pa was always the same loving father, but business cares seemed to weigh on him heavily.

New Orleans: Reconstruction

THE WHOLE TENURE of life seemed and was, changed. Conditions were so different that one felt a stranger in one's own land. Of course, Father could make a living. He knew too many ways and was past master in so many avenues that he must be able to support us. But, once in New Orleans, we found very few of the old friends and those had lost their positions and influence. It was almost like coming to an unknown land. It was life to begin over with six children and the prime of life past. I could not help yet. I intended to teach, as soon as my diploma gave me a right, on the roll of expectant public school teachers. I determined to be as self supporting as possible, as soon as possible.

Full of those serious thoughts, we landed in New Orleans early in April. There were very few houses for rent. Uncle and his family were soon to move to the third district. He had obtained to be in charge of the insane in New Orleans and the place had fine apartments for his family. Pa was to take the house then occupied by Uncle, on the corner of Galvez and Esplanade. The house was a little small but we had no choice. For two weeks both families occupied the house, the men and Léon sleeping at the insane asylum.

Our stay together brought no disturbances, as our former two days stays had done. We were all very busy. The spring sewing had to be done. I had grown some four inches in the last year and all my clothes had to be changed.

Léon soon found employment in a crockery establishment as clerk for Mr. P. Maloche. That was not precisely what he had been to college for, before the war, but things were changed. Pa rented an office and announced himself as surveyor and architect and we began our Reconstruction life. Ma taught the children as always.

We found the Bercegais seven blocks from us, the Carrejolles five blocks off, and the Tacons next door to them. The Pikes from Baton Rouge were also here but they were still rich and . . . well, we could not go with them yet. We had to build up a little. Mrs. Pike, lonely as ever, called on Ma repeatedly. Ma went a few times but the children grown to be young girls were too fine and too proud for me. Their father had employed the four years of war speculating; their brother had escaped conscription by going to Europe and was not yet back. They were friends we had to gradually drop. We had little time for visiting, anyway. Two months later the Tacon family moved to Mobile and we took their house on Dumaine Street next door to the Carrejolles.

The two months of our stay on Esplanade Street brought forth only one episode. The Bercegais had called and the old friendship had resumed. There was only one thorn, and that was Camille. He had been in the Yankee army. Not voluntarily, it is true, but once in, he had stayed in until he had been wounded and sent home. He was looking coarse, his employment was coarse, his associates those of his employment.

I had come to know that I was not obliged to consider myself betrothed to him, and I hoped there would never be a necessity to refer to the past or to a now absolutely impossible future. A few weeks passed. One Sunday I went to church with Féfé. I borrowed Ma's prayer book. I took dinner at Bercegais', came home later and returned the book into Ma's hands. The next Sunday I borrowed it again. Mine had no Gospels in it. I went to church with Mémé [Aimée Frémaux] and Sister. On standing for the Gospels, the book opened at the place of itself. There was a note there. I knew the handwriting at once. I hid the note in my glove and did not hear a word of the rest of the Mass. I was in a veritable tumult. It was quite two hours after I got home before I managed to be alone and read the note. It was just what I feared. Camille wanted to know how I felt about him, if I was willing to accept his devotion. I was to let him know, by note or by word, through Féfé. If it was *no*, well, I was to make no sign and he would understand. I cried a good bit, then had to dodge the folks for fear they would notice my eyes. Mémé had stayed to dinner. She asked several times what worried me. Finally, we both looked out of the window on Bayou Street and safe enough from intrusion, I brought forth the note. Of course, it was not to Camille, but the question was, was it my duty to show it to Ma. My French raising said it *was* but my absolute knowledge was that Ma was going to make Sister a third party to a confidential note. Mémé was very positive that the note was mine and I had a right to keep it and not show it. As return confidence Mémé said that she was in love with a boy named Henri St. Clair who was now at college, that he sent her notes by his sister occasionally, etc., etc., that no one should know anything about it until he left college and asked her in marriage of her father.

Finally, I decided that if it was *yes* I intended to answer, it would be my clear duty to tell Ma and show her the note, happen what may. But as it was *no* I had better destroy the note, which I did on the spot, and saying nothing, thereby avoiding complications between the two families. It was easy enough to make no answer. Avoid him for a few months, he would understand and no one be mixed up in it, and above all, his pride would be saved. I could not consider accepting him. I remembered his years of devotion and I wanted to spare him all I could. The name Henry St. Clair was never to pass my lips. I naturally believed that Aimée, who was my same age, sixteen, felt and would act as I intended to do.

It was several weeks before I saw any of the Bercegai family, but on the day of our move they came to help us. I avoided a tete-a-tete with the boy, but late that evening Féfé asked me if I had no answer for her brother—so she knew. She said she had put the note in the book the Sunday before and we both trembled at the thought that a whole week it was in Ma's keeping. What would have happened if she had handled the book? When I told Féfé that I had no word to send, she cried and said the War had done it, the fighting on the other side, etc., etc., but that time would efface that feeling and may-be later I would forget it. I said no, I would never forget; how could I? "There is no one else, is there, Céline?" she asked gently. No, there was no one else, and there it ended for many months.

On Dumaine Street life was much more gay. In the evenings there were a number of girls, all friends to the Carrejolles. I was introduced to the crowd and all were friends from then on. They were:

Cecile Smith (Carrejolles)	Bébé Geux
Eveline Jaufroid	Amelie Molezan
Louisa Jaufroid	Lélia Esnard
Emelie Beauregard	Alida Roy
Louisa Troxclair	Marie Huant
Adrienne Troxclair	Alice Huant
Mimie D'Aquin	Esther Smith
Adine Jacob	Solimi Revail
Léonie Guex	Blanche Marionneaux
Sophie D'Aquin	Cornelia Blanchard
	Maria Rabouin

and their brothers and younger sisters, quite a crowd to begin with.

When September came round again Ma sent me to the public high school. I entered the senior class at once. Madame Blanc was the principal and a poor principal she made. She was soon changed and replaced by Miss Mills, a lovely woman.

Life at this time was hard, very hard in every way. There was poverty and pride, work and study, and hardships at home, and the ordinary hardship of a growing girl, the readjustment of society, the dropping of some, the picking up of others.

Father was very busy but the pay was not much as we would have needed to be as we used to be. I had known how to make tatting, a trimming, for several years. When I learned it, I was eight years old. I learned it from Ma. Old Mrs. Gashet-de L'Isle had taught her maybe ten years sooner. It had been a fashionable trimming in the dear old lady's girlhood. Now it happened that it came into fashion again. Very few persons had ever seen any before the ceasing of hostilities brought over fashion plates from Paris. Being very familiar with the shuttle, I immediately announced myself as willing to make tatting, for pay. This was the first swallow of the old time pride. Orders came in almost faster than I could fill them. Plain scallop tatting was paid 20¢ a yard. I managed to make 1 or 1½ yards a day. Insertion paid 35¢ a yard, medallions from 5¢ to 25¢ a piece. There were forty of the 5¢ ones to the yard. These prices were for thread No. 30.

A lady making a baby trousseau had me make many trimmings with No. 60 or No. 80 thread. She paid accordingly. I got up every morning at five o'clock, dressed, made tatting and had breakfast—a cup of coffee and bread, no butter—before going to school. The high school then occupied the basement of a church on Casacalvo Street and Elysian Field Street, twenty-six blocks from our house, Dumaine Street near Miro. I walked to school, tatting all the way, going and coming, and tatting at the thirty minute recess at twelve. I ate one or two dry crackers for luncheon. It took no time and did not soil my hands or my work. I studied at night, sewing, mending, or tatting in the evening. We retired at ten P.M. On Saturday after house cleaning, I gave the day to Pa's work, finishing maps, plans, etc., under his direction. Sunday, I only studied my lessons, wrote my next Friday's composition, and enjoyed the company of girls.

I was growing tall and perforce very slender. I was somewhat overworked. To earn and make all my own clothing, do one half of the house-work, go to school, study, teach the boys arithmetic, help Father, and try to get a little amusement with it all was a great deal for an undeveloped girl. Besides, the home was so strict. Sister was growing very tyrannical and Ma let her grow without check. In June 1867 for some reason, the time of graduation was put off to the following December. I was very disappointed. It was for me losing four months from September to the last part of December. In the summer my health had become very irregular, but mostly bad. When school began again in September I frequently fainted on arriving at the school. The old German portress was kind and knew what to do. She would wet the corner of her apron at the cistern, wipe it over my face and fan me a bit, and by the time school took in, I was ready for the day's routine. The last two weeks were very hard to me. I often felt faint all the day. Twice Miss Mills, who had married and was now Mrs. Tewell, had me taken home by one of the girls, Miss Mary Ballard. I should have gone in the car at least one way. Those fifty-two blocks were too much, but I was so extremely timid that I could never beckon to stop a car and if I once got in with other parties I would get out when someone else stopped as I would never have dared to stand up to reach the bell strap. My timidity was a great worry to me and a great inconvenience.

There were no cars then on Dumaine St. I walked to Esplanade St. often in hopes that someone would be waiting for the car and I could get in with them unnoticed like. Once I started in the car with several persons. I sat down, very red in the face, and looked for my purse—no purse. I opened my books one after the other in hopes of finding a car ticket there. I often had them there, but, alas, there was no ticket. At any moment the car driver might call for the fare. I got up, pulled the stop strap and before the car was stopped I was at the steps and down the street I flew. In the evening I found my little purse on the rug in my room where it had slipped my pocket.

There were many uproars and riots all over the city in those days of readjustment. In 1866 there had been quite a bloody fight between the whites and the negroes at the Mechanic's Institute on Dryad St. near Canal.[1] Quite a number of negroes were killed and for a while they seemed more subdued and rational. Brother had taken no part in anything of the kind but we feared to see Léon mix up in that sort of affair. His friend, Joe Garcia, had come to live in New Orleans early in 1867. He lived up-town but we saw him now and then. Ma liked him very much and always praised him to our boys for his extra polite manners.

My brother Henry was now six years old and Ma bethought herself to have him regularly christened. She had expected to have her friend Zéline Lafosse as his God Mother and Pa had thought of Mr. Gallimard, but after Mr. Gallimard's death he picked no other. Henry took upon himself to choose his own sponsors. He chose Joe Garcia and Eveline Jaufroid, and so it was settled and his many names were Henri Joseph Edmond Frémaux. Joe gave him a suit of clothes as a christening present. Henri was very fond of Joe and almost in love with Eveline and in some way he had made up his mind that she and Joe would some day marry. His little speeches to that effect were quite embarrassing to her at times. She had had a sweetheart and his name was Edmond, but Henry did not know that. In fact, nearly all the girls seemed to have one best friend among the boys. All these little affairs did not turn out in marriages but many did wind up that way. Their mothers did not seem to have much faith in the durability of all these love affairs. They seemed a poor, but happy, set of girls and the crowd made me one of them, as much as they could. My time with them was so short and Ma so different from the other mothers. Uncle Justin, too, was a sort of martinet about his girls.

One Sunday Féfé came to breakfast. She was just from Mass. She laid a fancy looking envelope near me and said old Mrs. LeBreton had given her that to give to cousin Mémé and would I, if I was going there soon, hand it to her. Cecile Smith, Aunt Julia Parra, and I intended going there that very day so I took the letter and seeing it was so fancy, I ventured to say that perhaps it was an invitation to some party or wedding. Pa thought it looked more like a valentine, only it was in June and not Valentine time. Just then Cecile came in to say that she could not go but would go the next Sunday. Ma then told me I had better wait a week also and to go on and tell Aunt Julia that our plans were changed. I hurriedly wrote a note to Mémé explaining our change of programme. My note was on a torn off scrap of paper and the only available envelope was quite large so I put Mrs. LeBreton's letter in it to keep my scrap note company, put on my hat and went to Julia's. She was dressed and waiting for us. I gave her the letter, told her it explained our change of plans and said I was sorry. She was disappointed but hoped she would go back again with us the next Sunday. We loved Julia Parra who was not *our* aunt at all but Aunt Honorine's much younger sister. All went as usual for three days. Thursday evening I was at Mrs. Carrejolles.

We were all enjoying some music and singing when Léon called me aside. "Céline," he said, "there is hard time ahead for you. What have you and Mémé been plotting? Uncle sent for Pa at his office, and Pa has just come home and is talking to Ma, and Ma is like a fury. I came over to warn you." I was so frightened that I almost fainted. I sat down on the front steps and tried to think. I had not seen Mémé for a month or more. I did not feel guilty at all but I was scared well and good.

At that moment Paul came for me. "Gee," he said, "what did you do? Ma is going to beat you for sure this time."

I came into the house. Pa was walking up and down the room with his hands in his pockets, looking worried. Ma was livid. I can not exactly recall how the scolding began. It was a half hour or more before I understood what it was about.

After Ma had called me all the vile names she knew and said I would bring her grey hair in sorrow to the grave, and I was no fit companion for my innocent sister, etc., etc., Pa finally said, "Stop crying long enough to answer me one question, please. Where did you get the letter you sent Mémé?"

"Well, Pa," I said, "you know as much as I do about that letter. You all saw Féfé fetch it last Sunday, saying that old Mrs. LeBreton had handed it to her at church to be given to Mémé. I have not seen or heard anything of it since."

"Well, Caro," Pa said, "I thought Céline could not have known anything about it. Let's let it drop and say no more." I wanted to ask him to stay but I did not dare. That was my trouble, I never dared. It seemed to me that asking Pa to stay would be like asking his help against Ma. I let him go without a protest. Then the scolding began anew.

It turned out that Mrs. LeBreton was Henri St. Clair's grandma. I had not known that or that the letter was from him, that in it he told Mémé that vacation was near but he could not come to Louisiana. His father had decided that he should go to Canada immediately and stay until he graduated. Then he would be a young man and he would come and ask her hand of her father, etc., etc. Julia had forgotten the letter till they sat at table, and thinking of it, handed it to her, telling her it was from me explaining my absence. Uncle saw Mémé get red and tears come in her eyes. He leaned across, took the missive and read it. His comment was, "Well, when the young man comes, I will see what he is like. In the meantime, I do not want any writing between you. Nice girls do not get notes from boys and I forbid it." Mémé, in her confusion to excuse herself, said she was not the only nice girl it happened to, that I, Céline, had a written proposal long ago and did not show it to my mother or anyone but (she), Mémé, etc.

That was what Uncle had sent for Pa to tell him. So it was out. Poor Camille!! I had spared him in vain. Ma said Pa *must* go and speak to him. How dared he presume to address me, with his record. As to me, I was a plotter, a nobody, a girl who could be in secret correspondence two years, palming herself off for a decent girl in the midst of an honest family. It went on and on. I was not allowed to say a word that night. I was sent to bed and hours later when I was supposed to be asleep, my "innocent" sister was brought to the room, Ma enjoining her not to wake me and say a single word to me.

As soon as Ma was down-stairs, Sister exclaimed, "Céline, you're a fool. Why don't you marry Camille and leave this infernal house? I'd go live with you." I said nothing. I had promised not to speak that night.

Next day while Ma was busy, Pa asked me why I had not told about the note and I explained to him just why. He sighed and said it was all very sad about his old friend's son falling beneath his rank, that he was happy to see that I had understood that the families might yet be friends but that Camille did not count at all. Then he asked, "What is his attitude to you since the note?" I told him that I never saw him. He was never in when I called on the girls, or if he was, he went out at the gate. My eyes had never met his in all that time. Then Pa said that was all that was necessary and that he was sorry I had told Mémé. So was I, for I spent an awful two weeks. Ma kept her eyes on me all the time as if I was about to do some very dreadful thing. As I went to school each day she hoped that I would go about my business and not go galivanting around picking up love letters from every Tom, Dick, or Harry. I was very unhappy.

The time for our graduation was approaching. Ma had very little money when our uniform was agreed upon: a white cashmere dress looped up on one side with a japonica, showing a white satin petticoat, another japonica in our hair and a third at our belt. It was not very expensive. We bought the flowers at wholesale. I think they came to 25¢ apiece. To get my dress Ma broke into a $20.00 gold piece she had since before the war. The satin underskirt had been Ma's wedding underskirt. I felt badly that Ma had had to sacrifice part of her gold piece for me. I did not feel loved and did not feel happy at the expense made for me. One thing I knew, that Ma was proud of my school success. That year the three high schools of New Orleans graduated together, two girls' schools and the one boys' school. As a class, our school was ahead of both the others and I was, by some margin, ahead of my class. I could not have done better. I knew that even if nothing was said about it, Ma must be proud of me.

The day set for graduation was the 22nd of December. A few days before that Cecile had asked Mr. Carrejolles to give her her Christmas present, a broach and earrings, representing grapes and leaves, of pearls and gold enamelled leaves. As I was dressing she ran over and asked me to wear them as they would look so well with my dress. I was very confused at her kindness, but she would not be refused. I wore them. My wrap was red but it really did not matter as Ma would take care of it while I was on the stage. As I left the house, Evel ran after us and insisted on changing my wrap for hers, a new opera cloak of white chenille and swan's down with white rosettes and flowing ribbons. It was so kind of her, too. I wanted to refuse but it could not be done, and beautiful in borrowed finery, we went along, the whole six of us with Pa and Ma. Henry carried my immense bunch of violets. The uptown girls were to fetch white flowers, and the boys, red roses to form the red, white, and blue of the country's flag.

Well it was that I had memorized my valedictories, one in French and one in English, for I was so frightened that I could not have read a line.

When it was all over, Pa presented the violets to Mr. Rogers, then superintendent of public education. He promised to keep me before the Board for the first vacancy and my hopes rose high. On leaving the hall, we met Joe Garcia. He said he had been there with his cousin, but they had been separated in the crowd, so he walked home with us, that is with Sister. Léon and I were having a very serious talk all the way back.

While waiting for an appointment and having more time for fancy work, I made a little more money and helped Father a little more. He told me once that my help was worth from $7.00 to $8.00 a week to him, that is, he could take that many more orders and fill them.

In the spring Mr. [Louis] Surgi became City Surveyor and he took Father as his first clerk. That was much better than what Father was doing. Two months after our graduation, I was appointed as supernumerary at the Barrack St. School, then at the St. Ann St. school and also at the Bayou Bridge school. Between the three I should have done pretty well, but we were paid in "scrip" and lost anywhere from forty to sixty cents on the dollar. It was infamous, so that with all I made I averaged no more than $5.00 a month in that first year. Then, of course, there was my needlework that helped out some. I joined the girls a little more in their amusements. Ma believed in making life a thing of duty only, and always. Amusements *she* never took and seemed willing that I would have just as little as was possible. For instance, at Mrs. Jaufroid's they were to play a parlor comedy. The girls were all asked to come over and choose or to be chosen for the different parts. I could not go but it turned out that a certain part suited none of the available girls. I was sent for.

Ma explained that they could go on with the parts, send me mine to copy and that when the rehearsals began, she would send me, and so it was. Those evenings were frolics to the other girls, to me only glimpses of *possible* good times, impossible to me. We lived just across Dumaine St. Ma told Mrs. Jaufroid to ring a little bell when they were ready to begin and to send me home directly when my part was over. I did not appear in the last scene and it was only at the last rehearsal that I stayed to the end. As Pa was to be stage manager, he stayed on and I with him.

So little was my intercourse with the others that Mr. Paul Lacaste, who for his part spoke with an awful twang, was a subject of pity to me. I thought he was afflicted with that defective voice. Only after the comedy was over did I discover my error. I enjoyed the evening, but how much more enjoyment could have been my share if Ma had let me go freely to the rehearsals.

After leaving school my thoughts turned often to the possibility or impossibility of seeing my Jackson friends again. I planned and thought and devised many ways, always to come back to the impossibility of it all. I was too poor and Ma, I was sure, would not let me go even if I got the money. Yet a sort of hope held me to the purpose of saving the required amount. I could not think of going with less than $20.00 and that was about as hard to save from my earnings as $100.00, or seemed so then. However, Léon had been having his shirts made by "Aunt" Julia and paying her her price. He came to me one day and asked if I would make him six. I thought he wanted to economize and I said, "All right, furnish the cloth." He did so the next day, remarking that he would pay me as he did Julia. I felt myself getting red in the face. To be paid by my brother for what I thought was almost his due upset me quite a good deal. When they were finished, I refused the pay. I was loth to take the money. It was the old pride of the slave holder's daughter. Pay had never been heard of at home "before." Ladies, "before," were not paid. Oh, that pay! How often did my pride rebel against putting out my hand for my pay and many dollars I lost by it, too. I often sent the boys with my needlework. *They* had not known any "before" and did not mind taking money and fetching it in their naked palm. A few of the "old time ladies" who gave me work, put the money in an envelope and laid it near my parasol or other belongings and I took it as I left. It was foolish? It was delicate; we had not yet learned to be other than delicate. We had been taught to deposit our alms silently in an extended palm or a little tin cup, not to let it fall noisily as women untaught were want to do. We were gradually being reconstructed, rebuilt, re-taught, and the readjusting was painful and often made us wince.

Yet, my necessities called for money. We were woefully poor. So were the rest of the neighbors and money had to be made. That spring of 1869 I made a very fine baby dress of tatting and the boys raffled it for me. Finally, I had my $20.00 put aside. Now came the other part—get away. Girls, then, never dreamed of going anywhere alone. I mean unaccompanied. Sallie had written to Mother to ask if I could come up if she could get an escort agreeable to Ma. There were many and many parleys, Ma and Pa and several of the neighbors, to discuss the propriety of this, that or the other guardian. Finally, late in June, Mr. J. G. Miller, an old man, a minister and father of many girls, besides being one of our best Jackson friends, told Father that he would see me safely in Sallie's care to go up there, and to return I would be placed in care of someone just as reliable. Many were the recommendations made me, many instructions given Mr. Miller, and finally, accompanied by Pa, Ma, Sister, and Joe Garcia, I went aboard the boat that was to take us as far as Bayou Sara.

Just as the boat was about to leave, Léon came to me quickly, thrust a letter in hand, and said, "Read it after you are started." It contained money, $6.00, and a note explaining that as I would not take the shirt money, he offered this as pocket money to spend, or waste, or have, as a "backbone" prop.

A moment later I was very much disturbed when David Miller came up and said I was in *his* care as his uncle had gotten off at Carrolton. Business was keeping him unexpectedly and not wanting to make me miss my trip, he had said nothing to my parents and quietly substituted David in his place. David was a little older than I was. We had been classmates for three years, but all the same, I worried to know if it was my duty to tell or not. David proved very unobtrusive. I only saw him at our start and when we landed at Bayou Sara. There Mr. Zackie Lea was awaiting me with a carriage and we were soon at the old plantation. I spent six happy weeks with my friends. Oh, such happy, free weeks, so different from the war time days of constant apprehension. I considered that I belonged entirely to Sallie, did and went only according to her advice.

She sent me to a party at the Taylors'. A young man asked to be my escort. Mr. Worthey told him, "No, you can follow the carriage but 'Frenchy' goes with the family." He later explained that Mr. Austin was a queer young man and would embarrass me more than please me as an escort. A moment before we got off for the dance, Mr. Bob Austin arrived, his head and beard entirely shaved off, dressed in white from head to heels, riding a white horse, and leading a black one side-saddled, begging that I ride out with him. I was dressing upstairs and saw him. I also saw Mr. Worthey go and meet him at the gate. Presently, the black horse was turned in the lot and Mr. Austin went his way. He did not go far, for as we reached the crossroads he was at the carriage window. Willie Worthey was at the other, and in that way we proceeded.

I had fixed it with Willie that I would enter the house on his arm, but somehow, Mr. Austin was quicker than Willie and I had to enter with the conspicuous man. The surprise of the guests was all he could have desired. We made a sensation but it was very short. I spied a seat between two of my old schoolmates and got rid of my conspicuous cavalier. I did not dance with him at all and we gave him the slip on our return. I was already in bed when I heard him come for his black horse.

I attended another party at the Stocketts', across the creek. We danced till three A.M. A number of us were in a big plantation wagon. After crossing the creek our wagon stopped. Pull, haul, back, everything was tried in the pitchy darkness but we seemed rooted to the earth. There we stopped till the first faint rays of daylight when we found our impediment to be a pine tree caught between the wheel and body of the wagon. We went on but the sun was stinging our bare heads, arms and shoulders ere we reached old Mrs. Miller's. Breakfast was almost ready and we hastened into our house garments in a hurry. We were all very happy and chatty and not feeling sleepy but Mrs. Miller sent us to rest and we really did go to sleep till wakened by the first warning for dinner.[2]

The whole six weeks trip was one of complete content. Sallie's sewing at that time was of dainty little baby things. I was very handy with my needle and many were the little garments I made or trimmed. It was a work of love and I did my best. From appearances they were not to be used very soon. No mention was ever made of anything. I saw her sew and sewed with her. Rhoda once took me to a closet and displayed two or three pretty little pieces and hastily put them away without a word. A few days later, the old lady called me in the very early morning. "You are the early bird, so I will show you something," she said, and from her armoir she took two pretty embroidered flannel shirts and a pretty little sacque worked in morning glories. I asked if Sallie had seen them. "No, indeed, child. I would not have Sallie think I knew she will ever need them." This was a strange thing to me, everybody knowing a thing and pretending to each other that they did not know it. Sallie sewed in her own room, never before her mother or sister. She did not seem to mind me but never made a remark about her work. But they were lovely friends and so kind to me.

When my time was up, Mr. Zack Lea drove me to Bayou Sara and left me in the care of 'Bertha Whiteman (Buff Taylor, that was) until Mr. Miller, the old gentleman this time, should be ready to take the boat. That was late at night. I had a very pleasant day with Buff and her little boy baby.

I found all well on my return.

When schools reopened in September or October I was employed two months straight at Bayou Bridge in the place of a Miss Chauchon who had typhoid fever.[3] That was $53.00 a month. I should have had $106.00 but we lost 63¢ on the dollar that session. Later in the fall, I taught two weeks at the high school, the French class in Mrs. Coiron's place. That was a situation of $85.00 a month. I worked pretty steadily those days. I got a little better acquainted with the girls and at times I was almost happy. Then, suddenly would come one of those jarring shocks in the way of a scolding of some kind, always accompanied by humiliating publicity. If Ma had only taken us in a room alone and lashed us physically or mentally, I could have stood it better, but her sudden flying at us in or out of company made me very miserable and increased my timidity tenfold.

Joe Garcia was a very frequent visitor at the house. He took dinner with us every Sunday. With him Mother never found fault.

We once were going to the convent to see one of my cousins boarding there when Ma abruptly said, "Why did you refuse the offer of marriage to your friend's brother?" It came as such a surprise that I did not know what to say. I did not know then how she knew of it. It afterward transpired that on a flying trip through N.O., Scott Worthey had met Father and told him that I had refused him, but that he hoped still to make me change my mind if my parents had nothing against him, etc., etc.[4]

After a moment's hesitancy I said, "Ma, I would have told you before but really I do not want Sister to know of this. She talks so inconsiderately." Ma said she (Ma) knew already and that I was not to put conditions to her, that she knew what to say or not to say and I was very impertinent to hint at a lack of tact in her, etc.

Just at first, I had meant to tell all the whys and wherefores, but I felt that they would be a terrible arm in Sister's quiver, so I explained that I did not love him and was not sure he loved me sufficiently. I could tell Ma was very much disappointed, but she really had nothing tangible to scold about so in silence we finished our short walk.

Ma had not taken off her bonnet on our return when she began to tell Sister all she knew about my poor little affairs, ending with a sort of insinuation that I would never do anything sensible that would be a credit or a help to the family. I cried all evening. This tearing out and bringing to light and discussing all that which I considered secret and sacred was about the hardest of the hardships which met me at every turn.

By night all the young crowd knew that I had refused another offer of marriage and I was miserable.

Mr. Joe

JOE GARCIA, so everyone said, was in love with me. I could not see it that way. I was more inclined to think he came for Sister, if for anyone besides Léon and friendship. I had had lovers, serious and not serious, but they acted very differently, so I lived my life planning a future of my own making whenever the existing turmoil of politics, upset of social positions, and racial riots would let our dear Louisiana settle into something like a civilized state.

In one of the many rioting fights, Mr. Garcia had been wounded, shot through the foot. Father, being on the scene, had him fetched home in Léon's room and there, after the bullet had been extracted in the street, he was made as comfortable as was possible.[5] We two girls were in bed.

We knew Léon, Pa, Oscar, and many of the neighbors were doing patrol duty that night. We heard a cab stop at our door, then Pa speaking to Ma. Doors opened and shut and the cab left. We thought Léon was hurt but presently I heard him clatter up the stairs, then down again. Well then, it was Oscar, and for some reason his old mother must not see him just then. We felt very sorry and very concerned, and we were all in a flurry. We caught many words, hurt, bullet, doctor, poor boy, but nothing definite came to us. We knew someone had been carried up and into Léon's room on the wing. The boys, in the room next to us, slept on undisturbed. Then all sounds ceased. Looking out of the window we could see a shaft of light from the wing room to the street. We knew better than to go out there to enquire so we woke Paul up and sent him to Léon for information. He was the longest time returning and told us in a very offhand way, "It's Joe. He was shot somehow on the leg or foot. I don't just know, but gee, Pa surely has him fixed up fine so his hurt won't dry. The water drops, drops, on a flannel all the time and gee, you—." There Ma's door was heard to open. Paul sneaked back to bed. Ma came as far as the landing, listened a moment and went down again. We did not talk again till morning.

I was hurrying my work to get to school, this time at Bayou Bridge school, when Sister announced that Ma said we could go and speak to Joe, or read to him if he so desired, as Léon had to go to work and the boys to school. Sister flew up there. She was pretty, bright, witty and good company. I finished up my and her share of house tidying and went off to teach.

In the evening I had boys kept in so I came home later than usually, then ate my cold dinner. By then Léon and several of the boys had come and were entertaining Joe Garcia so I did not go to see him. Next day, just as I was leaving for school, Ma called out, "Go speak to Joe, Miss. I told you to go yesterday and he will feel hurt at your neglect." I went for about half a minute and got off to school in a hurry. Things went on that way for two weeks. Then Léon carried Joe down every morning and carried him up again every night until he could help himself with the aid of a crutch and stick.

Just about then there was a very foolish game called Planchette that had just come in fashion. It was a so-called mesmerism game. The outfit for it cost $1.25. That was too much for our purse and I thought it foolish anyway. But one day, on my return from school, I found Joe and Sister deep in the game. After that, many were the hours that, for politeness sake, I spent trying *not* to understand the drift of Joe's mesmeric questions, but he was an invalid and must be humored. We were left a good deal alone with him, as the girls thought I would enjoy most *not* to have them drop in as was their want. It vexed me considerably but there was nothing to be done. I would not even have mentioned the subject to the girls. Joe stayed six weeks at our house, then went back to work. We saw nothing of him for three weeks or a month.

In these days of readjustment I had many enjoyable evenings in jaunts with Father. He took me to see all sorts of interesting things, the gas works (it was coal gas then), the cemeteries, the dry docks, ships, wrecks, crevasses, anything so it was a jaunt with him was a pleasure to me.

Many times we would go visit Father Turgis at the little chapel, corner of Rampart and St. Louis. Pa had profound love and respect for the brave and self-sacrificing soldier priest.[6]

Father had gradually become the general adviser and organizer of our set. He planned every little amusement any of us took pleasure in. Sometimes he chaperoned the lot of us to a very early Mass at some distant church. He was in demand at every picnic, all charitable tableaux, etc., etc. Thus it came about that our home was the general rendezvous of all the girls and, of course, of the boys of our set. In our poor little way, we had some very pleasant moments. Personally, mine were often marred by the conviction or absolute knowledge of an impending scolding.

Sister in some way managed to have a falling out with Uncle's family so no more visiting took place for ten months.

We were getting along a little better. Pa's employment paid him $150.00 a month. Léon was self-supporting. I was working some. Paul had employment. He gave Ma $10.00 a month, which money Ma never used but put away for him. She gave it all back to him when he left New Orleans in 1875.[7]

In the winter of 1869–1870, Edith, Mary Ward, Rhoda Worthey and also Mary Miller, visited New Orleans. Edith, Mary, and Rhoda came to us. Mary Miller went to a relative's house. I saw little of her. Edith was in charge of her music teacher, Miss Kokerno. She only remained one week.

Pa was happy to be able to return to these Jackson girls a part of the kindness their parents had shown us. He took them about to see things of interest, also twice to the theatre. I had never seen a play in English. The play was Mr. Scott Siddon's master success, *The Lady of Lyons*. The second play was a sort of medley, more of a show. There were acrobats, jugglers, etc.

On New Year's eve Rhoda sprained her foot badly and had to spend several days upstairs so we had fire in our room. I know that grate was astonished at the first heat since it had been put up. We had taken the house, corner of Tonti and Dumaine, when it was new, and no other room ever saw fire but the front room which was a combination dining and living room. That New Year's day was memorable in many ways. . . .[8]

We also had much company, New Year visits as was the custom those days. Every young man we knew called, if only for a few minutes. Most of them brought bonbons, as French candies were called. For my part that year, I got eleven packages, and a pretty satin box full from Joe Garcia, and several presents from the girls, little friendship tokens. Uncle gave me a ring, a circlet of gold, chased with little stars. I had brought about a reconciliation between the families. Rhoda and Edith had been invited with us to a midwinter reception at Uncle's and I was very proud of my friends. Rhoda was a magnificent young woman. Her jet black hair was braided, coronet style, intermingled with a chaplet of pearls and silver wheat. Her dress was white cashmere with many rows of white watered ribbon embroidered with wheat and field flowers in natural colors. Edith wore pale green, her magnificent hair hanging in long curls and a half wreath of tiny white flowers bringing out their gloss. Mary Ward wore a visiting dress. She did not dance but her sweet joyous wit made her a favorite before the party was half begun.

Joe Garcia tried hard to get a tête-à-tête with me but he was a bunglesome sort of a wooer and I had a nice time evading any complications which might have been followed by some outbreak with Ma. I did not want that, anything but that while the girls were with us. I preferred, at the time, to lose a lover, if needs be, to having Ma scold before our guests.

In February that followed he did manage to ask his question and said he would speak to Father at the first possible opportunity. I got no scolding when he did so. Pa did not accept exactly, told him that if in a year he was of the same mind and I had grown to feel as he wished, he could then talk it over. In the meantime, I was to be perfectly free that no engagement would be said to exist. Of course, in a few hours the whole neighborhood was informed of the fact that I was "promised" to Joe Garcia.

In this unsatisfactory state my affairs stood when I went to Jackson for my second visit. I went on the 25th or 27th of May [June] to be in time to attend commencement. It was well understood that I was not to correspond with Mr. Garcia. That suited me. I would not have known in just what manner to write. Not to write was easier and I was well content.

Edith was now full grown. She was a beauty, so also was Loulie, her sister. Sallie had a fine little boy, Jesse, by name. We became great friends. Sallie's health was not good, so that I was quite a help to her.

The commencement dinner was given in a grove near Millwood. The school on Miller's property was Mrs. Norwood's, hence the name Millwood. The pupils were in great numbers. We were having a very pleasant time. I was quite a while with Jane McNeely and she asked me to come and stay a few days at her home. I referred her to Sallie. Then Edith and

Loulie came in. One was with Tom Woodside, the other with her brother, Glancy. Then Leander McNeely almost took possession of me. He monopolized me to the extent of being a very uncomfortable escort. I went to dinner with another young man. This angered him. There was quite a fuss, almost a cutting affair. I left the grounds and was making my way to Mrs. Miller's when I came face to face with Scott Worthey.

He had returned just that morning from California and I had left his wife and Sallie eagerly awaiting him. I had intended staying away from Worthey's a week or more so as not to hamper the family gathering. My first words were of surprise at his being near Millwood. He answered that as I was there, he thought he ought to come and see me home. "You are running away from Leander, are you not? You had better let me take you home at once. Besides, you can not go to McNeelys' this week, I will not allow it." I no longer wanted to go to McNeelys' and I had reasons for not wanting to go back with him either, so I said I had promised to go home with one of the girls and would be with Sallie on the morrow. After much arguing, he consented to go back to his home immediately.

I went on to Millers', gathered my things, and set out to find Edith to make arrangements to go home—with her, that is. I drove out with Lulah, Glancy, and Emma Erwin. We passed by Mr. Worthey's and sent in a note to Sallie. She understood, and next day sent me some things by a negro. I stayed a week at Edith's. They came in that night for the debate but I stayed with Mrs. Jones and Ventress. I think it was the first time that Ventress and I had been for any length of time in each other's company. I found him very pleasant but he was very timid. So was I and I guess we were both glad that Mrs. Jones took on herself the burden of conversation.

There were some sort of exercises going on the next morning and yet some others at night. Edith came from the debate. She had soiled her dress and wanted it fresh for the next night. It was then past eleven at night. I agreed to help her so we waited until the house was asleep and we began our laundry work. There was an elaborate dress, waist and underdress of swiss. There was a cabin in the yard and to do this we repaired with all our needed paraphernalia. The washing was easy enough but the starching and ironing were done under difficulties. The only fire to heat the irons had to be made in the kitchen fireplace, a great blazing log fire. The irons would get smoked and soiled and have to be rubbed on the clay flooring of the cabin to cleanse them. Often they were too cold to use by the time they were clean. To and fro we ran across that big yard in the darkness, guided by the fire in the kitchen one way and the lamp on the other end. I guess it was an acre across. I have never done anything quite so inconveniently since. It was three A.M. when, reeking with perspiration and our hair full of ashes, we triumphantly carried the dainty suit into the house. The fluting had all been done by warming the fluting tongs over the lamp. It was nearly daylight when I fell into a troubled sleep but the next *day* at ten A.M. we were again in the college listening, or rather, *not*, to the Greek and Latin speeches which had cost the boys so much study and preparation.

One night Mrs. Jones told us, Edith and me, to sleep in Ventress' room. Loulie was sick. She said Ventress and Mr. Woodside had gone to the Woodside place near Port Hickey and would not return for three days. We were late going to bed as we always were. Edith fetched to the room a large dish of honey and a churn crock full of cream together with a few biscuits for our supper. We were just about to remove the things when we heard the boys in the lot. Ventress was instructing Tom Woodside to go in the window, make no noise, as the house was asleep, and he would put up the horses and meet him in a moment. Edith put out the light and told me to run up the stairway. We would sleep upstairs. All my clothes, shoes and stockings were on one chair. I picked it up and fled. Tom was at the window. Edith groped around, found some of her scattered apparel and came to me. Immediately we heard a crash. Tom had upset the honey into the cream. He struck a match, then we heard him laugh and throw himself on the bed. Then Ventress entered and there began quite a room cleaning mixed with exclamations of "Who on earth can Edith have here? Where did they go? How many do you think there were? I found only two saucers and two spoons. What could they have been doing at this time of the night? The lamp is hot yet. What will mother say about her ruined churning?" etc., etc.

We were as still as could be. I was holding that chair and getting tired too. The door at the top of the stairs was locked. When we were about sure that the boys were asleep Edith went down into her mother's room, found the key, but could find no matches or lamp. In the dark we groped to a bed. It was piled up with all sorts of rubbish. We could only guess at what the things were. Finally, we threw ourselves on the dusty mattresses. It must have been nearly two A.M. It grew cold by daylight. Edith got some old curtains. We covered with them and slept a little. I wondered why we were in that predicament. Had it been in our house I would have called out to Brother and there would have been no scramble at all, but Edith's way was always her own peculiar way.

In the morning we looked at each other. We were sights, dusty, sooty, streaked like zebras, in an attic with no water, towels or a clean spot to sit on. We waited an interminable time till we saw a piccaninny cross the yard. Her name was Minnie. With her aid we got what we needed and presently I was prepared to go downstairs and get from Mrs. Jones, who had heard nothing of the night's commotion, those garments and accessories that Edith had left in her brother's room. Breakfast was rather an embarrassed meal and later I returned to Sallie's.

There I had a strenuous week. Scott and his wife were there. They were casting about for a place to build their home. I was invited to go with them and do the choosing. I declined. I did not even go with them. I knew better. I could see how it was with them. They would never be happy. It was a case of marrying in haste, for spite, and repenting at leisure. In their possible seventeen months of marriage they had been perhaps three months together and she knew and he said, that his old love folly was all he meant to live for, etc., etc. It was awful.

Father and Sister were to come up and we would go home together. Pa had some surveying to do at Prophet's (or Profit's) island. It would take him ten days, then he would visit for three or four days. He came on time, fetched Sister. Right there my fun stopped. Pa took with him, among others, to the island, Willie Miller and Mr. Lawrence Miller and quite a number of negroes.

While he was away, Sister began her vexations. She wanted to visit at Mrs. Miller's and was very insistent about it. I would gladly have taken her there, walked over some evening, but she had sprained her foot in coming and we had to wait for a conveyance. No one had any but she made her desire known so plainly that two horses were at last procured but *Miss* would not go horseback. Then some friend passed, going to town in a carriage, and she went. Two days later Sallie suggested I should go and see what Sister might be doing for that foot.

Docile to hints, I went. I found her with quite a little court around her, girls and boys vying with each other to entertain her. She was on a sofa, her bandaged foot on a stool. Seeing her so quietly comfortable, I went over to Millwood to spend the evening. There was quite an impromptu musical going on. In a half hour or so who should come in but Sister, carried by two of the Miller boys. She sat on their crossed hands and seemed quite content. They deposited her on the sofa and the evening's amusement went on. They drifted into charades, then songs, then some persons executed a few fancy dances. Someone asked, "Who can dance the Varsovienne?"

One of the girls announced that I could do so. She had seen Sister and I do so several times. To dance at a party was one thing, to stand before a crowd and dance *to* them, quite another. My embarrassment was short. I said I would like to oblige them but Sister was hurt. We would show the step at some other time. I was getting composed after my little speech, feeling remorseful that I should be glad that Sister was crippled, when lo, the little vixen got up and called out so that all could hear, that she was willing to try. If it hurt her too much, why she would stop. She was so sweet about it that had *I* refused, after, I would have seemed unkind. I went cold all over, then red to the roots of my hair. We got up and Sister started like a fairy. She never danced better and more lightly. Twice the length of the room was all I could stand. I got out on the dark gallery and fairly silently cried. Lilah Carter came to me there and said many nice things. They did not think badly of Sister's little tricks. She was young and, of course, full of mischief. The boys would not mind having carried a mock invalid or even carrying her back. But I knew Sister was just past seventeen, no child, and I was greatly mortified.

The next day several letters were brought to me, one from Ma, one from Mémé Beauregard and one from Joe Garcia. It was the second; the first I had not answered. This one I fondly hoped Sister would know nothing of. I opened none of them until I was perfectly alone and put them in the pillow-slip at the back of the pillow I had used the day before. Then it was time to say good-bye and get back to Wortheys's. Rhoda had come for us. As I was putting on my hat, Sister called out, "You must not forget your love letters you are so secretive about." Then the girls began to tease. I had to take the letters. I could not leave them and all the way in the carriage Mr. Zackie teased and Sister gave little snatches of information, drawn largely from her imagination, but with enough truth to show that she knew the contents of the missives. I was most miserable. Next day I had to give Sallie an account of things. She said she would see to it that my letters be delivered privately but no more came from Joe. Sallie said if I wanted to write privately I could go to her room and do so. No, I did not wish it. Mother's orders were to be obeyed. It awed me to think that Joe would have written against Ma's absolute command but, of course, he was not under Ma's rule. He was not her child.

Pa arrived the next day very strongly emotioned. He was pale to the lips and his voice trembled as he narrated the following: Late the night before they had come, in the course of the coast measurement, upon several bomb shells, unexploded. One was very large. Pa suggested the next morning he would have a boat rowed to the middle of the current and throw them in. The negroes heard him and before he was up they carried them under a tree, managed to uncap them and were extracating the powder from them. It was not so very easy and a deal of digging with a stick had been done. That in the large shell was more difficult. Pa heard some clicking, clicking, as of iron against iron. He went to the door to see what caused the noise and found that seven negro men and three children were gathered close together, looking at one of their number who sat astride the big shell and with a spike nail and hammer was working to dislodge the caked explosive. "Don't do . . ." Pa said no more. An explosion had taken place. Willie Miller was knocked senseless by something which turned out to be the head of a negro baby. Every one of the niggers was as a mass of quivering flesh, most of them headless. Several were blown to atoms and never accounted for. All work had, of course, been postponed. Pa had come in to take Willie to his parents. He was about sixteen years old and was quite unnerved.

The next day Father went out again. He took Sister to town where she stayed two days visiting without me. Glancy had been sent for me and I was about to start on horseback to visit Edith when Sister put in an appearance. "I want to go, too," she declared.

"All right," Glancy said. "I came for both of you. Get up behind me." That would not do. "Well, I'll get behind you," Glancy offered. That would not do either. She was afraid to be pulled off by the boy so we tried to make her satisfied to ride alone and Glancy and I would take the other mount. She tried that but got frightened and jumped off. Then Mr. Scott said he would lead her horse all the way, two and a half miles, and return, if it would make me look less miserable. Of course, I could not allow *that*. Finally, after I had offered not to go, at which Glancy began to cry, and after Mr. Scott told her she ought not to go if she was afraid of a horse, at which she cried and said the best of life was always for me; Edith knew she could not ride and sent horses to suit me, not caring if she was suited or not. She talked and talked. Finally, Mr. Scott decided I should go with Glancy and when he or Ventress could get, hire, make, borrow or steal a conveyance, Sister would be taken to Monk's Corner, as the Jones' place was called. It was through the kindness of Mr. Ray that Glancy got the loan of a gig and went for my wayward sister the same evening.

She brought the news that little Johnnie Miller, the baby, eighteen months old, was reported very sick. Next morning the child had died. A negro brought the news to the different plantations. Immediately, Sister *must* go to the funeral. Mrs. Jones expostulated. It was impossible. She, herself, would like to go but could not. The horses and mules were all in the field and so on and so on. Sister then declared she would walk in. To this we all objected but she put on her hat and started, so Mrs. Jones stopped a mule from the field, borrowed a nigger's jumper and sent Glancy to catch up with Sister and see her safely as far as the Miller's home. I never asked whether or not she went to the burying ground. I never mentioned the affair to her but my vow was made then and there that my friends would never have another visit from me unless Sister could not come. I was perfectly miserable all the rest of our stay, not very long, for in a few days, Father's work being finished, he came for us. He bid all our friends a hearty farewell, invited them all to come to us at any time. We left. As we passed through the town we saw Mr. Dell-Pianne, who bowed very coldly, turned, and went into a store. I was very much surprised. Of all well-bred gentlemen, none could be advantageously compared to Mr. Dell Pianne. Father was hurt and asked if we had offended that family. "No," I answered, "I paid my respects once before you came, and Sister called the time you fetched her in alone."

Father was rather worried for another reason so the incident passed with less investigation than would have been at another time. This was the worry. On landing from the island the day before, Lawrence Miller had disappeared. No one knew anything about him. Father was talking to him, walking just in front of him on the narrow gang-plank and not getting an answer, turned and missed Lawrence. He asked, called, looked, no Lawrence. His wife was awaiting them all at dinner. They all went in expecting to see him come in any moment, but he never came. That is, it was three years before he quietly walked in at his mother's where his wife and baby had been cared for. As far as I know, he never gave any account of himself, just moved his family back to their house on the river and took up his life where it had been interrupted.

We reached home as usual, by boat, from Bayou Sara. Aboard we had quite a pleasant time. We met Evariste Landry. He was returning from his vacation. He played the piano and many of the ladies danced. Others played and still others sang and the hour was nearing midnight before we retired.

I knew well enough that Ma would hear of Joe's letters so I might as well tell her myself. I put the two letters in my pocket as I went downstairs next morning. I was very much excited. I did not want to show my letters. They were mine. They were not at all "love letters." The second one, especially, narrated quite at length a little trouble Mémé had had. That was not Ma's secret. She really had no right to *that* one. I thought of burning them but I knew I would be scolded for that or maybe punished, to the knowledge of the whole neighborhood. Still, I put off the evil moment. "After breakfast will do," I thought. Then, "After the boys have gone to school;" then, "After I have straightened the downstairs."

I don't know how long I would have waited, but Ma swooped down on me with a loud, "Well, Miss, have you not something to tell, something to show me? Why do you always wait till others have done their duty before you say what you ought?" I was appalled. When had Sister told? I thought I had kept her in sight every moment of these twelve hours. Evidently I had not. I slowly took out letter number one and handed it to Ma.

At the same time I found courage to say, "Mother, there is hardly anything in that letter, believe me. Don't read it, please." But she read every word, then folded it up and handed it back with a smile, which I understood only years afterward. She handed her hand out for another.

"How many have you?"

"Only two, Mother."

"Well, give it here." I was desperate. Mémé's affairs were going to become public property, for Ma would tell Sister, and Sister the whole crowd.

"Mother," I pleaded again, "This letter has even less in it than the other, of my own affair. It treats of other people. It was not meant for other eyes than mine. I will feel disgraced if you read it. Father knew I got it. He did not ask to see it. I wish I had never gotten it." By then I was in tears. Ma took it out of the envelope. I began to tear number one into bits and to drop it into the empty grate. Then Ma returned number two.

She had only glanced at the first line, "I am honorable, as you know. I do not read other people's business." She angrily told me, "Now, pick up the litter you have made and be wiser next time."

I picked up my scraps, put them back in their envelope and they are there yet after these many years. I was months getting reconciled to that letter episode. There was no bullying Sister. I was too timid. There was no begging her to mend her ways as far as I was concerned. She would mock and laugh and say that she was learning at my expense how to manage her bark when her time would come. I amused her. My wretchedness was always an incentive to her to do some outrageous thing. Through her my troubles never ceased. I could never thoroughly enjoy anything. She was as the sword of Damocles ever hanging over my timid head.

In the early fall one of my cousins married. Both Sister and I were bridesmaids. Then Edith wrote that she would soon be married, asking me to be bridesmaid some time in December. Ma said Yes. She emptied an armoir that I might have the whole place for my dress. I could not have afforded another so soon. I was simply delighted and a little surprised.

In the meantime, the French and Prussian war had ended so disastrously to Father's native land.[9] All the French residents of New Orleans united to give a monster entertainment, the produce of which should be sent to help with its little mite toward the immense sum to be paid by France into the coffers of Prussia. We were poor. All New Orleans was poor. All the south was poor. Yet we must do our best. Father, for his share, undertook tableaux. Let me say here that they netted $1172.30. We worked, Pa and I, four months, taking all our spare time to get things ready. We made whole armors, gold, silver, or marble white, all appurtenances of every conceivable God or Nymph. Glue, paper, buckram, paints, flowers, etc., etc., cumbered every spare place of our house and we even borrowed place from our neighbors. I do not think Joe Garcia enjoyed those four months as much as we did. He was not French. His interest was not much. When he came to see me he generally found me glueing or fitting some child with some sort of costume, and he was too polite to say anything but always left early.

When the "Bazar" took place, it lasted ten days or rather ten nights. The tableaux were done by thirty-two children from eighteen months to twelve years. I enjoyed those ten nights as Pa kept me with him after Ma and the children went home right after the tableaux. Joe Garcia was there most of the time in uniform. He belonged to the militia and they did guard duty, turn about, during the duration of the "Bazar."

December arrived in the midst of all this. Léon had planned his marriage for January 1871. Edith had written me to get their wedding rings, hers and Tom Woodside's, and fetch them when I came. Then she wrote that the marriage would take place on the second of December, that Mr. Woodside would be in New Orleans on the thirtieth of November and would see me safely to Monk's Corner.

I got my trunk packed. The pretty dress, all fluffed out with knots of silk paper, occupied most of the space. Mr. Woodside came in the morning and said he would return at "boat time," five P.M., with a carriage as it was rather a rainy day. He had hardly gone when Ma concluded that I had pleasure enough for the winter, in the Bazar. Besides that, Brother's marriage was approaching and that ought to be interesting enough to keep me from wishing to go to a stranger's wedding. And that was final.

Mr. Woodside came. I gave him the rings and a present for Edith. Ma told him very politely and very positively that I could not go. I said not a word. My throat was so pinched that I could not have talked without screaming. I kept up appearances till I got in bed that night. But what a night I had of it. Disappointment was so hard to bear. I was so very bitterly disappointed. The trip, the wedding, the three affairs to follow, all danced and grinned in my brain all the week. Then I settled to it. It was over but the soreness lasted long, very long.

On the first of January, 1870, I was formally engaged to Joe.[10] This fact in no way changed the manner of our relation to each other. We were very little at ease. I felt very miserable all the time, knowing that Joe was an American and that their way of intercourse when engaged was quite different from the way of our house. Many and many times I resolved to ask him not to call again, just to come on our wedding day when I would be ready. Of course, I never asked him. How could I when I never spoke to him without at least three other persons around?

Once Jan. 15th, a person, Mr. Lemarie, invited Sister and me to dinner. We went about twenty minutes before the dinner hour. We found on arriving that the baby was sick, the lady staying upstairs with it. The gentleman received us in the parlor. He seemed in high glee. I wanted to go back home but he insisted to keep us. Just as someone came up the porch steps he called to Sister that his wife wanted her upstairs and they both went up. The person was by that time knocking at the front door. I could see through the shade that it was a man. I went and opened. It was Joe Garcia.

"You here?" he said in surprise.

"Yes," I answered. "What did you come for?" I asked. "Did Ma send for us?"

"Why no, I was invited to dinner. I thought I was to be the only guest. I had understood it that way but I am glad you are here."

Then I told him that I was not glad, that I wanted to go home only that I was afraid Ma would scold. I saw only too plainly that it was a sort of trick to bring us together and give us a moment alone. I felt caught, tricked. Joe offered to retire but I could not counsel that either. I felt miserable. I was not by any means intimate in this house. Sister was. I had been very much surprised at the invitation but Ma had accepted for us and I had to come. So there we sat, Joe and I each on one side of the fireplace. It was cold and had begun to rain. The dinner was not being served and all the others upstairs for a half hour or an hour. The time seemed very long. Then Mr. L[emarie] came down noisily, coughed, called for dinner to be served, then entered the parlor, jubilant. "Oh," he said, "why did you not sit on the sofa?"

"It is too far from the fire," I said, "and Mr. Garcia was a little bit wet. It is raining, you know."

"I had not thought of you two being cold," he coarsely remarked. That silenced me. I never volunteered a single word all the remaining hours in that house. The dinner was served, the wife came down, so did the baby, so did Sister. She was genuinely surprised to see Joe, so I know she was not in that plot.

It was still raining when we went home. Joe sheltered me with his umbrella. Mr. Lemarie sheltered Sister under his. When within a few paces from our door he called to Joe that perhaps it would be best for him, Joe, to wait a moment outside before coming in. "I will do as Miss Céline wishes," replied Joe.

"Come in *now*," I said, and so we did. It happened that there were several visitors at the house. Ma did not notice Joe's entrance and all went well till we were alone before retiring. Then Ma asked if I had enjoyed the dinner to which I had gone so reluctantly. "The dinner was all right, I think, Ma," I replied, "but excepting if you *order* it I will never again set foot in that house."

For once when I had told my tale I got no scolding. Pa put his hand on my head as I kissed him goodnight and remarked, "Timid girls make their own lives hard, dear, but you need never go there again. Your mother will pay the dinner call with your sister."

Things were not always so easy.

Once, I had gone to spend the evening at my aunt's. It happened that Mr. Garcia came to call. One of the neighbors' little girls saw him step from the car. She ran up to him and said, "I bet you don't know where Miss Céline is today."

"No, where is she?"

"Over there," said the child, pointing to Aunt's house. Joe turned face about and came to Aunt's. I never thought to ask him who had sent him or if anyone had sent him. He very often visited my cousins. We spent a pleasant evening and later Ma sent one of the boys to accompany me home. Joe came too. I thought Ma was going to strike me. In her fury she accused me of clandestinely making appointments to meet *men* away from home. I had a home. That was the place to see my betrothed, etc., etc. Joe hated to leave me with Ma in that humor. I wanted him to go.

Finally, one of the boys said, "Joe, you better go. Ma will scold you next." He looked at me. My eyes said go while Ma was reaching for Henri's ear to punish him for his insolence.

The week before Léon's marriage, Joe came to Ma with a letter from his sister, saying he would like to speak to me about it. "Go ahead and speak to her," Ma said. "I do not prevent you talking, do I?" So, there, in the sitting room, where Ma and Pa were reading and the children studying, Joe came to me and said that his sister desired to leave her home and come to make her home with him. I had many questions to ask about his sister. I knew he had a sister, but I also knew that she had been taken in the home of a rich uncle at his mother's death when she was about eight years old and that Joe had not seen her or heard from her in some nine or ten years. So to most of my questions he could not answer, but the upshot of the affair was that I told him that I was sorry his sister wanted to come, but that if he felt it his duty to care for his sister I would do a good part by her and try to make her happy.

We were to be married in the spring. The exact date was not picked out but Joe thought the end of March or early in April he would be ready.

I had sent my resignation to the just obtained situation as teacher and was giving private lessons half the day so as to reserve time to make up my trousseau.

Léon married Miss Irène Mürr.[11] I was not at all delighted with the alliance, but personally she was a pleasant girl and gained our friendship. She made Léon a good wife and he was happy with her. Nothing more can be asked of a wife. Mr. Garcia was a best man. I was the only bridesmaid. It was an evening of marriage. It so happened that old Mrs. Pollack died and was to be buried that twenty-seventh of January. The funeral was some way delayed and the marriage had to wait nearly an hour.

At the house after the ceremony there were absolutely no guests except my brother's employer. Nevertheless, with her three sisters and the eight of us, Mr. Garcia, and Mr. ———, a very pleasant evening could have been spent from seven to ten or eleven o'clock or later. Ma insisted that Mr. Garcia send off our carriage. Léon had sent his off as he was going to live in the house with his people-in-law. Mr. ——— did not understand French and strangely enough Mrs. Mürr led the conversation wholly in the idiom, so Mr. Garcia and I took especial care to entertain the stranger. It was a sort of languishing evening, a "split" crowd. I think everyone was uncomfortable. They were splendid musicians, all of them. Pa, seeing a chance of reviving the lot of us, asked for some singing. On that, Mrs. Mürr looked at the time, declared it was nine o'clock and good time for the newly married to retire!! Mr. ——— skipped out so quickly that he only bid Léon good-bye. We were all very much confused by Mrs. Mürr's announcement. It was a warm, balmy night such as we often have in New Orleans between two cold spells. The windows were all open and I could see people sitting on their door-steps enjoying the beautiful night. I thought with a shudder of the carriage having been dismissed and having to walk in full dress through the street full of curious people. A full dress wedding ending at nine o'clock, it was absurd. Everyone would be set wondering at what was wrong, but, of course, we had to go.

We had been dismissed and go we did. Very politely and even amiably we made our "adieux." Not a word was spoken on the short way home. Joe did not come in but left us at the door and went to his boarding house.

Two days later, he left New Orleans for his sister in Greenville, Alabama. The same day I went to see my new sister-in-law. As I went in, Mrs. Mürr ran to me, threw her arms about me and said she was so glad to see me. They had feared they would never again see me. How far had I gone? Where had I left Mr. Garcia? And I can not remember how many other puzzling questions she asked. When I could take breath, I made it plain that I did not at all know what she was driving at. Finally, she said a Mrs. Wiltz, whom she had seen very early in the morning, had told her that she had seen Mr. Garcia and me elope aboard the Illinois Central railroad and that they all had been so grieved for Ma, etc., etc. I was very much taken back on the first moment. Being so very timid, I had a good cry, then it came to me that *I* had seen old Mrs. Wiltz, an invalid, sitting in her wheelchair in her garden, as I passed a few moments before. We had exchanged a few words. The old lady had looked perfectly calm and natural. I began to wonder if Mrs. Mürr had invented the whole thing. I had never met a lying grown person but I knew Mrs. Mürr was of a kind I did not know very well, so I just wondered. All the while she kept me in the front room.

Then I asked if I could see Irène. Oh, yes, I could see her, but she hoped the emotion would not prove too much for her, etc. I must have looked astonished, for she added, by way of explanation, "Brides are always very nervous, my child, You will find that out soon enough, if, however, Mr. Garcia still wishes to wed a girl reported to have eloped." I made no answer but walked into Irène's room. My "nervous" sister-in-law was very quietly eating a ham sandwich with mustard and pickles. She welcomed me very quietly. I became convinced that she had not heard the elopement episode and indeed it took several of Mrs. Mürr's startling announcements to make me realize that she manufactured her news entirely in her own brain, whenever the feeling came over her, to gush over anyone. She had precious few opportunities to gush over me after that and none at all after I was married. Such persons I considered dangerous and whenever we were forced in the course of events to be in the same room, I was most exquisitely polite, but equally distant and cold.

When Mr. Garcia returned with his sister, he boarded her at Mrs. Arsiore Soniat's on Ursuline St. Then he came and asked mother if we would call on her. Ma acceded to his wish. We put on our bonnets and went with him. It was only six blocks away.

I found the girl rather well shaped in her petite size. She had a wealth of beautiful, glossy, black, curly hair hanging below her waist held by a ribbon around the head, child fashion. She wore a trailing dress of very fine material. She looked like a child with a "grown-up's" clothes on. She was rather good looking but too dark for beauty, to my idea. Mr. Garcia's hair was the same as hers but his skin is very fair. All that night I wondered how I would like her as a constant companion, would others find her nice and would she find a sweetheart and marry when the time came. I thought her at that time to be seventeen years old but later I found she was almost three years my senior.

She told me that first day that she had a few purchases to make so I took her out the next day with Mrs. Soniat. I had never gone shopping alone. It was not the right thing for girls to do those times. Two or three girls could go but I felt much better going with a lady.

About three days later, on Sunday, we had a number of friends at the house as usual. About noon Joe was up in the boys' room when, like a whirlwind, Miss Sara Garcia came in the parlor without knocking. She wore a house dress of dark purple calico, all one half of her beautiful hair was well curled, the other half not yet untangled. She was bareheaded and held her comb in her hand. Unabashed by the crowd, she asked, "Is my brother here? I must see him right away." She would not sit down and seemed to be much troubled. Joe was called. When he saw her accoutrement he flushed very red and wanted to take her from the parlor. No, she would not go. She could say what she wanted before anybody. "Mrs. Soniat's little child is sick. Mrs. Soniat *pretends* it is teething fever but I am afraid it might be yellow fever. I know they always have it in this city. Joe, I want you to take me away from there. I shan't go back. I did not leave home to come and die of fever in New Orleans." And she rattled on.

Joe picked up his hat and turning to Ma, said, "Please let Miss Céline take her upstairs. I will go and investigate." The poor boy was in haste to get out away from the crowd. I felt dreadfully sorry for him. Such an exhibition of unreason, then yellow fever in February! Several of the girls came up with us. We quieted Sara. She finished combing her hair, but that was all we could do. None of our clothes could be adjusted to fit her. We remained upstairs to await Joe's return. He came back very sober looking, embarrassed, and out of sorts. He called his sister. They had a little talk on the porch. I lent her a hat and he took her back. He was to have taken dinner with us as he did every Sunday but he did not come back. It was a week before we saw him again.

When Sara had departed, Féfé said to me, "Céline, if you were not such a timid fool, as I know you to be, I would tell you to write to Joe that you cannot have that girl live with you. Let him send her back or board her several miles from wherever you live. But I know you, you will not do anything so radical. For heaven's sake, girl, if she really has to live with you, put your foot down the first day, the very first day, you understand. Let her know that you are first and will be first at all cost. But lo," she added disgustingly, "don't I know you are too soft. You will feel sorry for Joe and not know you are bruised till she makes a door-mat of you. Fortunately, I am there. I will fight for you." All of the girls laughed uproariously at that speech. I laughed a little sickly laugh too but I was deeply disturbed. Strangely enough, it was not Sara that frightened me but Féfé's offer to fight for me. Poor dear Féfé, how wise she was, nevertheless, and how her inalterable love for me made her see just where I would suffer and which of my faults would be a foothold for undoing my promised freedom and happiness.

A few weeks later it became very apparent that Sara needed all the spare money Joe had. Her board was $40.00 a month. She needed a complete spring outfit, her washing, her car-fare, etc. So it was agreed that we would marry later, maybe in the summer or fall. I did not want to marry in debt.

My father was to give us our bedroom set. He had bought one to his liking, costing, with the mattress and pillows, $215.00. He had to go and have it stored until such time as we were ready. Father was then employed at a salary and this present was made with extra money for drawings which he made at odd times, mostly in the evenings by lamplight.

Sara soon had another row with Mrs. Soniat so Joe boarded her uptown at Mrs. Lambourne's. She had been two months at the Soniat's.

My trousseau was about completed so I lived on as before helping Pa with his work and his extras and making a little money with my needle. I called at the Lambournes' once to see Sara. Mimie Beauregard was with me. Sara was not in. Mrs. Lambourne entertained us quite a while about her boarder and I gathered that she was not fully satisfied there and that soon poor Joe would again be looking for a place for his sister. She came down to see us quite often. She did not know how to cut or fit or put together, but she sewed very neatly as to the stitch, so all that she needed made was made at our home.

Ignace Hebert was now Mimie's betrothed. They were to be married a year later than Joe and I. Léon's wife began to know that she would be a mother. She and Sara met very often on Sundays. They cordially disliked each other. My own sister took very little notice of Sara, one way or the other, at that time. It would have been well for me if this enmity had remained at that form after my marriage.

My marriage had, I think, gotten on Ma's nerves. She was more than ever strict with me. I had my way in nothing. The most trifling things, a visit, a present, to give, or to receive, were often the cause of terrible scoldings. Yet, Ma was pleased with Joe for a son-in-law. She had liked him even before I knew him. He was a friend of the family even while I was at school in Marion, Alabama.

After a time Sara began to be dissatisfied with her life. She had fallen in with a confessor among the Redemptorists who induced her or encouraged her to become a nun. When the project was mentioned to me, it found me indifferent. Not so my friend Féfé. She was delighted. There was a solution to the Sara problem, as she called it. Then came the trousseau to be made. She had just been fitted out very lavishly, now nun's clothing had to be made. Had I been older I would have known that postulants need very little. The real trousseau comes at the time of taking the veil.

We made a complete outfit, twelve of everything, two corsets, two pairs of shoes, two veils, yards of linen for the guimpes, etc. which would be needed, two habits. We made up only one of the dresses. Then the time came to leave for she would not join the order in New Orleans. She wanted to go to Emitsburg but Father Neightheart was not sent there.[12] He was sent to Vicksburg so to Vicksburg Sara took herself. Pa, Joe, and I went to the depot to see them off, two girls and the Father. The priest seemed out of humor. *I* thought the other girl very quiet. Sara, quite buoyant, told her brother good-bye "for life," she said. They left.

On the way home it was decided that we would marry early in November. We were then in August.

Six days later Joe received a letter from the Superior of the convent saying that if she had known the state of things regarding Miss Garcia she would never have taken her in, a moment even. She was not a fit subject for a religious and she must be come for immediately. The letter was very ambiguous.

Joe could not get a leave of absence from his work. He looked up his brother, who could get off, and sent him for Sara. Of course, Joe had to pay the expenses. Four days later Sara arrived. Ma, in speaking to Joe of his sister, told him that he had better fetch her to live with us. It would not be quite three months and would be so much less expensive than to install her in another family. The Lambournes did not want her again and her aunt and cousins said no amount of pay would induce them to have her in their home. So to our house her brother brought her. She was very pale as one who has lost a lot of blood. She volunteered that she had had a hemorrhage. Ma told me it was best not to talk to Sara at all of her illness, that I would have plenty of time for explanations after I was married, if I ever married at all. By the way, I never did enquire about it. It turned out that Sara had only the clothes she had on. On leaving she had given all her clothes to her washwoman and others. On leaving the Convent after eight days stay, she left everything. Again we had to make her clothes.

Sister and Sara began to fairly dislike each other. As I was no longer teaching I was home all day. Sara helped me in my share of household work but she did not help Sister with her tasks. That began it. Besides, Sister began to gall at Ma's strict rules. Sara got on Ma's nerves too, so that I had a rather hard time all round.

One day Ma was scolding me about something, it was really nothing very bad. I had been to Aunt's for an evening and instead of coming home straight the two blocks, we went four blocks out of the way with Aunt's sister, then home. There were ten of us boys and girls and my aunt and uncle. It seems that Ma sent for me while we were on our round about route. It angered her that I should not be just where she had sent me, hence the scolding. Aunt tried to say a word in my behalf. Ma ordered me in the house and shut the door on the crowd. Sister was never very patient. She was not in this at all but she broke in with some remark about being tired of our "being always scolded before people," etc. It made Ma furious and she sent both of us to our room "for a month."

Sara had been uptown to visit some of her people. Joe came home with her and great was her astonishment when Ma told them I was punished for a month so Joe need not come back for that length of time. Joe took his departure immediately. Sara came upstairs. This was in mid-September. I was to be married in the first days of November.

The next Sunday Joe came to dinner as usual. He had not been at the house a half hour or so when he found I was still "punished." He left. Sister concluded that six days punishment was an ample sufficiency and began to plan to get out. She called to Esther Smith, one of her friends, to come in and spend the rest of the day. Esther came at dinner time. We went down to the meal. Afterward, we returned to our room. Sister dressed elaborately. The "crowd" was going to the City Park for a walk that evening. As they passed, Sister had Esther run down and tell Ma good-bye and at the same time to make the announcement, "Mother and Mrs. Huant are taking us all to the Park. We are leaving now."

Ma said, "Good-bye, go and have a nice time." So Sister, Esther and the others went. Upstairs, Sara and I were, of course, very quiet.

Sister came in at bedtime and only called "Good-night all," as she crossed the sitting room and that was the end of her punishment. Ma never mentioned it to her. I continued in penance. At every meal I came down. After breakfast I stayed down to do my part of the work and went up and sewed at my wedding things. At dinner I again went down then straightened the dining room into a sitting room again and went up.

Joe came several times. Sara saw him and he brought me candies that he gave Sara. They were opened and passed around, then Sara would fetch them to me. When I think of it now I am tempted to laugh at the ridiculousness of the whole thing. But I did not laugh then. I was too horridly mortified. As the last days of "my month" arrived I was more and more unhappy and embarrassed. How would I face Joe? Would he be there that very first day or would he kindly stay away? I did not dare send him any word but hoped he would not come. If we had lived like we read in books it would have been all easy sailing. It might have been quite romantic. I could think of many ways that would make the day quite worth a month's separation. But we emphatically did *not* live like in books. It was meet him for the first time in the sitting room with all the family around the reading table, with no word in private, no explanation possible, then or at any time, till we were married, unless I got in some other scrape and was in penance again in November. I spent several days thinking about that eventuality.

Well, all things come to an end and so did my month. I stayed up thirty-one days to the hour, then came down with my tatting, sat at the table and began to work. Ma looked up and said, "Well, is that all? Are you not going to apologize?"

"Apologize for what?" I asked.

"Why, for not having asked my pardon long ago, Miss. You are a rebellious, ungrateful child. I can not think what has come over you. Your pride, young lady, will be your undoing yet. I will break your spirit yet, never fear. I will conquer you," etc., etc.

"Ma," I finally said, "I am sorry you are angry. I am sorry I walked those four blocks out of the way, a month ago, but I am *not* rebellious. You laid a penance on me which you thought in proportion to my fault. I obeyed you without a word. What do you want me to beg pardon for? I can not ask a pardon when I do not consider that I gave offense." Then she said she supposed my approaching marriage was what made me so independent. "I do not think so, Ma," I said. "If I was Joe I would not marry a girl who is bad enough to be scolded and punished at nearly twenty." Then I burst into tears and sobs and went upstairs to bed. For several days relations between Ma and I were very strained. Then it gradually wore off and things were as usual. I soon came to grief again.

Mother and I had watches exactly alike.[13] She kept hers in a watch case on her mantle shelf. I kept mine upstairs or was wearing it. Both were always wound regularly, mine, every morning. One day Paul touched Ma's case and it fell to the floor breaking the crystal of Ma's open faced watch. I walked in the room at the very moment. The boy was very much frightened and asked me to put my watch in the case for a day while to took Ma's for repair. I consented. He was so scared, poor little chap.

In the evening Ma found "her" watch wound. Then there was a row. She wanted to know who had wound *her* watch. Well, no one had, so everybody had their part in a general scolding. A few days later Paul brought back Ma's watch, when the same thing happened again. This time one of the other children had seen the transfer and piped out, "That is not your watch, Ma. I saw Céline take the one on your mantle piece and carry it out." I looked at Paul. His very lips went white at the idea of an exposure. I could not feel it right to drag him in, and after all, Ma, herself, had put the idea in my head. I would be married in two weeks so I could stand a little longer as sort of protection to those youngsters. I took the scolding and begged Ma's pardon for having touched her watch "in a moment of idleness." A few days later Ma said I was so mean to the boys that if she was not across a wide table she would slap my face. I had told Paul that he would never have friends if he did not form binding friendships at school, advising him to make up a difficulty he had had with Jules and Mano De la Marinière.

That was the last scolding of my girlhood days. I wish it had been the last of my life. As a husband, Joe did not take Ma's irascibility at all so well as he had before I belonged to him. But that does not come in this narrative.

My marriage was approaching. The cards were being sent out. I would have liked to invite to the church a few of the girls I had gone to school with and also a few of the teachers at the schools where I had replaced them at times, but Mother would not hear to it. She did not know them and saw no necessity for their presence at the church. Of course, as my children have suggested since, I could have asked Joe to send those eight or nine cards but it did not occur to me at that time. It would have been thwarting Ma's authority and I was incapable of such actions as regarded Ma and I would never have dared ask a favor of Joe. It would have seemed bold at that time.

Father had had a regular situation for a year or more and things were a little easier about us. [14] My trousseau had not been such a strain as it would have been two years sooner. Dry goods were very expensive. All the cambric used cost 17¢ a yard; cotton (domestic), 15¢. My sheets, 7 yds. to the pair, cost $5.00. I had four pair. A pair of wool blankets were $15.00, curtains for the house, $15.00; a mosquito bar, $7.00. Mr. Garcia bought the crockery, glassware, tinware, curtains, blankets, and furniture. Only my bedroom was a present to me and cost $215.00. Our friends also gave us many presents in the form of ornaments for the beautifying of our little home which was being built. It belonged to a baker named Seiner who, knowing that we were soon to be married, offered to have the openings to suit us if Mr. Garcia thought of renting in the neighborhood. He rented it at $25.00 a month. It was soon evident that we could not occupy that house for a month to come so Mr. Garcia rented, for one month, the other half of the house we lived in rather than put off our marriage.

I had chosen my bridesmaids many months back when Sara was supposed to be a nun. They were first, my sister; second Mémé Beauregard; third, Aimée Frémaux; and fourth, my friend, Féfé. A few days before the marriage, a distant relative of Mémé's committed suicide so that she could not be one of the maids. I did not replace her. There were three others and Sara's toilette was already made, so she did not take the place.

I had engaged a young servant who came on the first of November. She was very proud to be the bride's "maid" and for the three days preceding the fourth, she did all she imagined would be agreeable. I had never had a maid so did not need her at all, but she was quite a help to Ma in fixing my future rooms. I did not enter that side at all till after the ceremony.

Through some unfortunate misunderstanding between Ma and Aunt Honorine, the latter did not come to my wedding but Mémé and Hortense did so. Léon's wife had a girl baby eight days old, so, of course, she was not there, but Léon came and his mother-in-law sent her little girls with a servant to "sit around and watch Léon to see if he was enjoying himself while his wife was kept at home."[15] Such were their instructions. As there were no children of their size invited and as Ma resented the intrusion, she had them stay in the kitchen with the servants. Only once or twice did they come forth and peep in at the parlor door.

The guests present at home that night were not very many. On Joe's side of the family [were] his brother, Ben; his sister, Sara; Mr. and Mrs. David Williams and baby (they were cousins); Mr. Duggan, from the firm Joe worked for; Mr. Charlie Carson, one of Joe's fellow clerks; James Legeai, Leo Blanchard and Ignace Hebert, groomsmen and friends of both families. Mr. and Mrs. Isidore Pinsard, cousins of Ma; Mr. and Mrs. Martin and two children, cousins once removed; Mr. Bercegai and two daughters, Féfé and Franka; Aimée and Hortense Frémaux, my first cousins.

✑ Afterword ✑

ÉLINE ended her memoir with her wedding, but of course neither her life nor her story ended there. Her marriage with Joe Garcia seems on the whole to have been a happy one. After the tragedy of losing her first son at birth, she bore and reared four children: Anita Caroline, Céline Marie, Florestine Louise, and Joseph Francis. With Céline's assistance in managing their finances, Joe's career prospered; he was able to buy out his employer's printing firm and build it into a large and successful business. Joe was already active in the Knights of Momus by 1872 and, owing to deep involvement in the Crescent City White League, the family enjoyed a respected position in New Orleans life after the Reconstruction period. By the time of Joe's death in 1920 the Garcias were an established part of uptown New Orleans society, and Céline continued to enjoy a favored social position until her death some fifteen years later.

Not everything went as Céline would have wanted it, however. Marriage did not free her from the people who had caused her the most pain during her youth. Her sister-in-law Sara whom she disliked and distrusted came to live with them in 1873 and remained a member of the household for the rest of her life. So too did Céline's parents. In the same year Joe invited them to come live with him and Céline because Léon Joseph could not support his family.

Céline's father's financial circumstances never provided him and his

243

wife more than a fragile material security; only for a short period toward the end of his life were he and Caroline able to afford their own home. However, due to his deep involvement in the White League in the 1870s, after the return of Democratic control of the state, he was appointed register of the state land office and in 1880 was commissioned lieutenant colonel in the newly organized Louisiana National Guard. He served in this largely honorific position until shortly before his death in 1898. Caroline, who survived him by ten years, spent the remainder of her life with Céline.

The other members of Céline's family were more successful in creating new lives for themselves. In 1875 her brothers Léon and Paul decided to leave New Orleans in order to homestead near Mermentau, Louisiana. They were later joined in southwest Louisiana by their brother Edouard. Paul took easily to farming, but Léon proved a poor farmer and eventually obtained an appointment as surveyor for Acadia Parish. His death in 1890 left Irène a widow with eight children. Francine married Georges Henri Granjean in 1879 and settled in New Orleans, as did Henri, the youngest, who married Ida Jung in 1884.

In later years, moved perhaps by her father's death, Céline devoted herself increasingly to social activities connected with Confederate veterans' organizations: the Ladies Confederate Memorial Association, and the like. Léon Joseph's death probably also inspired her to begin writing about her family and her youth. Throughout Céline's long life she had written brief autobiographical sketches. Now these began to grow into the memoir, a memoir which would not present a historically accurate picture of her past but which would serve as a private meditation, from the perspective of a New Orleans society woman well into middle age, on her life as she remembered it.

Céline's life had been darkened by family tension and rivalry, and as she neared death she hoped that her children would not suffer the same divisions and conflicts that had plagued her for so many years. Her last written words, painfully typed out at the end of the personal testament in which she divided up the mementos which meant so much to her, were a plea to her descendants to avoid what she had experienced: "Be friendly to each other, Children. Please be friendly in dividing this very little estate. It will please me if I can see you from the other shore."

✐ Notes ✐

Abbreviations

ASC   Register of baptisms, marriages, and burials, Ascension Church, Donaldsonville, Louisiana. Diocese of Baton Rouge, Department of Archives.

CD53   New Orleans City Directory, 1853.

CD57   New Orleans City Directory With Baton Rouge City Directory as Appendix. Mygatt and Co. 1857.

CD70   New Orleans City Directory, 1870.

FFP   Frémaux Family Papers. Private collection, Baton Rouge, Louisiana.

Introduction

1. Mary Chesnut, *Mary Chesnut's Civil War*, ed. C. Vann Woodward (New Haven, 1981).

2. Lucy Breckenridge, *Lucy Breckenridge of Grove Hill: The Journal of a Virginia Girl, 1862–1864*, ed. Mary D. Robertson (Kent, Ohio, 1981). While middle-class southern women such as Céline have been largely ignored except by such scholars as Bertram Wyatt-Brown, there exists a great and growing literature on elite southern women and their families. See in particular Daniel Blake Smith, *Inside the Great House: Planter Family Life in Eighteenth-Century Chesapeake Society* (Ithaca, 1980); Anne Firor Scott, *The Southern Lady: From Pedestal to Politics, 1830–1930* (Chicago, 1970); and most recently, Catherine

Clinton, *The Plantation Mistress: Woman's World in the Old South* (New York, 1983).

3. Sarah Morgan Dawson, *A Confederate Girl's Diary* (1913; Civil War Centennial edition, Bloomington, 1960).

4. One awaits with real interest the results of Professor Dorothy Brown's current research into "lost" women authors of pre-1935 Louisiana.

5. Céline's grandchildren, however, remember her as a quite different person—a warm, loving figure quite devoted to the family.

6. See Paul Lachance, "Intermarriage and French Cultural Persistence in Late Spanish and Early American New Orleans," *Histoire sociale/Social History* 15 (1982): 47–81.

7. This information is contained in the marriage contract dated 6 September 1813. Copies of the de Montilly marriage contract and their separation of goods (see below) were presented as evidence in a settlement made between the two before public notary Jules Mossy in New Orleans on 13 November 1840. I am grateful to Wanda Frémaux Harris for providing me with a photocopy of these documents.

8. Legal separation of 8 November 1822 (FFP).

9. "Succession of Jean Dominique Marion Victor de Montilly," New Orleans Notarial Archives, vol. 35, no. 454, Second District Court.

10. On the low status accorded spinster-governesses in the Old South see Bertram Wyatt-Brown, *Southern Honor: Ethics and Behavior in the Old South* (New York, 1982), pp. 238–39.

11. See Wyatt-Brown, *Southern Honor*, pp. 231–34.

12. Wyatt-Brown, *Southern Honor*, pp. 138–48, 231–33.

13. On the growing importance of discipline and the mother's role in enforcing it, see Jacques Donzelot, *The Policing of Families* (New York, 1979), pp. 20–21; and more generally, Edward Shorter, *The Making of the Modern Family* (New York, 1975), pp. 205–54.

14. Clinton, *The Plantation Mistress*, pp. 123–37.

15. See James W. Mobley, "The Academy Movement in Louisiana," *Louisiana Historical Quarterly* 30 (1947), and, more recently, Raleigh A. Suarez, "Chronicle of a Failure: Public Education in Antebellum Louisiana," *Louisiana History* 12 (1971).

16. On the war in Louisiana see in general John D. Winters, *The Civil War in Louisiana* (Baton Rouge, 1963), and most recently, on Port Hudson, David C. Edmonds, *The Guns of Port Hudson: The River Campaign, February–May, 1863* (Lafayette, 1983). On Reconstruction see Joe Gray Taylor, *Louisiana Reconstructed, 1863–1877* (Baton Rouge, 1974).

Beginnings

1. Céline's great-grandmother was Marguerite Françoise Grimpreau, 1750–1828.

2. The Prince was presumably Duke Jules de Polignac, 1749–1793.

3. Jean Louis Joseph Leveque was comte de Fleury.

4. Céline's "great grand aunt" was Yolande, duchesse de Polignac. The actual relationship between the Grimpreau and Polignac families is obscure.

5. The phrase "a la lantèrne" means "To the lamp post."

6. A "ci-devant" was a supporter of the *Ancien régime*.

7. Céline's grandmother was Anne Françoise Levêque de Fleury, 1798–1857.

8. The son was Etienne Joseph Vicomte de Fleury, 1759–1841. In 1865 Caroline received an urgent letter from M. La Vallée informing her that her great-uncle had died in 1841 and had left her and her sister an inheritance worth seven or eight thousand francs which he had directed to be divided only after the death of his "femme de confiance." This woman enjoyed the income for twenty-two years, and only died in 1863. Because of the Union blockade La Vallée had been unable to contact Caroline until after the war (FFP).

9. Céline's grandfather was Jean Dominique Victor Marion de Montilly, 1794–1849.

10. The three children were Ernest Marion de Montilly, 1813–1847; Flore Caroline Marion de Montilly (Frémaux), 1818–1908; and Marie Céline Marion de Montilly (Schmidt, then Frémaux), 1815–1848.

11. The identity of this family is unknown and complicated by the poor transcription of the name. A more likely version is Shevelev or Shuralov. Lizette's family name was probably Durnov.

12. Napoleon Joseph Frémaux, 1821–1898, would become the father of Céline Frémaux.

13. Caroline was employed by Gabriel S. Shields, who had married Catherine Surget in 1838 (Adams County Marriages, Marriage Book 6, p. 269).

14. The baby was Léon Victor Frémaux, 1847–1890.

15. Céline died on 27 February 1848. In June 1848, Caroline wrote a brief poem to her infant nephew:

> Helas! insoucieux enfant
> Plus heureux que ta vieille tante
> L'heure pour toi passe en jouant
> Sans regrets, comme sans attente.
>
> Ignorant le trésor perdu
> Tu souris, et ta bouche rose
> N'aura pas un basier rendu
> Charmée ta mère qui repose. (FFP)

16. Caroline went to her mother in New Orleans and then took the position as governess with the Bercegeays in Donaldsonville so she could be near her nephew. Jean François Aimi Bercegeay (died 1887), a native of Belgium, had married Victorine Blanchard in 1842 (ASC, vol. 10, p. 124).

17. They were married on 25 April 1849. Caroline and Léon had already become acquainted when she had visited him and her sister in 1847 following the birth of Léon Victor. Following that visit he had sent her a humorous letter in the form of a rebus thanking her for a gift to the infant (FFP).

18. Léon's father was François Etienne Frémaux, 1787–1841. The cross of honor was actually awarded by General Bonnaire at the battle of Condé, 20 June 1815 (Archives de l'Armée de Terre, Service historique de l'Armée de Terre, Vincennes, dossier Frémaux).

19. Mrs. Frémaux was née Aimée Adélaïde Lebrun, 1790–1842.

20. In 1831 Mme Frémaux advertised herself as "Madame Frémaux, midwife, regularly admitted at the school of the Maternité at Paris, and acknowledged as such by the medical board of New Orleans." (See Rudolph Matas, *History of Medicine in Louisiana* vol. 2, ed. John Duffy [Baton Rouge, 1958], p. 64). What role, if any, she might have had caring for French troops is impossible to determine.

21. Only in 1855 did he change his name to Léon (FFP).

22. Justin Frémaux was apparently born on 7 December 1831, just after the arrival of the Frémaux family in Louisiana. He died in 1901. Aimée Frémaux, 1833–1845, was the youngest child.

23. Victorine was the daughter of Mrs. Bercegeay by a first marriage to Siffroy Blanchard. The younger Victorine married A. W. Warren of Massachusetts on 20 November 1851 (ASC, vol 10, p. 329).

24. The sisters were Marie Louise Frederika (Féfé) Bercegeay, ca. 1843–1874, and Marie Francisca, born in 1845. The brother, Camille Theodule, was born in 1847 (ASC, vol. 6).

Donaldsonville to Baton Rouge

1. In her diary, Céline records that in 1874 Féfé died "of irrepressed anger" (FFP).

2. "Mrs. Supervièlle" was possibly the wife of M. E. Superville, editor of *Le Drapeau de l'Ascension*.

3. Francine Josephine was born on 3 August 1852.

4. In Louisiana the Know Nothing or American Party opposed the anti-Catholic position of the national party and attracted French Catholics opposed to recent Irish and German immigrants. See Marius Carriere, "The Know-Nothing Movement in Louisiana" (Ph.D. diss., Louisiana State University, 1977), especially pp. 6, 18, 54, and 65. Justin apparently had a varied career. In 1861 he was captain of the Parish Prison; in 1866 he was in charge of the insane asylum in New Orleans; in 1870 he was a stockbroker; and in 1876 he listed his occupation as jeweler.

5. Paul Octave Hébert, 1818–1880, was governor of Louisiana from 1852 to 1856.

6. Louis Hébert, a graduate of West Point and member of the state legislature, was a planter in Iberville Parish. He served as chief engineer from 1855 to 1860. He entered the war as a colonel of the Third Louisiana Infantry and was promoted to brigadier general on 26 May 1862.

7. J. Joubert is listed as residing at 275 St. Ann in the CD53.

8. Paul Eugène was born 14 September 1854.

9. Mme G. Avril resided at 283 St. Ann (CD53).

10. Pauline Adam de Fontenelle Pinsard (born in Rimogne, France, 1822; died in St. Gilles, Belgium, 1901) was the second wife of Isidore Pinsard (born in Paris, 1819; died in Brussels, 1886), the son of Eugène Pollas Marion de Montilly, Caroline's aunt.

11. Marie Honorine née Lenfant was born in 1833.

12. Victor Pinsard died in 1877. Isidore had married and then divorced his first cousin Adrienne Felice Marion de Montilly. Adrienne is never mentioned in the memoir or in any other family records.

13. Aunt Honorine's daughters were Aimée (Mémé) and Hortense.

14. This was the family of Benito and Florestina Maura Garcia, Joseph Garcia's parents.

15. The old maid was Mme Aimée Gautier (CD53).

16. The *Algerine*, a "snag boat," was completed and left New Orleans on 12 April 1854. *State Engineer's Report*, January 1855, p. 177.

17. Léon Joseph Frémaux was frequently involved with the supervision of work being done on state boats between 1854 and 1860 both as special assistant engineer in 1854 and then as assistant state engineer. Frémaux's activities as assistant state engineer are chronicled in detail in the annual state engineer's reports covering the period 1854 to 1861. Much of his time was spent inspecting the Mississippi and Red rivers and keeping the channels navigable. Thus he was away much of the time, leaving Caroline to care for the children alone. In 1854 the state engineer G. W. Morse reported that 103 slaves were employed in state works in his department (*State Engineer's Report*, 1854).

18. Isidore and Martha Larguier had five children: Cora (b. 1844), Emma (b. 1846), Carry (b. 1849), Isidore (b. 1852), and William (b. 1854). (Birth years are calculated from the 1860 census.)

19. Edouard Charles was born 12 September 1856.

20. The state penitentiary, built in 1834, held three hundred convicts in 1858. It was operated by a private company which paid the state one-half of the net profits from the prisoner's labor. (F. M. Kent to Moody Kent, 9 March 1858, Amos Kent family papers, Louisiana State University Archives.)

21. *Grande tête de veau bouilli* means "big boiled calf's head."

22. This short account was written in 1900.

23. She died on 6 July 1857 at the J. A. Sigur plantation in Iberville Parish.

Childhood

1. The inventory of Mme de Montilly's estate describes Odile as "A negro slave named Ordela alias Odile, aged about 34 years and her child named Alice, a griffone, aged about 18 months," and values her and her daughter at $800 (FFP).

2. This was presumably the family of A. Delpeusch, 120 Toulouse (CD53).

3. This was presumably the family of A. Choppard, St. Peter (CD53).

4. Jean Jacob Farnet lived at Rampart near St. Phillip (CD53).

5. "Oh, how we amused ourselves at Mr. Godichon's. We were neither men nor women, we were Auvergnants."

6. One must doubt the accuracy of this statement about emancipation. After 1857 a slave could not be set free in Louisiana except by act of the legislature and there was no such act.

7. Caroline was the daughter of Hypolite Tacon, 175 Toulouse (CD53).

8. Trevanion Lewis was later second lieutenant of Company A, Creole Guards, Eighth Louisiana Infantry, in which Céline's father served as captain. He eventually reached the rank of colonel. He was killed in action at Gettysburg on 2 July 1863. Jim Cooper was employed as a governor's messenger (CD57).

9. Adolph Kent was the son of F. M. Kent who was employed in the state engineering department in the 1850s. Adolph attended West Point, served as second lieutenant and then first lieutenant in Companies C and A, First Louisiana Infantry. He was killed in action at Murfreesboro 31 December 1862.

10. Valentine Gorlinski was the wife of Joseph Gorlinksi. She was a music teacher. He, a native of Poland, was a civil engineer and parish surveyor (CD57). In 1858 he was in charge of the Lafourche valley (*State Engineer's Report*, 1859).

The War in Baton Rouge

1. Thomas O. Moore was governor from 1860 to 1864.

2. Major Joseph A. Haskin, a native of New York, surrendered the garrison on 10 January 1861 (Winters, *The Civil War in Louisiana*, pp. 9–10).

3. Charlie Ilsly later joined the Pointe Coupée Artillery and rose to the rank of first lieutenant. He died at Macon, Georgia, on 11 August 1864 from wounds received in Atlanta.

4. Major Kelly was later Colonel Henry B. Kelly.

5. Henri Edmond Joseph was born on 16 November 1861 in New Orleans.

6. The two men were in C. E. Fenner's Battery of the Louisiana Light Artillery.

7. The Baton Rouge Academy was chartered in 1820, closed ten years later, and went through various reincarnations. See James William Mobley, "The Academy Movement in Louisiana," *Louisiana Historical Quarterly* 30 (1947): 766–70.

8. On 28 May 1862, guerrillas opened fire on a small party of Union sailors from the *Hartford* attempting to land at Baton Rouge. Admiral Farragut responded by shelling the city (Winters, *The Civil War in Louisiana*, p. 104). One should note that Céline's account of the events leading up to the Battle of Baton Rouge and of the battle itself are considerably confused.

9. Mary Gill was a native of England (1860 Census).

10. Father's friend was Valentin Dubroca. In the 1860 census his real property was valued at $25,000. Even allowing for the inaccuracies of the census returns from West Baton Rouge Parish, Céline must have greatly exaggerated the wealth of his plantation.

11. Maurice later entered Company D, Eighth Louisiana Infantry, as a private and was paroled on 11 June 1865.

12. Sasthène Allain was one of the wealthiest planters in West Baton Rouge Parish, with real property appraised in the 1860 census at $300,000.

13. On 5 August, just four miles above Baton Rouge, the Confederate ram *Arkansas* developed engine trouble and, rather than allowing its capture by the enemy, her commander, Lieutenant Henry K. Stephens, ordered the crew ashore, set her on fire, and cut her adrift. The loss of the *Arkansas* made it impossible for the Confederates to drive the Union forces from Baton Rouge (Winters, *The Civil War in Louisiana*, pp. 120–22).

14. William S. Pike was a wealthy Baton Rouge banker.

15. Céline's chronology of the battle seems somewhat confused. It actually took place on 5 August, the same day as the loss of the *Arkansas*, and ended

inconclusively because the Union forces, although forced to retreat, could not be routed because of the protection of the gunboats (Winters, *Civil War in Louisiana*, pp. 113–24). Both Céline and Sarah Morgan, who had taken refuge across the river, seem to have believed that the battle took place on the sixth (Dawson, *A Confederate Girl's Diary*, pp. 146–47).

16. This was on 11 August. Some time later, to judge by the difference in handwriting which indicates the progression of Céline's arthritis, she added in parentheses: "Mr. [Bennet] Barrow, Colo (Dubroca) told me yesterday—1914." Still later she added: "I have reason now to believe that the house we were in and was told was the Barrows' was really the Lobdells', for we met the Morgans there and I see by Miss Morgan's diary that it was at the Lobdells' that they refugeed that night." The reference is to Dawson, *A Confederate Girl's Diary*, pp. 166–67.

17. Colo's song was "The Young Sailor's Lament."

18. In his 1889 military autobiography Léon Joseph Frémaux wrote, "At Tupelo, I was designated to accompany General Bragg in Kentucky; but my knowledge of the Mississippi River in Louisiana, caused my orders to be changed to the Command of Genl. Breckenridge at Baton Rouge. I brought to the General a recommendation from Gen. Bragg to permit me to select a point on the River to intercept the enemy's vessels plying between New Orleans and Vicksburg. Baton Rouge had been recaptured; but no point could be selected that offered the advantages of Port Hudson. I therefore brought my orders to Gen. Ruggles and immediately mounted in barbette 4 siege pieces, 24 pdrs. and made some temporary earth work for the light artillery. The front being somewhat defended, the work for the heavy guns 8 and 10 inches Columbiads was begun, as well as the line of breastworks in the rear and several redoubts, at the principal roads entering Port Hudson" (FFP). On Port Hudson, see Edward Cunningham, *The Port Hudson Campaign, 1862–1863* (Baton Rouge, 1963).

Port Hudson, 1862

1. The home of James H. Gibbens in Port Hudson is still standing.

2. The *Essex* first appeared near Port Hudson on 24 August 1862. On 7

September it was fired upon and withdrew with minor damage. It was never disabled. Which engagement Céline remembers is unclear and her information erroneous. On the night of 14 March 1863, Admiral Farragut ran the fort and in the process lost the *Mississippi*, a side-wheeler, which exploded, and the *Richmond*, which was crippled. She may have confused these two separate engagements. See Cunningham, *The Port Hudson Campaign*.

3. This aside suggests that at least this portion of the memoir was written prior to Caroline's death in 1908.

4. Lieutenant Fred Y. Dabney was the chief engineer who prepared the plan of defense (Cunningham, *The Port Hudson Campaign*, pp. 128, 121).

5. L. Bonnecaze owned a dry goods store at the corner of Lafayette and Florida streets (CD57).

6. Potts must have been either Nelson or Oliver Potts, both of whom were masons, (1850, 1860 census).

7. General Franklin Gardner assumed command of Port Hudson in late December 1862 (Winters, *The Civil War in Louisiana*, p. 166).

War Time in Jackson, La.

1. Mrs. Wiley was the wife of G. H. Wiley, professor of Greek and Latin at Centenary College.

2. Rev. J. C. Miller was president of Centenary College from 1855 to 1865 (E. W. Fay, *The History of Education in Louisiana*, U. S. Bureau of Education Circular of Information, no. 1 [Washington, 1898], p. 140).

3. A. G. Miller was the principal of the preparatory department at Centenary College (Fay, *The History of Education in Louisiana*, p. 140).

4. Black troops were extensively engaged in the siege of Port Hudson, particularly in the Third Massachusetts and the Twelfth Regiment of the Corps d'Afrique recruited largely from local blacks (Winters, *The Civil War in Louisiana*, p. 304). Who the "Mexicans," to whom Céline refers here and elsewhere, were is entirely unclear.

5. According to his own account, Léon did not leave Jackson until after the surrender of Port Hudson on 9 July 1863: "After the surrender of Port Hudson,

9th July, 1863, with the help of friends, I was able to reach Mobile, where I was laid up for nearly a month" (FFP).

6. No Confederate general was named Ogden. Presumably Ogden was Major Fred N. Ogden, who commanded the Eighth Louisiana Heavy Artillery Battalion at Vicksburg until he was taken prisoner there. He was later paroled and was in command of Scott's First Louisiana Cavalry after that unit was brought back to Southeast Louisiana in 1864. After the war Ogden headed the Crescent City Democratic Club, a paramilitary unit described by Joe Gray Taylor as "a terrorist organization," to which Céline's father belonged. On 27 February 1873 the Fusionist party gubernatorial pretender John McEnery appointed Ogden brigadier general of the first division of Louisiana militia and in this capacity he led the attack on the Metropolitan Police Force supporting Governor Kellog. Presumably Céline's post-war experiences led to confusion. See Taylor, *Louisiana Reconstructed*, pp. 163, 254.

7. While on leave from Virginia, Captain John McKowen captured General Neal Dow who was convalescing at the Heath plantation (Cunningham, *The Port Hudson Campaign*, p. 115).

8. After his recovery, Léon Joseph was placed in charge of the Mobile defense works. Later he was sent to Fort Gaines to take charge of the fortifications at Grant's Pass and on Dauphin Island. He later supervised the preparation of defenses of Mobile, Spanish Fort, Blakely, and the Tensas River.

9. Dr. Thomas S. Jones, a physician, was professor of natural sciences at Centenary College and on the board of the Insane Asylum. Dr. Jones was the first of four generations of the family to practice medicine. (Fay, *The History of Education in Louisiana*, p. 140).

10. The Thomas Worthy family had a large plantation in East Feliciana Parish valued in the 1860 census at $43,000.

11. Céline's memory is incorrect by one year. On 2 August 1863 General George L. Andrews sent a detachment of 250 black infantry and 50 cavalrymen and a section of artillery to recruit blacks for the Twelfth Regiment of the Corps d'Afrique. The next day Colonel John L. Logan with 500 men surprised the federals at Jackson and routed them with significant Union losses (Winters, *The Civil War in Louisiana*, p. 304).

12. The Campbellites were at that time a quite new indigenous American

Protestant denomination called The Christian Church, founded on the western frontier ca. 1830.

13. Logan placed the casualties at one hundred Union troops and twelve Confederates (Winters, *The Civil War in Louisiana*, p. 304).

14. Asphodel, the home of the Fluker family, is still standing.

15. Dr. J. D. Barkdull was the administrator of the Insane Asylum in Jackson in the 1850s until his murder in February 1865 (Richard Lawrence Gordon, *The History of East Louisiana State Hospital, 1847–1934* [Master's thesis, Louisiana State University, 1974], p. 67).

16. On 25 May 1865 large quantities of recently surrendered Confederate ammunition which had been stored in Mobile cotton warehouses accidently exploded. The cause of the accident was never determined, although it was blamed on careless handling of the ammunition on the part of black soldiers assigned to the depot. The actual number of casualties is unknown although property loss was in excess of $700,000 (Charles Grayson Summersell, *Mobile: History of a Seaport Town* [University, Ala., 1949], p. 42).

17. Here Céline added, "This phase of my life explained at length in a smaller manuscript." Presumably this is her "A Love unto Death." See Introduction, p. xxxvi–xxxvii.

Reunion in Alabama

1. A heading, "On the River, Aug. 14, 1865," suggests that much of the details from this section of the memoir came from Céline's diary.

2. Although the number of deaths in the explosion is unknown, Céline is certainly exaggerating enormously. See above, page 153, note 16.

3. Helen F. Smith was the daughter of Colonel A. Y. Smith of Pratteville.

4. Miss O. P. Talbird was the governess of the home department.

5. O. L. Shivers was the steward of the home department.

New Orleans: Reconstruction

1. The Mechanics' Institute riot which took place on 30 July 1866 contributed significantly to the urgency for a congressional reconstruction program.

Approximately 37 Unionists were killed and 136 wounded. Only one fatality occurred among the whites assaulting the Institute (Taylor, *Louisiana Reconstructed*, pp. 109–11).

2. Céline added later: "Scott's Wooing, elsewhere recorded under the name of 'A Love Unto Death.'"

3. Bayou Bridge was an integrated school until 1868. In May of that year the school was the scene of a significant setback to postwar integration. A number of "colored" students had been attending the school. Following a complaint, the superintendent William O. Rogers wrote to the principal, Mrs. S. Brigot, ordering her to find out if any non-white students were attending. The result was that on 27 May, twenty-eight students were transferred to an all-black school (Roger A. Fischer, *The Segregation Struggle in Louisiana, 1862–76* [Urbana, 1974], pp. 111–12).

4. Scott Worthy had proposed to Céline during her visit to Jackson in 1868. She refused him because she had heard that he had begun to drink.

5. Both Joe and Léon Joseph Frémaux (and, in minor capacities, Léon Victor and Paul) were involved in the social and political organizations which would give birth to the Crescent City White League. In 1874 Léon Joseph was captain and Joe lieutenant of Company C of the Fifth Ward White League, composed largely of residents of Dumaine Street and the surrounding neighborhood. On 8 September of that year, seventy-two guns allegedly destined for Frémaux's company were seized and he and Armand Guyol were arraigned before Judge A. H. McArthur on charges with conspiracy to assault officers of the Metropolitan Police Force (Stuart O. Landry, *The Battle of Liberty Place, September 14, 1874* [New Orleans, 1955], pp. 77–79; Taylor, *Louisiana Reconstructed*, p. 292–93).

6. Here Céline inserted a long article clipped from the *Morning Star* of 4 June 1908. Turgis was born in Brittany and served as a chaplain in the Crimean War before coming to New Orleans. During the war he was chaplain to the Orleans Guard and became a favorite of this and other Louisiana units for his generosity and bravery. Céline concluded the newspaper account: "Such was the life of Pa's old comrade. I revered the noble old man and always enjoyed our visits to him."

7. On 23 August 1875 Paul and Léon Victor left New Orleans to homestead in lower St. Landry Parish on the Mermentau River.

8. In her diary, Céline recorded the announcement of the engagement of her

cousin Hortense Frémaux. More personally, reflecting on her rebuff of Scott Worthy and of Camille Bercegeay (whose family she had visited on New Year's Day) as well as on Joe Garcia's earnest but bumbling courting, she wrote: "How different are my feelings today from what they were a year ago. Then, my mind, filled with folly, could engender no other thought than that of a realization of my silly dream. But now I have banished those thoughts and for a time my heart and mind were both at rest. Here of late I suffer from the suffering I impart. Last year I begged in my immature soul for a love I could not have: this year, it is I who am begged and can not give my heart. Make oh my God, that I share the love he has for me. If it must be that I can not love him, make that he forget me. Thy will be done" (FFP).

9. The war ended on 18 January 1871.

10. Actually 1871. Her diary entry indicates none of the continuing hesitation that she suggests here. She wrote: "This year I can at last write it in full: 'I love; I am loved.' The Lord in his almighty said to *him,* 'Forget not'; and his justice whispered to me, 'Love him,' and I loved, and I now love him, yea love him. I may well write it here, why not? None will read it, none will hear me whisper my prayer of gratitude to the Most High. Could I but once, only once, be alone with *him* and say, 'Joe, I love you,' and I think it would throw off all restraint between us so far as love confidence concerned. I seem outwardly cold even when at midnight he slipped on the first link of the binding chain. Even then when my heart was leaping forward to meet his, a sort of fear calmed down the foaming tide."

11. Irène Mürr was the daughter of Auguste Mürr (born in Strassbourg, 10 November 1825, killed at Shiloh, 6 April 1862) and Joséphine (Delphine) Guth, (born at Lyon, 23 April 1832, died in New Orleans, 30 April 1883). They were married in New Orleans in 1850. Irène, one of seven children, was born in Mobile, 10 March 1851. Her brothers Felix and Edmond Auguste died in their infancy as did a sister, Florentine Marie Sophie. Her surviving sisters, Sophie Marie Andréa, Delphine Marie Lizzie Joséphine, and Gabrielle Marie, whom Céline tutored prior to her marriage, were respectively thirteen, eleven, and nine at the time of Irène's marriage. The loss of three children as well as her husband and the difficulties of caring for those who survived must have contributed to the "peculiarities" noted by Céline, whose own family had known hardships but no loss of life either before or during the war (FFP).

12. Father Neithart later returned to New Orleans in 1876 and held a number of important positions in the Redemptorist order (Roger Baudier, *The Catholic Church in Louisiana* [New Orleans, 1972], p. 458).

13. The two watches, made by the Lépine firm in Paris ca. 1825, had presumably been given to Caroline and her sister Céline. That of Céline passed to Céline Frémaux and later to her brother's daughter likewise named Céline.

14. He was then working as an assistant draftsman in the office of the City Surveyor (CD70).

15. Léonie Sophie was born on 27 October 1871.

✑ Index ✑